Poetry's Knowing Ignorance

Poetry's Knowing Ignorance

Joseph Acquisto

BLOOMSBURY ACADEMIC
NEW YORK • LONDON • OXFORD • NEW DELHI • SYDNEY

BLOOMSBURY ACADEMIC
Bloomsbury Publishing Inc
1385 Broadway, New York, NY 10018, USA
50 Bedford Square, London, WC1B 3DP, UK
29 Earlsfort Terrace, Dublin 2, Ireland

BLOOMSBURY, BLOOMSBURY ACADEMIC and the Diana logo are trademarks of
Bloomsbury Publishing Plc

First published in the United States of America 2020
Paperback edition published 2021

Copyright © Joseph Acquisto, 2020

Cover design by Eleanor Rose
Cover image © Getty Images

All rights reserved. No part of this publication may be reproduced or transmitted in any form or by any means, electronic or mechanical, including photocopying, recording, or any information storage or retrieval system, without prior permission in writing from the publishers.

Bloomsbury Publishing Inc does not have any control over, or responsibility for, any third-party websites referred to or in this book. All internet addresses given in this book were correct at the time of going to press. The author and publisher regret any inconvenience caused if addresses have changed or sites have ceased to exist, but can accept no responsibility for any such changes.

Library of Congress Cataloging-in-Publication Data
Names: Acquisto, Joseph, 1975- author.
Title: Poetry's knowing ignorance / Joseph Acquisto.
Description: New York, NY : Bloomsbury Academic, 2019. | Includes bibliographical references and index.
Identifiers: LCCN 2019009564 (print) | LCCN 2019020605 (ebook) | ISBN 9781501355233 (ePub) | ISBN 9781501355240 (ePDF) | ISBN 9781501355226 (hardback :alk. paper)
Subjects: LCSH: Poetics. | Poetry. | Ignorance (Theory of knowledge) | French poetry–History and criticism.
Classification: LCC PN1043 (ebook) | LCC PN1043 .A28 2019 (print) | DDC 808.1–dc23
LC record available at https://lccn.loc.gov/2019009564

ISBN:	HB:	978-1-5013-5522-6
	PB:	978-1-5013-7837-9
	ePDF:	978-1-5013-5524-0
	eBook:	978-1-5013-5523-3

Typeset by Integra Software Services Pvt. Ltd.

To find out more about our authors and books visit www.bloomsbury.com and sign up for our newsletters.

What we need is not more knowledge but the willingness to forego knowing.
—Stanley Cavell

L'homme qui ne médite pas vit dans l'aveuglement. L'homme qui médite vit dans l'obscurité. Nous n'avons que le choix du noir.
—Victor Hugo

Contents

Note on Translations	viii
Introduction: "That Key That You Must Always Keep on Losing"	1
1 Knowledge, Truth, and Ignorance in Nineteenth-Century Poetry (Hugo and Baudelaire)	23
2 Saying the Ineffable: Poetry Is Poetry (From the Romantics to Valéry)	53
3 Non-knowledge, Limit, and Productive Impossibility (Bataille and Blanchot)	85
4 "Moving Forth from Uncertainty All the Same" (Jaccottet and Maulpoix)	121
5 Poetry, Community, Relation	163
Notes	186
Works Cited	204
Index	211

Note on Translations

Unless otherwise indicated, translations are my own. Quotations from published translations are indicated by citation of title and page number.

Introduction: "That Key That You Must Always Keep on Losing"

What kind of knowledge, if any, does poetry provide? Does it compete with, substitute for, or merely exist alongside philosophy or other systematic or non-systematic attempts to characterize our relationship to the world and to delineate the limits of our attempt to know it? These questions are certainly not new, and answers to them have been proposed far more frequently than any single book-length study could possibly account for. And yet there is something that happens in the nineteenth and twentieth centuries that inaugurates a new way of posing this relationship or framing the problem of the relationship of poetry to knowledge. This has something important to do, I will argue here, with a shift in the use of the term "poetry" whereby there is a newly reinforced distance between poetry as a concept and as the collective name given to poems.[1] Working out exactly what this means, and what this means for poetry as a way of knowing, will take the whole of the book to flesh out, but this dual change—a shift in the meaning of "poetry" and a reconsideration of its relationship to knowledge—is still very much present, as modernism's heritage, in poets' and thinkers' discussions of poetry and knowledge of the world. In a recent study, Angela Leighton does maintain the more standard use of "poetry" to refer to actual poems, affirming that "to help us to know *differently*, in all the word-bound, sound-bound, rhythm-bound ways of poetic language, is what poetry, as opposed to philosophy, can offer" (178; emphasis original).[2] But for so many of the poets I will be considering, there is at the very least a slippage between this use of the word to refer to actual poems and a more abstract and generalized term that represents some kind of alternative to philosophical knowing but also meanwhile seemingly removed from the "word-bound, sound-bound" nature of poems on the page.[3]

And so I will often speak of poetry in this study, but far less often about poems, since my claim is that modern poets themselves, beginning in the mid-nineteenth century and to this day, have created the category "poetry" as distinct from the poems they write and about which they make a variety of claims about the relationship of the poet or reader to the world as mediated by the category "poetry." That latter use of the concept has as point of both comparison and contrast such concepts as "philosophy" or, more broadly, "thought."[4] Poetry thus conceived is a slippery concept, and that is part of the point: the difficulty that poets have both in defining it and in separating it (or not) from the practice of writing and reading actual poems is inherent in the kind of concept that "poetry" is, and it could not be otherwise without simply becoming, if established with conceptual clarity, a variant of philosophy or, if more directly associated with poems, a traditional term that does not make any particularly new kind of knowledge claim.[5] In this sense, the proliferation of definitions of poetry in the modern period, the many instances in which poets writing in prose declare that "poetry is …," is indicative of the new impulse to attempt to define something that resists definition. As Henri Meschonnic has written, "la poésie commence par échapper à toute définition, tout lieu, toute question d'origine ou d'inscription. Elle échappe au verbe être…. Pourquoi elle est question, non pas réponse" ("poetry begins by escaping all definition, all place, all question of origin or inscription. It escapes the verb 'to be.'… That's why it is question and not answer") (11).[6] And yet the impossibility of defining poetry leads not to a refusal to define it but to a proliferation of attempts to say what poetry is. The vast variety of predicates that these "poetry is …" statements take on also reflects the situated, contingent, and infinitely revisable nature of poetry according to this new conception. It hints too at the fact that this very malleability is part and parcel of "poetry" as a form of knowing. As Jean-Luc Nancy has claimed, poetry's non-identity to itself is part of what is poetry:

> La poésie est par essence plus et autre chose que la poésie même…. La poésie ne coïncide pas avec elle-même: peut-être non-coïncidence, cette impropriété substantielle, fait-elle proprement la poésie…. Ainsi l'histoire de la poésie est l'histoire du refus persistant de laisser la poésie s'identifier avec aucun genre ou mode poétique. (*Résistance* 10–11)
>
> (Poetry is by essence something more and other than poetry itself…. Poetry does not coincide with itself: perhaps non-coincidence, that substantial impropriety, makes poetry properly speaking…. Thus the history of poetry is the history of the persistent refusal to let poetry identify with any poetic genre or mode.)

By expanding what "poetry" is to areas far beyond actual poems on the page, modern poets borrow of course from the older etymological sense of *poiein* in the sense of making. Poets, I will argue, make poems, but they also make meaning, they craft a kind of learned ignorance, and they forge the conceptual space for the creation of a community that would attempt to provide an infinitely revisable answer to the question of what poetry is.

The expanded definition, in this case, would shift what is meant by "making" not by broadening it to other kinds of artistic creation but by applying the activity of making to meaning itself, i.e. seeing it as an active and changeable activity rather than a process of discovery of something immutable. This is a distinction underscored by Jacques Maritain in 1927 when he contrasted metaphysics, in its "contemplation of truth," to poetry, which "stands in the line of *making*" (*Art and Scholasticism* 128). He goes on to remark that

> Poetry thus understood is clearly no longer the privilege of poets. It forces every lock, lies in wait for you where you least expected it. You can receive the little shock by which it makes its presence known, which suddenly makes the distances recede and unfurls the horizon of the heart, as much when looking at any ordinary thing or cardboard cutout… as when contemplating a masterpiece. (129)

Such an approach, as it would go on to be developed throughout the twentieth century and beyond, expands the realm of the "poetic" to other kinds of experiences and at the same time gives poetry a privileged role to play in what used to be metaphysics' territory. This is not to say that poetry provides access to truth by metaphysics' definition, but rather that poetry is better able to make room for contingency and, via the emphasis on making and thus potentially on remaking, can bring metaphysics closer to the realm of the poetic. It might even suggest that the kind of traditional distinction that Maritain evokes here may no longer be tenable when this new sense of truth is at play.[7]

Any attempt to solidify or clarify such an approach to poetry risks missing the point of the kind of knowledge that these poets collectively shape. This, admittedly, makes the task difficult for a critic who wishes to do more than point to this variety of discourses about what "poetry" might mean, both as a source of meaning about itself as a linguistic practice and as a mode of knowledge about the world that intersects with other modes of thought without being reducible to them. But being willing to approach the contingency and to embrace the sometimes halting and tentative meanings that are available from poetry as a way of knowing is part of taking its approach seriously. My claim throughout the book will be that the restless definitional urge that first emerged in the Romantics is still an important aspect of the way poets and critics talk about poetry; in that sense, my argument will be historical while at the same time suggesting the continued relevance of triangulating among poetry, knowledge, and ignorance as a way of continuing a poetic and critical conversation about poetry. The considerations of the poets and thinkers I study are, necessarily, unsystematic and sometimes reluctant to supply precise definition of the terms they employ. That sometimes vague use of terms such as "poetry" or "knowledge" or "experience" is precisely the point. To define such terms precisely is impossible while remaining within the kinds of claims that these writers make about the necessarily ungraspable, irreducible aspect of these words and the ideas to which they relate. While readers may wish for definitional precision, my providing that here in this study would be a violation of the letter and spirit of the approach to poetry and knowledge that these poets collectively espouse. The fact that these meanings are fleeting, temporary, and open to infinite revision is a key aspect of poetic experience for these writers, and the urge repeatedly to say more about them, which stems from a kind of productive ignorance that I will explore, is what drives the interhistorical conversation about poetry that I hope to facilitate here.

In that sense, perhaps the best starting point is Philippe Jaccottet's characterization of poetry in *La Promenade sous les arbres*:

> La poésie est donc ce chant que l'on ne saisit pas, cet espace où l'on ne peut demeurer, cette clef qu'il faut toujours reperdre. Cessant d'être insaisissable, cessant d'être douteuse, cessant d'être ailleurs (faut-il dire: cessant de n'être pas?), elle s'abîme, elle n'est plus. Cette pensée me soutient dans les difficultés. (*Œuvres* 139)

> (Poetry is thus that song that you cannot grab, that space where you cannot dwell, that key that you must always keep on losing. Ceasing to be ungraspable, ceasing to be doubtful, ceasing to be elsewhere (should we say: ceasing not to be?), it spoils, it is no longer. This thought sustains me in difficult moments.)

The notion of a key that one must always lose again suggests not simple contingency but rather a complex play of certainty and doubt, arranged in a temporal succession and a process that actively resists coming to a conclusion. At the same time, this definition eschews placing poetry in the domain of an eternally inaccessible form of knowledge, and makes room for insight both about poetry and about the world as seen poetically, while also maintaining the imperative to lose the key. The French construction retains some ambiguity about whether one must actively lose the key (a kind of imperative: "one must …") or whether the key ends up lost without action on the part of the agent ("a key that must always be lost again"). And Jaccottet imbues this process of losing and finding with a comforting function, a guard against despair in the nature of this process that is subject to constant contextual shifts and that will never come to rest. Defining poetry this way invites us to expand our notion of what counts as truth, a concern that links Jaccottet's concerns with a long history of thinking literature and philosophy together that stretches back to the Romantics.[8] Andrew Bowie has repeatedly underscored the continuity of the Romantics' attempts to remap truth, esthetics and subjectivity, and our own:

> [I]t does seem to me possible to try to think of truth, in Romantic fashion, as a goal which we can never say we have reached, but which we understand via our very sense that anything we determinately assert is open to potential revision; something like this view has, for example, recently been advanced in Hilary Putnam's notion of truth as idealised consensus. This, however, does not mean we can *assert* that the ideal of consensus is even potentially realisable: all we can assert is that our experience of truth is of an ongoing insufficiency which yet sustains the continuing demand for a better account…. [T]his can be turned into an account of the intrinsically normative nature of truth, which can be importantly connected to questions of art. (*Romanticism* 204–5)

I will have much more to say throughout this study about this infinitely revisable model of truth. It is important to note the collective "we" that emerges in Bowie's account here, as a caution against considering this approach to poetry as a deeply personal or even solipsistic one. An idea that will emerge most fully in my last chapter is that the model of knowledge about the world that the poets and critics I consider advance is only conceivable within a community of readers and writers, of subjects who conceive themselves as such by virtue of their relation to others, and who create that community by virtue of that conception.

This notion of poetry as a "key that you must always keep on losing" thus has the potential to include actual poems but also expands that purview to include other types of writing and thinking, since it poses itself as a mode of interpretation more than a set of texts or a system of knowledge. It is in this sense that a poet such as Lautréamont could write that "les jugements sur la poésie ont plus de valeur que la poésie. Ils sont la philosophie de la poésie. La philosophie, ainsi comprise, englobe la poésie. La poésie ne pourra pas se passer de la philosophie.

La philosophie pourra se passer de la poésie" ("judgments on poetry have more value than poetry. They are the philosophy of poetry. Philosophy, thus understood, includes poetry. Poetry will not be able to do without philosophy. Philosophy will be able to do without poetry") (Lautréamont 283). In light of twentieth-century developments in speaking about poetry, one can read Lautréamont's statement not as merely suggesting that philosophy surpasses poetry but rather that the categories of "philosophy" and "poetry" are ripe for expansion when one begins to consider "poetry" as something other than written poems. This sense both of a tension between philosophy and poetry and of their unquestionable interconnectedness goes back to the Romantics. Friedrich Schlegel famously claimed that "where philosophy stops, poetry has to begin" (98), but also that "whatever can be done while poetry and philosophy are separated has been done and accomplished. So the time has come to unite the two" (104). Poetry, as it begins to take shape in the modern period, is something that diffuses, or at least complicates, distinctions between "poetry" and "judgments on poetry," and in that sense, we can witness a new kind of ideal for poetry that may indeed subtract actual poems from the meaning of what one calls poetry.

This kind of split continues to resonate, to the point where the author of a book called *The Hatred of Poetry* can write in 2016 that "the fatal problem with poetry" is "poems" (Lerner 23). The remark comes amid a discussion of the defense of poetry as a genre that "is itself a kind of virtual poetry" (22). Such a view reinforces a certain heritage of the idealist tradition whereby actual manifestations of an ideal type cannot possibly reach the perfection of that ideal. As ancient an idea as this may be, it has been reinforced by a tradition that places increasingly heavy metaphysical demands on poems, and no doubt part of the reason for the split that I have identified between poetry and poems is that increasing conceptual burden that may force us to idealize our conception of what poetry is. Poets over the past 150 years have given us access to a new category or way of thinking by their—at least temporary, perhaps at best only tentative—separation of poetry from poems. On the one hand, we have actual poems, verbal creations whose meanings and sound patterns can be subject to formal analysis. On the other hand, the more philosophically inflected notion of "poetry" includes, but also in important ways surpasses, actual poems in order to invite reflection on what we mean when we speak of such a thing as poetry, in its relationship to itself, to the reader, to the external world, and to an imaginative world which it creates or whose creation it makes possible when poets and readers write about what such a thing as "poetry" could be. The first move toward articulating what poetry is, as Jacques Derrida has written, a destructive one, a renunciation of knowing: in order to answer the question of what poetry is, "on te demande de savoir renoncer au savoir. Et de bien le savoir, sans jamais l'oublier: démobilise la culture mais ce que tu sacrifies en route, en traversant la route, ne l'oublie jamais dans ta docte ignorance" ("they ask you to know how to renounce knowing. And to know it well, without ever forgetting it: demobilize culture but what you sacrifice on the way, crossing the way, don't ever forget it in your learned ignorance") (109). Writing by poets about poetry both preserves a kind of idealism and also, by constantly reminding us of the hesitant and tentative nature of any kind of declaration we want to make about poetry, ultimately cancels any notion of a transcendent, definitive, or ahistorical ideal.

What is at stake is the way poetry and thought relate within the context of, and not despite, significant doubt on the part of poets and readers alike about the exact nature of that relation or our ability to say anything meaningful about it. But that is, precisely, the kind of question that modern poetry could always be said to be taking up, and so the question of poetry's relation to thought or meaning is always present in any discussion of poetry to begin with. And the limits, or potential failures, or only temporary and contextually situated nature of that knowledge are always part of the answer that poetry has to offer to such questions.[9] As Claude Ber has observed, "le poème est lié à la question de la pensée, de la possibilité même de la pensée, parce qu'il est le lieu où la question du sens prend forme hors discours, dans la chair de la langue" ("the poem is linked to the question of thought, of the very possibility of thought, because it is the place where the question of meaning takes shape beyond discourse, in the flesh of language") (18). The kind of meaning that is at play here "inclut sa propre défaillance, que l'on nomme cette dernière 'indicible' ou conscience d'un rapport rien moins que transparent entre le langage et le réel" ("includes its own failure, whether one names it 'unsayable' or consciousness of a relation that is nothing less than transparent between language and the real") (18). This awareness of the limits of one's understanding expands our consideration of poetry to something much wider, which Gabriel Trop has called poetry as a way of life. The kind of openness that operates in Jaccottet's notion of the "key that you must always keep on losing" has been, since early Romanticism, "constitutive of [the esthète's] existence" and is "drawn instinctively toward expansiveness" (Trop 41).

The poets on whom I focus in this study establish themselves in continuity rather than rupture with modern lyric poetry; I do not engage in this study with the often depersonalized poetry of the twentieth-century avant-garde.[10] While this is partly for reasons of establishing an appropriately narrow scope, I also hope to suggest that the relation of poetry to knowing and unknowing, as it was fashioned in and after Romanticism, retains important unfinished business in terms of the poetic subject as he or she constitutes him or herself in conjunction with the kind of knowing or unknowing that lyric poetry may be said to produce, and the relationship to other kinds of lived experience that it generates. Jean-Michel Maulpoix underscores that the new lyricism of the late twentieth century is not related to Romantic self-absorption or excess expressivity; he articulates the project of the new lyricists this way:

> la persistance d'un certain type de rapport à la poésie, pour lequel la scène de l'écriture est moins importante que l'expérience humaine qui la précède ou la prolonge.... [Le lyrisme] implique l'affirmation renouvelée d'une inter-dépendance étroite entre l'écriture et la vie. Ce rapport se traduit tout d'abord par un nouveau rythme, un nouveau « régime » significatif de la remise en mouvement du discours poétique. ("Existe" 261–2)
>
> (the persistence of a certain type of relationship to poetry, for which the scene of writing is less important than the human experience that precedes or prolongs it.... [Lyricism] implies the renewed affirmation of a narrow inter-dependence between writing and life. This relationship results first of all in a new rhythm, a new significant "regime" of the putting into movement once more of poetic discourse.)

Since poetry and poetic subjectivity are, on this model, mutually constituted, the presence of the poetic subject in the poetry is crucial to the ongoing question of what or how poetry may be said to know.[11] The poets and thinkers with whom I engage here see themselves in some kind of lineage, however critical or even transformative they may be of that lineage, that stretches back at least to the nineteenth century and that addresses a kind of poetic language that seeks to understand poetry, the world of lived experience, and the experiencing subject simultaneously even as these categories sometimes exist in tension with each other. And of course, even within that narrower range of poets, there could never be enough space to account adequately for poets and thinkers who have made important contributions to the kinds of questions I am posing here. Some are treated only in passing, such as Stéphane Mallarmé and Michel Deguy to name only two,[12] and some, such as Francis Ponge and Martin Heidegger, are not addressed at all.[13] This study, like any study, is partial and tentative rather than all-encompassing in what it hopes to accomplish.

That tentativeness and partiality is also a mark of the argument I am making, and necessarily so, given the nature of that argument. It is not in a strict sense systematic, because what I am claiming about the kind of knowledge with which these poets engage is itself a refusal of systematic thought that would aim at an all-encompassing approach to knowledge.[14] The ideas that this kind of thinking and living yield are, as Rodolphe Gasché puts it, "ideas that can always only be realized in finite form, as individualities, as fragments, and in a process of infinite, endless approximation" (161).[15] As I shall have repeated occasion to demonstrate, poetic knowledge or non-knowledge as I understand it here is characterized by its tentative nature, its willingness to lose the key (to return to that image of Jaccottet's), to conclude only provisionally and in a way that is dependent on the context of a particular experiencing subject bound by the limits of a community of interpreters of which he or she is a part. Knowledge of this kind should make us suspicious of claims to totalizing and unrevisable absolute knowledge, and it would be paradoxical and disingenuous to claim to offer a definitive analysis of a kind of knowledge that refuses such an approach. Nor am I proposing a kind of secularized negative theology whereby poetry and/or poetic knowledge is defined by a series of claims about what it is not. The poets and thinkers I include here have made many statements of what poetry is; what their approach also implies is that we need to see the truth or success of those claims as partial and temporary at most, and above all as an invitation to respond and to participate in the ongoing attempt to understand poetry, and the world through poetry, by adding to the discourse through which that understanding is tentatively worked out.

While more definitive conclusions may feel more satisfying and thus worthy of aspiration, on the part of the poets themselves and especially in academic discourse about literature, we have to see definitive conclusions as a temptation that risks being unfaithful to the literary projects they attempt to characterize. Robert St. Clair has described "such spots… where a text reaches down in the *inconnu*" as potentially "downright disturbing" (128). He claims that this discomfort can cause "something like 'hermeneutic anxiety': the desire to exhaustively provide totalizing responses" (128). For St. Clair, there is an ethical imperative to avoid such totalizing readings:

> if there is an ethics to/of reading, it consists in assuming one's *lack* as a reader (if not more simply as a human being), and in relinquishing the authority of definitive claims and accounts in favor of the *conversation* that all properly theoretical "views" on literature (or anything else) involve. (128; emphasis original)

Appropriate response to this ethical imperative risks saying too little by resisting the urge to conclude, or at least to conclude definitively. And yet the poets and thinkers I consider here would very much endorse this model of reading and interpreting poetry. For to resist concluding does not mean avoiding saying anything at all. It is, rather, and as I will argue throughout the book, to identify and embrace a kind of productive ignorance, a knowledge that is first and foremost a knowledge of poetic knowledge's own limits, an appreciation of which should not shut down response but rather enable it. It is this dialogue in response to a constant questioning, to an answer-turned-question, that continues to blur the boundary between poetry and writing about poetry, and between poetry and criticism at least if, in our criticism, we attempt to honor this stance of poetry's productive ignorance.[16] As poet Lorand Gaspar puts it:

> Ce que les poètes ont à dire de la poésie, c'est encore de la poésie. C'est la poésie et rien d'autre…. C'est dire que cette réponse non répondante est du même ordre que l'activité, que la propriété qu'on cherchait à cerner dans les paramètres d'un langage. Si cette « substance » nous apparaît volatile, comme toutes les substances, c'est tout simplement qu'elle est indissociable de ce qui ne s'exprime pas dans la langue. (52–3)

> (What poets have to say about poetry is still poetry. It is poetry and nothing else…. That is to say that this answer that does not answer is of the same order as the activity and the propriety that one was seeking to enclose within the parameters of a language. If this "substance" appears volatile to us, like all substances, it is quite simply that it is indissociable from what cannot be expressed in language.)

On this model, the critic's task is to be faithful to poets not by attempting to reproduce their work but by seeing the critical act as itself creative, and in the same way that poetry is.

Tracing this heritage takes us back once more to the Romantics. Friedrich Schlegel writes that "one can say that it's a distinguishing mark of poetical genius to know a great deal more than he knows he knows" (*Philosophical* 40), but he also indicates, in a general statement that is no doubt applicable to the poet, that it is possible to cultivate a knowledge of one's ignorance: "The more one knows, the more one still has to learn. Ignorance increases in the same proportion as knowledge—or rather, not ignorance, but the knowledge of ignorance" (*Philosophical* 55). One of poetry's characteristics is, on this view, the impossibility of its being captured by anything we could say about it. As Werner Hamacher puts it, quoting Schlegel's *Athenaeum Fragments*:

romantic poetry—and "in a certain sense all poetry is, or ought to be, romantic"—cannot be exhausted by its theory, which is to say, by a discourse that speaks about it. Something is always left over, and this remainder cannot be grasped by theoretical reflection, for every theoretical articulation has to be, for its part, a moment of that poetry itself. (Hamacher 226-7)

Efforts at saying what poetry is thus have the potential to reinforce the unknown rather than eliminating it; both poetry and critical or theoretical writing about poetry forge this space of creative ignorance and, in so doing, develop a relation of interdependence that might go so far as to call into question the very split between poetry and writing about poetry, in a way that is not unrelated, as we have seen, to the positing of the subject who attempts to know poetry. Hamacher underscores the way genre, like poetry and the subject itself, necessarily exceeds itself:

By positing itself, genre poses for itself a limit and posits itself, as self-positing, beyond this limit. It does not therefore take place: it must always designate its completion as completion, but with this designation it deposes itself from its own activity and is thus always at once before its end and beyond its end. Genre is an irreducible duality: more and less than itself. (230)

Andrew Bennett, in his insightful study of literature's relationship to ignorance, claims that ignorance "may be said to constitute the very condition of poetry, of literature" (16). What Plato denounced as a weakness of poetry can be turned, Bennett argues, into its strength:

After all, literature has been, from the first—from Plato onwards—not only designated as the realm of ignorance but designed as that mode of writing in which paradoxical, self-refuting or "impossible" statements such as the confession of ignorance ("I know that I am ignorant"; "We are all ignorant"; "I know that nothing can be known") are seen simply not as self-contradictory (and therefore paradoxical, absurd, nonsensical, scandalous, a threat to rationality or reason, to good sense, a tragedy or folly, hysterical) but also as *possible*—and possible to take seriously. The position of ignorance, indeed, may be said to drive literature or a certain thinking or certain traditions of thinking of literature. (21-2)

On this model, ignorance is the motor of poetry and of its interpretation. Rather than a linear model whereby we move from ignorance to knowledge, this view suggests a constant re-energizing of the impulse to understand poetry, and to understand the world "poetically," through a constant questioning of what it would mean to do that. By doing this, we open up possibilities previously unavailable to thought. While philosophy and literature are often portrayed as at odds in terms of the ways in which they define and assess claims to knowledge, this opening up to previously unconceived and inconceivable possibilities has been considered by philosophers of literature.[17] Catherine Wilson, for instance, provides a definition of "learning," and by extension, of knowledge, that can encompass works of literature. With reference to the novel but in an article that considers poetry and other forms of literature more generally, she claims:

> a person may learn from a novel... if he is forced to revise or modify, e.g. his concept of "reasonable action" through a recognition of an alternative as presented in the novel.... [T]he term "learning" applies primarily to a modification of a person's concepts, which is in turn capable of altering his thought or conduct, and not primarily to an increased disposition to utter factually correct statements. (327)

Whatever is possible is an incitement to engagement, and the discoveries of new kinds of ignorance, not least about questions such as what poetry is and the relationship it has to the world from which it springs and which it shapes, are what push us toward the next attempt to articulate provisional answers to these questions.

This is not to say that poetry provides consolation for non-knowledge. Georges Bataille and, echoing him, Maurice Blanchot characterized "inner experience" as both necessary and anguishing. Refusing the lie of totalized and totalizing knowledge yields a subjectivity defined entirely by questioning, as Blanchot writes:

> L'expérience intérieure est la réponse qui attend l'homme, lorsqu'il a décidé de n'être que question. Cette décision exprime l'impossibilité d'être satisfait. Dans le monde, les croyances religieuses lui ont appris à mettre en cause les intérêts immédiats, les consolations de l'instant aussi bien que les certitudes d'un savoir inachevé. S'il sait quelque chose, il sait que l'apaisement n'apaise pas et qu'il y a en lui une exigence à la mesure de laquelle rien ne s'offre en cette vie. Aller au-delà, au-delà de ce qu'il désire, de ce qu'il connaît, de ce qu'il est, c'est ce qu'il trouve au fond de tout désir, de toute connaissance et de son être. S'il s'arrête, c'est dans le malaise du mensonge et pour avoir fait de sa fatigue une vérité. (*Faux pas* [French edn] 47–8)

> (Inner experience is the answer that awaits a man, when he has decided to be nothing but question. This decision expresses the impossibility of being satisfied. In the world religious beliefs have taught him to call into question immediate

interests, consolations of the moment as well as the certainties of an imperfect knowledge. If he knows something, he knows that appeasement does not appease and that there is a demand in him that nothing in this life answers. To go beyond, beyond what he desires, what he knows, what he is—that is what he finds at the bottom of every desire, of every knowing, and of his own being. If he stops, it is in the disquiet of the lie, and because he has made his exhaustion into truth. (*Faux pas* [English edn] 37–8))

Lived experience informed by this kind of approach to poetry cultivates an acceptance of questioning, or of *being* "nothing but question," and makes us renegotiate what it might mean to live conscious of an ignorance that can be remediated only tentatively and temporarily. Poetry is a spur to a certain kind of knowledge, according to Andrew Bennett, not because it provides more knowledge or a different kind of knowledge but because

> instead it offers "chaos" or "wonder," or it offers something (a universe) made "anew." If the universe is made "anew"—and this is the point of the claim—it will be new to us, unfamiliar, *not* known. Poetry doesn't so much produce knowledge as make us aware that we don't know what we think we know, what we know or think we know only too well.… Poetry doesn't just begin in wonder, as Aristotelian philosophy does, but ends there, it ends up, if we are to see as poets do, in or with our ignorance of things. (74)

Poetry, on the view I will develop here, extends this awareness of what we do not know to include itself, and perhaps especially itself, to the point where this questioning becomes an integral part of the way we understand what poetry is. As Gerald Bruns indicates:

> Poetry meanwhile does not use words; it contemplates them from the outside as if they were things—but to what purpose? There is a good chance that poetry does not know what it is, much less what it is for. It cannot be traced back to a reason…: it exists in the form of a question, inaccessible to theory or redemption, divided against itself (without identity), opaque, gratuitous, and *unwirklich*. Whoever enters into this condition enters into an absolutely singular mode of existence, one that cannot be separated into a before and after or subsumed into contexts, categories, or totalities of any kind. (*Anarchy* 156)

The slippage is crucial here between the discussion of what poetry is, its identification as a question, and the description of a state of being, one which refuses categories and totalities. This is the link I hope to develop in the chapters that follow, whereby a definition of poetry as question leads to an approach to poetry that is simultaneously an approach to lived experience in a mode of constant questioning, so that to live in poetry is necessarily at the same time to live in the world beyond it. Exactly what this might mean is in fact part of the question of what poetry is, and attempts to categorize or summarize it definitively, here or in the conclusion, would necessarily violate the nature of poetic knowledge and poetic ignorance. Nor can we be content, however, to fall into silence about this unknown. Poetic non-knowledge invites, rather, a proliferation of discourse to propose provisional answers to the questions that poetry generates or that poetry is.[18]

Making such claims about poetry complicates the construction of an academic argument, because if what I am saying about poetry is correct, one should be more than suspicious of linear arguments and confidently asserted conclusions about it, since these are allied more typically with philosophical discourse about which the poets with whom I engage here are skeptical, and to which they oppose their conception of poetry as a mode of knowledge or non-knowledge.[19] I have sought to let the poets speak as much as possible in their own textual voices here, and to put them into implicit dialogue when they have been independently pursuing similar paths in terms of attempting to articulate poetry's relationship to knowing and non-knowing while linking that pursuit to the question of what "poetry" itself could be said to be. I aim to be faithful to the spirit of the claims I am making about knowing poetry, and I seek to intervene in the ongoing conversation about poetry's relation to knowledge and non-knowledge without making definitive pronouncements about it. My argument is not genealogical, since many contemporary poets continue to engage explicitly with the words and ideas of their nineteenth-century precursors in order to establish an intertextual and interhistorical conversation about poetry.[20] For, as Philippe Lacoue-Labarthe and Jean-Luc Nancy have argued, "nous apperten[ons] encore à l'époque que [le romantisme] a ouverte… Il y a aujourd'hui, décelable dans la plupart des grands motifs de notre « modernité », un véritable *inconscient* romantique" (*L'absolu* 26) ("we still belong to the era [Romanticism] opened up…. A veritable romantic *unconscious* is discernible today in most of the central motifs of our 'modernity'" (*Literary* 15)).[21] This means that the progression of the argument may not always be linear and that the conclusions may seem less than definitive by some standards. What I do hope to demonstrate is that, according to the conception of poetry established by the writers I consider, these provisional conclusions are as far as we can hope to go; those conclusions should invite us to lose the key once again, to echo Philippe Jaccottet, and to continue the conversation, and thereby create communities of sometimes divergent voices and those who read them and/or respond by continuing the dialogue.

In that sense, the approach I take here diverges from two other twentieth-century takes on the relation to knowledge. It is opposed to the disclosive model of Martin Heidegger in that it does not suppose any truth about the world that is there to be revealed via the operations of poetic thought.[22] But it also opposes the view whereby poetry has nothing to say that is not simply reducible to the words of a poem themselves. This perspective is illustrated by these remarks by Jacques Réda in the development of his assertion that "la poésie se prouve d'elle-même ou… elle n'existe pas" ("poetry proves itself from itself or… it does not exist") (55):

> Car en fait il n'y a rien à dire. Ce qui s'énonce dans le poème doit suffire si c'est rempli, si la limite réellement atteinte est celle de l'indicible qui ne se monnaye pas. Mais surtout *il ne faut* rien dire, le fond des choses étant une solitude abrupte qui n'a pas à encourager le tourisme. (56)
>
> (For in fact there is nothing to say. What is enunciated in the poem must suffice if it is filled, if the limit that is truly attained is that of the unsayable that cannot be bought. But above all *it must not* say anything, the bottom of things being an abrupt solitude that does not need to encourage tourism.)

Such a view reduces readers to appreciative silence of a poem and risks canceling meaning. As I will discuss further in chapter four, we can draw on recent engagement with the notion of "absolute music" in order to articulate the importance of words about poetry: for music to be meaningful at all, that meaning needs to be expressed in words about it. The same holds, I contend, for poetry: it is ultimately fruitless to argue for the self-sufficiency of poetry independent of any discourse about it, since the meaning of poetry is necessarily tied to the articulation of that meaning in words different from those of the poem itself.[23] As John McKeane has noted in the context of a discussion of Philippe Lacoue-Labarthe, "to comment on [the] reflexivity of poetic discourse is not necessarily to endorse it" because "poetry, then, represents a language that it is impossible to speak, one representing a danger of drowning to those who would enter it" (134).[24] Poetry means nothing without the commentary through which that meaning is brought into being, and, therefore, commentary on poetry by both poets and readers is an essential intervention in poetry rather than a secondary appendage to it.

What I hope is clear is that I am not seeking to demonstrate how poetry (or literature more broadly) can come to turn in on itself via its pursuit of its own definition. This is because the definitional impulse that I am tracing always posits poetry in a relation to the world rather than attempting to remove itself from it. Poetry predicates itself on its existence within a world of relations that cannot be a mere exclusion, and, as I will argue in the final chapter, creates community by virtue of its resistance to closed meanings or identities. If poetry is able to contribute to our knowing of the world, it is because poetry as these poets conceive it automatically overflows its bounds to affect the world of lived experience by altering either the way we experience the world or the way we understand our experience. That change in understanding can result from the changes that reflection on poetry can provoke when we return to the world of experience changed by our encounter with poetry and our attempt to make sense of it. Dorothy Walsh, in her classic study of literature and knowledge, puts it this way: "The experience expressed, articulated, formalized, or, one might say, incarnated, in the poem, is the object of our apprehension when we read the poem and our experience of the poem is an experience of this experience" (88). As I explore in more depth later in the book, poetry's relationship to knowledge is characterized by a parallel duality in the subject and in our notion of poetry itself. Through this duality, we gain insight about poetry by needing to unpack and interpret what it might mean to say, following Novalis, that poetry is poetry. Articulating what that might mean is an activity that is intimately related to the question of what it might mean for a subject to be, like poetry, equivalent to or identical with itself.[25] Walsh poses similar questions when she distinguishes between experience and *an* experience:

> the essential difference between what is just experience and what is *an* experience is that *an* experience involves duality. *An* experience, as actual experience, is self-consciously recognized by the experiencer as his. This involves a duality of the self: the I-me duality. Thus *an* experience involves the apprehension of what is experienced, together with the apprehension of the manner in which what is experienced is experienced. The importance of literary art, from the strictly cognitive point of view, is that it provides an enormous extension and elaboration of this kind of knowledge. (Walsh 137)

To be able to claim an experience as meaningful or important, it needs to be removed from the continuous flow of lived "experience" and identified by the subject as meaningful, which is an act that removes the subject temporarily from that flow of lived experience and causes the subject to turn back on itself.

Literature, on Walsh's view, plays an exemplary role in our ability to engage in this contemplation which is also a division within the self. Likewise, for poetry to be meaningful, it cannot simply be experienced but rather must become the subject of reflection, so that reflection on poetry becomes itself a creative act parallel to the writing of poetry itself. As writers and readers work out the way poetry thus becomes double, they themselves become double, a subject and object simultaneously, the I-me duality that Walsh evokes. As poets articulate definitions of poetry, they attempt to be faithful to the experience of reading, writing, and thinking about poetry in terms of the kinds of productive ignorance it can inspire and to which it calls for a response. There is thus a dialectical relationship between the construction of subjectivity and the understanding of poetry, both of which try to account for the incomprehensible. Christian Doumet has signaled, in the context of the debate between Stéphane Mallarmé and Marcel Proust on obscurity in poetry, the homology between the obscurity of poetry and the obscurity of being itself, which can be revealed and named through poetry: "il existe deux sortes d'incompréhensible: celui qui réside au fond de l'être et celui qui, si j'ose dire, a trait au langage... [L]'obscurité éprouvée à la lecture du poème y est vécue comme la révélation de l'obscurité de être, qui en retour la justifie" ("There are two kinds of incomprehensible: one that resides in the depth of being and one that, if I dare say, concerns language... [T]he obscurity experienced when reading a poem is lived as the revelation of the obscurity of being, which in return justifies it") (Doumet 13–14). The dialectic between ontological and literary obscurity sets readers on a quest for understanding which, I hope to demonstrate, yields productive ignorance which takes the place of the impossible clarity or comprehension of that which must, ultimately, remain incomprehensible.

Chapter 1 begins by considering Victor Hugo's approach to poetry and knowledge of the universe. As Hugo portrays it, knowledge often seems either immediately accessible in visionary moments or absolutely impossible. I analyze early texts where he insists on Nature's knowledge and humanity's ignorance without positing poetry's ability to bridge that gap. By contrast, the later work *Les Contemplations* complicates the earlier picture of a strict dichotomy between knowledge and ignorance by introducing the idea of reading, and by extension, interpretation into the model. I examine scenes of reading in *Les Contemplations* in order to trace how Hugo sets up a network of relations among translation, interpretation, and knowledge, which upsets the strict dichotomy visible in his earlier work and turns answers into questions. If the role of the poet and reader alike is that of the translator, with all of the imperfect non-transparency that translation implies, Hugo's poetry is ultimately reticent when it comes to giving an account of how translation and interpretation lead to knowledge about the world. By claiming knowledge without an indication of how poetry generates it, he risks writing a poetry of *reportage* whereby knowledge and ignorance are merely indicated rather than worked out in the poetry itself. By contrast, Charles Baudelaire's critical writing and poetry demonstrate a move away from the question of revealed or unrevealed truth and toward a more complex account of the relationship between poetry and the experiential world. Baudelaire's attempt to remove poetry from philosophical concerns can be shown, on the contrary, to incite epistemological questions by requiring us to define exactly what poetry is and delineate the ways in which poetry might be said to be separate from other kinds of lived experience. The more one seeks to describe poetry in order to attempt to separate it from notions of truth, the more one is caught up in knowledge claims about what poetry is. Surface claims to a certain poetic naïveté hide a conceptual framework that makes important assumptions about what poetic knowledge is and is not, and in that sense, epistemological issues are deeply woven even into approaches to poetry that call on the surface for its strict separation from philosophical concerns. I show how this move from explicit engagement with knowledge in Hugo to the implicit poetic epistemology in Baudelaire ultimately leads, in the early twentieth century, to a more explicit poetics of ignorance that explores the creative potential in acknowledgment of non-knowledge.

Chapter 2 pursues the implications of modern poets' attempts to define poetry by framing them as a series of responses to the tautological proposition of Novalis, "poetry is poetry." Rather than dismissing a relationship between poetry and the world, such a tautological definition makes the question of the nature of poetry's relation to the world of lived experience all the more central, since the lived world of experience is implicated in, and not divorced from, the concept of poetry. I appeal to Pierre Reverdy's notion of "le lyrisme mouvant et émouvant de la réalité" ("the moving lyricism of reality") to show that the question of whether such an idea represents a harmony or tension between poetry and other kinds of experience has animated poets' reflections on poetry throughout the modern period. Our inability to know poetry as anything other than a permanent state of creative crisis itself represents a kind of knowledge; what prevents poetry from being a source of knowledge about the world is that poetry is unable to separate itself *from* that world of which it is a part. Any poetic account of the world would also need to be an account of poetry itself in both its sameness and difference vis-à-vis the world of experience. Thus the infinitely revisable answers to questions about poetry also become questions and answers about our subjectivity as shaped by the experience of reading and writing poetry, and encourage us to ask whether the self is best defined in a tautological relationship, as Novalis claimed poetry is. Since unpacking the tautological definition implies negotiating the gap between the reality of the thing and our attempts to define it, the tautological definition becomes a fertile starting point rather than an ending point that risks shutting down further discourse about poetry. Working out the implications of the tautology becomes a creative rather than a descriptive or analytical act, on a par in that sense with poetic creation itself. The second half of the chapter illustrates the way that the writings of Paul Valéry encapsulate the problems of the relationship of a supposedly "pure" or ineffable poetry to discourse about what poetry is and how it distinguishes itself from other kinds of thought and experience. The productive dissonance or restlessness of his characterization of poetry and what he calls the "poetic state" point to the way the constant reframing of the question of poetry becomes far more important than the affirmation of a definitive answer. Valéry performs the unraveling of a neat distinction, one which he often wishes to uphold, between poetry and what he labels philosophy. Sometimes implicitly and sometimes explicitly, Valéry sees poetry as a way of being in and understanding the world. The tension inherent in "pure" poetry and the world from which it seeks distance thus results in epistemological claims about the productive value of ignorance.

Chapter 3 probes ignorance as a neutral site of unknowing and identifies a dynamic tension between knowledge and ignorance in the context of modern poetry. To build on the new knowledge of ignorance that poetry unveils is to reorient former approaches to poetry rather than canceling them altogether. In fact, the inaccessibility of knowledge about the world could be said to be what gives rise to poetry as a space where the consequences of that non-knowledge are explored without having to arrive at definitive conclusions. To question the knowledge vs. ignorance dichotomy is to act poetically on the two terms and to apply the same interrogatory method which poets have applied to the term "poetry" itself. As in the question of poetry itself, calling knowledge and ignorance into question involves the risk of meaninglessness or tautology, but here too, that crisis or risk is actually productive because we come to see that ignorance, like poetry, needs to be articulated in discourse in order to be meaningful. In this way, it becomes different to itself and provides the springboard from which we can continue to articulate the ways poetry, knowledge, and ignorance continue to function interdependently. The bulk of the chapter is devoted to the ways in which Georges Bataille and Maurice

Blanchot arrange the constellations of these terms in their work on poetry. In Bataille's nonsystematic and paradoxical approach, poetry provides a kind of voluntary estrangement from ordinary experience and thus constitutes a form of non-knowledge. Bataille presents a sacrificial account of poetry whereby both words and meaning are the victims. The sacrifice can never be fully carried out, however, and the result is that poetry, unlike mysticism, tries to articulate its own meaning as part of the experience itself, thus bringing us to an awareness of the limits of poetry, a move that produces a knowledge of non-knowledge. On this view, poetry can never coincide with itself and so, despite what Bataille would like to affirm, poetry is what occurs at those moments when its own impossibility is posited. Since that positing can never be silent or wordless, poetry becomes, despite itself, an ordering principle. A poetics of impossibility results from engaging with notions of what we might mean by "poetry" but it also goes further by accounting for, and perhaps attempting to cope with, poetry's incapacity to deliver on its own demands. And in that sense we can say that poetry produces knowledge about what it cannot produce knowledge about, and thus points to its own limit. Bataille's "hatred of poetry" thereby becomes a moment of renewed possibility in the always incomplete sacrifice.

For Maurice Blanchot as well, poetry opposes itself to other kinds of thought by remaining question rather than answer. The role of the writer and reader of poetry thus becomes one of responding to the ways in which poetry becomes question and gives voice to its own impossibility. This view, rather than isolating poetry from other kinds of lived experience, constantly sends us back to it and challenges us to respond not only to poetry but also to the dialectical relation among ordinary language, poetic language, and the world of lived experience which is never separate from that language. We are unable to seize and describe that relationship precisely because there is never a moment where it ceases being in flux long enough for us to stand outside the relationship and describe it. Blanchot's project thus becomes one of making sense of poetic language while affirming that meaning is ultimately undefinable. Poetry thus becomes the question that is inaccessible to certain kinds of questioning, and thus we cannot grasp poetry but only respond to it. Blanchot thus shifts the question of knowledge vs. non-knowledge by showing that poetry is ultimately neither knowable nor non-knowable; thus poetry is a stimulus to what Bataille had called "inner experience" by guiding us to an acknowledgment of what it might mean to be only question.

Chapter 4 brings the discussion back to poets and analyzes how a poetics of knowing ignorance can translate into a way of life informed and even generated by Philippe Jaccottet and Jean-Michel Maulpoix's approach to poetry. Jaccottet is on guard against nostalgia for a Romantic poetics even as he implicitly asks what remains of that heritage for the contemporary poet. His poetics of doubt, uncertainty, and conceptual restlessness, which I have characterized above via his formulation of poetry as "key that you must always keep on losing," implies that to fail to lose the key would be to abandon poetry. Total affirmation and total negation of poetry are both overly facile simplifications for Jaccottet, so he posits the task of the poet, as Blanchot does, as negotiating a space whereby we can formulate knowing ignorance that is dynamic because it is always seeking a temporary (and only a temporary) release from itself. Poems, on this model, become doubt-given-form and records of fleeting meaning captured in its flight and proposed to readers for reply. By emphasizing the way the reading and writing of poetry correlate to a kind of lived experience in the world, Jaccottet harkens back to Baudelaire's anti-systematic approach to experience and crafts a poetry that amplifies and extends the lived experience of doubt. Ignorance thereby has the potential to yield temporarily to wonder so long as we accept the abandonment of the pursuit of conclusive insights and to continue instead the ever-renewed questioning to which poetry thus conceived necessarily invites us. In similar ways, Jean-Michel Maulpoix's extensive writings on poetry pose the question of how the modern lucid subject can continue to write poetry. His notion of a "lyrisme critique" ("critical lyricism") has as its goal an elucidation of what remains to us of former poetic traditions and how we might know that it remains. He establishes in his writings an implicit and explicit dialogue with the poetic and conceptual past and asks how to engage with it in whatever forms still remain accessible to us. His poetics are grounded in the notion that poetry would not have much of a role to play if we knew conclusively whether the world has meaning; it is the task of what Maulpoix refers to as "le poète tardif" ("the tardy poet") to explore that question. In so doing, the *poète tardif* transforms or consumes the self rather than expressing it. What emerges from that process is "un savoir fait de lignes brisées" ("a knowledge made of broken lines") (*Perplexe* 41), a form of knowing that resembles the broken lines of poetry and a drama of sorts whereby the poet-critic works to fill a void that language itself has created, and in a way that generates neither total skepticism nor definitive knowledge. Giving form to a question that must remain without answer creates a kind of dwelling that is a non-dwelling and has the potential to inform lived experience more broadly by presenting at least the possibility of a less absurd world that poetic processes may have the potential to create.

The final chapter takes on, by way of conclusion, the question of human relations and community as these are shaped by the practices of reading, writing, and defining poetry as the writers I have considered have described and carried them out. My analysis expands here from the epistemological to the ethico-political realm, and I begin by considering what it would mean for identifying the other to be, as Michel Deguy puts it, "une tâche poétique" ("a poetic task"). It is not that a pre-determined notion of poetry helps define the other but that both poetry and our relationship to others are mutually and simultaneously defined and redefined. The practices of reading, writing, and defining poetry as a tentative, open, and infinitely revisable task generates an open form of community, since poetry cannot, on this view, address itself to a preexisting community. Rather, it forms the community by calling for a response and an attempt to make meaning. The subject is thus constituted by relation cultivated by reading and by entering into conversation about meaning. I appeal to Jacques Rancière's expansive notions of "literary community" in order to show how poetry necessarily points toward itself and is entangled with other kinds of lived experience because in both cases we are challenged to make meaning from the experience through a verbal response that implies a relation to others. This is a precarious characterization of community, but working out exactly what it means is in fact, as Deguy had claimed, a poetic task, and thus one that does not lend itself to systematic delineation. In closing, Jean-Luc Nancy's notion of the "inoperative community," which for him is intimately related to literature conceived in a very broad sense, helps bring the strands of my argument together. His is a non-identity based community which never quite coincides with itself, and thus the work of the community becomes, in an operation that Nancy recognizes has much in common with the literary, an attempt to work out the meaning of words such as community even while recognizing that community's non-coincidence with itself is in fact constitutive of it to begin with.

Like poetry, community raises these questions and calls out for response even as we realize that no response could be adequate or definitive, and in fact, for Nancy, definitive answers are potentially aligned with fascism as the antithesis of community as he understands it. What has the potential to delineate a community is a constant reaffirmation of the need to rethink the delineation, to remake it. That remaking is, at base, a poetic task, one where the negotiation of meaning takes center stage in a process of finding the key and losing it again in an activity toward which poetry has pointed the way.

1

Knowledge, Truth, and Ignorance in Nineteenth-Century Poetry (Hugo and Baudelaire)

In Victor Hugo's poetry, knowledge seems to be by turns transparent or impossible. Both conditions pose interesting problems for the poet, because both the transparency and impossibility of knowledge seem to preclude a role for poetry as a vehicle for knowledge. In this chapter I trace a move from Hugo's earlier poetry, which offers this sort of all-or-nothing approach to knowledge, to later works such as *Les Contemplations* which complicate this schema by introducing the notion of reading, translation, or interpretation into the equation. Still, as I shall argue, Hugo's poetry is ultimately silent about exactly how poetry might translate an otherwise ineffable experience, leaving us with more questions that answers about the way Hugo's poetry does or does not serve as a vehicle of knowledge production. By contrast, Charles Baudelaire, at first glance, wants to divorce poetry completely from philosophical concerns with truth. His concern with beauty and with art for art's sake, however, entrenches him, perhaps unwittingly, in epistemological concerns, since making assertions about poetry's (non)relation to truth depends on assumptions about what truth and poetry are and how we come to know that. By attempting to separate poetry from questions of knowing by placing it squarely within the domain of experience, Baudelaire actually provides a much more complicated model of poetry and knowledge than Hugo had, as I will demonstrate via Baudelaire's critical writings and the prose poems "Laquelle est la vraie?" and "La chambre double." This move from explicit treatment of poetry and knowledge in Hugo to implicit claims in Baudelaire will then lead us to an explicit concern, in Guillaume Apollinaire, with poetic ignorance as a potential vehicle for poetic creation and a new approach to knowledge that is ultimately a recognition of what we do not and cannot know with certainty.

If knowledge is transparent, as Hugo sometimes implies, then its relationship to poetry must be called into question because such transparency seems to cancel the essential aspect of reading and writing poetry: interpretation. If meaning is inherent, then poetry really ceases to be poetry to the extent that we characterize the poetic text as requiring an act of interpretation. Or at the very least, poetry would become divided from itself as a phenomenon sometimes requiring interpretation but at other times providing transparent and immediately accessible meaning. If we are to say anything at all about poetry, either in the larger sense or in terms of any particular poem, we need to be able to use language beyond the language of the poem itself, and in that sense, even a purportedly transparent poem will yield other words once we begin to talk about it, and thus even an immediately transparent poem would then become divided from itself once we seek to account for the poem in words other than those that comprise the poem itself. And this is necessarily the case if we are not to end up with poetry as an experience that is untranslatable and for which we cannot account in words without fundamentally altering and, presumably, demeaning the experience. Such an account of poetry would be an odd conception of a verbal art, as Stéphane Mallarmé would go on famously to demonstrate in his insistence that poetry's very existence depends on the fact that language is imperfect, in the sense of a lack of correspondence between sound and sense, which is the example he gives in *Crise de vers*: "les langues imparfaites en cela que plusieurs, manque la suprême" ("languages are imperfect in that, being plural, the supreme one is missing") (*Œuvres complètes* 2: 208),[1] and hence the word *jour* sounds somber whereas *nuit* sounds bright. If there were a perfectly transparent language however, "*seulement*, sachons *n'existerait pas le vers*: lui, philosophiquement rémunère le défaut des langues, complément supérieur" ("*only*, let us realize that *verse would not exist*, which philosophically remunerates the defect in languages, superior complement") (*OC2*: 208). Since language is imperfect, and since poetry is born of that imperfection, the interpretive act is part and parcel of reading poetry, and not an unfortunate addition to it.

In Hugo's early poem "Pensar, dudar," in the collection *Les Voix intérieures* (1837), there is no explicit evocation of poetry. Nature is presented as all-knowing and humanity as ignorant of its secrets:

> … Cette grande nature,
> Cette création qui sert la créature,
> Sait tout ! Tout serait clair pour qui la comprendrait !
> Comme un muet qui sait le mot d'un grand secret

Et dont la lèvre écume à ce mot qu'il déchire,
Il semble par moment qu'elle voudrait tout dire.
Mais Dieu le lui défend ! En vain vous écoutez….
Toutes ces voix ne sont qu'un bégaiement immense !

L'homme seul peut parler et l'homme ignore, hélas !
Inexplicable arrêt ! quoi qu'il rêve ici-bas.
Tout se voile à ses yeux sous un nuage austère. (*Œuvres poétiques* 1: 996)[2]

(This grand nature,
This creation that serves the creature,
Knows all! All would be clear for whoever would understand her!
Like a mute person who knows the word of a great secret
And whose lip foams at this word that it tears apart,
It seems at times that she would like to say all.
But God prevents her from doing it! In vain you listen….
All these voices are only an immense stammering!

Only man can speak and man does not know, alas,
Unexplainable stop! Whatever he dreams here below.
Everything veils itself to his eyes under an austere cloud.)

Humanity has language but not knowledge whereas Nature knows all but does not possess language, which suggests that knowledge is nothing without the language to communicate it. A knowing that would not be convertible to a human knowing is no knowledge in any meaningful sense at all. Even though one might suppose that Nature is imagined here as possessing absolute knowledge, the absolute is thereby indistinguishable from nothingness if it is not communicable. The poem ends with an exhortation to resignation about the impossibility of communication with Nature and the concomitant inaccessible knowledge:

Puisque Dieu l'a voulu, c'est qu'ainsi tout est mieux!
Plus de clarté peut-être aveuglerait nos yeux.
Souvent la branche casse où trop de fruit abonde….
Enfants ! résignons-nous et suivons notre route.
Tout corps traîne son ombre, et tout esprit son doute. (*OP*1: 997)

(Since God wanted it, it is because everything is better that way!
More clarity would blind our eyes perhaps.
Often the branch breaks where there is an overabundance of fruit….
Children! Let us resign ourselves and follow our route.
Every body drags along its shadow, and each mind its doubt.)

Poetry is conspicuously absent from this poem about humanity more generally. If knowledge is figured alongside language here, poetic language might have the potential to bridge the gap, in a situation that would place the poet in the position of intermediary between Nature and humanity. Much would ride, in that case, on the potential transparency of the poetic word and its ability to surpass ordinary human language. In his later works, Hugo turns more explicitly to questions of the way poetry may or may not bridge this gap between nature and humanity that he sketches in this early poem. I turn now to *Les Contemplations* (1856), which offers a more nuanced take on these questions and is not content merely to assert the gap between all-knowing nature and hopelessly ignorant humanity.

From the start of *Les Contemplations*, Hugo identifies reading and writing with the act of seeking understanding about the world and other people more generally; the text that is to be read is often portrayed as having been written by God himself:

> Et tout homme est un livre où Dieu lui-même écrit.
> Chaque fois qu'en mes mains un de ces livres tombe,
> Volume où vit une âme et que scelle la tombe,
> J'y lis. (« La vie aux champs », *OP2*: 492)

> (And every man is a book where God himself writes.
> Each time that one of these books falls into my hands,
> A volume where a soul lives and that a tomb seals up,
> I read it.)

In "A Madame D. G. de G.," the poet calls on fellow poet Delphine de Girardin and enjoins her:

> Fais pour moi transparents et la terre et les cieux !
> Révèle-moi, d'un mot de ta bouche profonde,
> La grande énigme humaine et le secret du monde !
> Confirme en mon esprit Descarte ou Spinosa ! (*OP2*: 505)

> (Make the earth and the heavens transparent for me!
> Reveal to me, in a word from your profound mouth,
> The great human enigma and the secret of the world!
> Confirm in my mind Descartes or Spinoza!)

It is unclear, based on this exhortation alone, whether the poet is merely expressing a wish that he knows cannot be fulfilled by this or any poet, or whether he holds out hope that the poet, dead or alive, can in fact provide independent and definitive confirmation about the nature of humanity and the world more generally. If the world speaks in this poem, Mme de Girardin can supposedly understand it, as is clear from the last two lines of the poem: "La nature éternelle, et les champs, et les bois,/Parlent à ta grande âme avec leur grande voix!" ("Eternal nature, and the fields, and the woods,/Speak to your great soul with their great voice!") (505). But can that vision be accurately and transparently communicated to her fellow poet? While not made explicit here, this question already underlies even the earliest moments in the text where the poet addresses the possibility of knowledge about the world communicated through the poetic word. Moreover, the very fact that the lines inspire the reader to wonder whether this transparency is a mere wish or the hope for a realizable possibility already underscores the role interpretation will have to play in even these apparently straightforward lines about the relationship of poetry to knowledge. As Aurélie Loiseleur has noted, the lyric subject attempts in vain in this poem to "imiter l'immédiateté de la Nature" ("imitate the immediacy of nature"). In place of that immediacy, we are driven toward interpretation: "c'est le temps de latence qui se creuse entre le signe, et ce vers quoi il fait signe, délimitant par ce fait la place et le rôle de l'herméneutique, et refondant en elle dans cet espacement croissant le lieu et le mouvement de la poésie moderne, comme une interrogation, une tension et une errance" ("it is the time of latency that digs itself into the sign, and that toward which it gestures, marking off by this fact the place and the role of hermeneutics, and reestablishing in it, in this growing area, the space and the movement of modern poetry, like a questioning, a tension, and a wandering") (Loiseleur).

Such skepticism about the possibilities of poetry's (or the poet's) revelatory powers are confirmed rather than vanquished as the reader moves on through *Les Contemplations*, and such early indications of the tension between a mere wish and a hope serve to make the reader alert to such moments even in what might seem to be Hugo's more confident pronouncements about the potential of poetry. As Gabrielle Chamarat has noted:

> Le désir de connaître a épuisé les possibilités d'atteindre une autre réalité que celle de murailles dont le sens ne peut être percé. Le questionnement demeure, mais se heurte à l'opacité des objets.... Aux poèmes du doute psychologique, moral, métaphysique répondent les poèmes assertifs où le moi se recompose en sujet de la connaissance et du progrès. Mais le principe du recueil joue ici un rôle essentiel: chaque pièce est objection à d'autres, l'ensemble se résolvant en un fragile équilibre. (177)

(The desire to know has exhausted the possibilities of attaining another reality than the one with walls whose meaning cannot be attained. The questioning remains, but runs up against the opacity of objects.... To the poems of psychological, moral, and metaphysical doubt, there is the reply of the assertive poems where the self recomposes itself as a subject of knowledge and progress. But the principle of the collection plays an essential role here: each piece is an objection to other pieces, the whole resolving itself in a fragile equilibrium.)

A key poem that presents a scene of the poet reading, and that illustrates the kind of questioning that Chamarat evokes here, is the eighth poem of the section entitled "Les Luttes et les rêves," "Je lisais. Que lisais-je? ... " The poem presents, but does not explicitly acknowledge, the complexity of the model that the poet seems to propose in terms of the relationship among reading, translation, interpretation, and knowledge. The poet presents himself at the outset of the poem as reading "le vieux livre austère,/Le poëme éternel!—La Bible?—Non, la terre" ("the old austere book,/The eternal poem!—the Bible?—No, the earth") (*OP2*: 584). He reads the landscape as he would a book:

> Et j'étudie à fond le texte, et je me penche,
> Cherchant à déchiffrer la corolle et la branche,
> Donc, courbé,—c'est ainsi qu'en marchant je traduis
> La lumière en idée, en syllabes les bruits. (584)

> (And I study the text thoroughly, and I bend over it,
> Seeking to decipher the corolla and the branch,
> So, hunched over,—it is thus that, while walking, I translate
> The light into an idea, and the noises into syllables.)

There is a tension in the way the poet describes what he does here, or rather what he is able to do. While he sometimes represents himself as attempting to decipher nature as text ("cherchant"), without any indication of the success of the effort, in the very same sentence he claims to be translating light into idea and sounds into syllables. This assertion, in terms of a knowledge claim, raises more questions than it answers. Is there some kind of knowledge content to be understood in nature, that is, is nature in the strict sense the equivalent of a book in that it has a communicable message? Or is this a simple case of inspiration, where nature leads the poet to compose his poetry? The claim seems to be stronger than that, but the status of translation is left undefined here. Given that translation is by definition not a perfect and transparent rendering of an original, there appears to be an unacknowledged rift between the possibility of transparent communication from nature and the necessarily deforming act of interpreting and then translating what nature says.

It is not, then, that this poem gives the lie to the claim to understand what nature says to us, or that we require a deconstructive move to undermine what the poem claims to say, but rather that Hugo has inscribed sharp irony into this poem where the explicit content of the poem, i.e. the act of interpreting nature transparently as a text, is met with more questions than answers in terms of what knowledge we may gain, through poetry, from nature. There is a fundamental silence in Hugo's implicit theory of poetry as it is laid out in this poem, a theory to which the poet refers, rather dismissively, as a "rêverie" (584). If such musings about the revelatory potential of nature via poetry are simply to be dismissed, however, how can we affirm any kind of visionary poetics? While it may be asking too much for a poem to provide the principles of its own interpretation, a poem such as "Je lisais. Que lisais-je? ... " does cast a long shadow over other poems that might make visionary knowledge claims, since in the very poem where these claims are rendered explicit, a full-fledged account of how this move can be anything more than mere "translation" of a potentially ineffable experience is missing. We arrive at the very opposite of the clarity that one might hope to find in this kind of "reading."

The poet's "reading"/reverie is interrupted by a swift speaking to the poet, and the poem then provides a direct rendering of what the bird "says." He encourages the poet:

> Lis toujours, lis sans cesse, ô penseur agité,
> Et que les champs profonds t'emplissent de clarté !...
> Lis. Il n'est rien dans tout ce que peut sonder l'homme
> Qui, bien questionné par l'âme, ne se nomme. (584)
>
> (Keep reading, read without end, oh agitated thinker,
> And may the deep fields fill you with clarity!...
> Read. There is nothing in all that man can probe
> Which, well questioned by the soul, cannot be named.)

The bird goes on to make cosmic claims about the possibilities to be found in this act of reading: since everything will presumably reveal (or "name") itself, truth will lead to virtue, since "Bien lire l'univers, c'est bien lire la vie" ("To read the universe well is to read life well") (585). While one might expect the poet to agree with, and find inspiration in, the swift's message, the poem ends with the poet's indication that the bird is mistaken and that, since the poet is human and mortal, "Mon âme ne sera blanche que dans la tombe;/Car l'homme, quoi qu'il fasse, est aveugle ou méchant" ("My soul will be white only in the grave;/For man, whatever he does, is blind or vicious") (585). He adds tersely: "Et je continuai la lecture du champ" ("And I continued my reading of the field") (585). The poet thus refutes the point of view expressed by the bird in what constitutes over one half of the poem, and casts doubt not only over the bird's message but also over the study, reading, and translating that he had been doing in this poem or any other. Knowledge claims are set up in this poem only to be refuted by the assertion, more plausible than what had gone before, that we are blind, and thus the only knowledge to be gained from such poetry is a negative one. Such is a rather astonishingly modern conclusion about the relation of poetry to knowledge, or, more accurately, ignorance, but as we shall see as this study progresses, poets since Hugo have needed to come to terms not so much with poetry's ability to communicate knowledge but rather with the way that poetry accounts for, and perhaps springs from, ignorance.

The kind of reading and translating that the poet attempts in "Je lisais … " is in the realm of private rather than shared knowledge. Even the bird's speech, after all, can only be the poet's own translation of the bird's song, unless we are being asked to imagine a magic talking bird, a possibility that the poem does not explicitly exclude but which it does not directly suggest either. To arrive at any definitive statement about what exactly the poet is doing when he is out "reading" the earth requires a considerable act of interpretation, and interpretation is the one category the poem refuses explicitly to name among the other verbs such as *lire*, *déchiffrer*, and *traduire*. The confidence of the vision that the bird announces suggests certainty but also ineffability. His last words are as follows: "Aussi tu deviens bon, juste et sage; et dans l'ombre/Tu reprends la candeur sublime du berceau" ("Thus you become good, just, and wise; and in the shadow/You regain the sublime candor of the cradle") (585). This assertion is, of course, exactly what the poet goes on to reject, but since in the final line of the poem he announces his return to "la lecture du champ," the reader is left to wonder whether other creatures will have contrasting messages to what the swift said, or whether the poet will go on stubbornly to reject any claims from nature about human beings' ability to read and understand life and live it well. If these claims are merely subject to continual rejection, they lose their status as knowledge claims, which would presumably call into question the entire enterprise of reading nature that the poet undertakes both at the beginning and end of the poem. While at first glance the poem seems to present a vision of transparent meaning and the almost mystical union of understanding, loving, and doing good, the very structure of the poem serves to call all of that into question and yet affirm the value of the (perhaps futile) act of reading nature. If there are knowledge claims at work here, they can be only negative ones, the categorical refusal of all the assertions in the long middle of the poem.

What is true of "Je lisais … " is just as true of some of the longest and most important "visionary" poems of *Les Contemplations*, such as "Magnitudo parvi." As in "Je lisais …," the vision here is presented under the sign of its impossibility:

> S'il nous était donné de faire
> Ce voyage démesuré,
> Et de voler, de sphère en sphère,
> A ce grand soleil ignoré…
> Ce qui t'apparaîtrait te ferait trembler, ange !…
> Et qu'il ne resterait de nous dans l'épouvante
> Qu'un regard ébloui sous un front hérissé ! (*OP2*: 616)

> (If it were given to us to make
> This enormous trip,
> And to fly, from sphere to sphere,
> To this great unknown sun…
> What would appear to you would make you tremble, Angel!…
> And in the fright nothing would remain of us
> Except a dazzled look under a bristling forehead!)

What poetry reveals is the impossibility of vision, the inaccessibility of extraordinary knowledge. As Jean Gaudon has remarked, the words of the poem seem to be attempting to fill a void that they are ultimately unable to fill:

> Dans un déchaînement de quatrains qui s'accumulent sans retenue, il s'abandonne à une sorte de fièvre mystique. Les strophes s'engouffrent dans le trou béant laissé par le monde sensible, comme si seul le verbe poétique pouvait remplir ce creux qui est l'image de la totalité, ce « Gouffre » qui est, en même temps, « Légion ». (379)

> (In an outburst of quatrains that accumulate without holding back, he abandons himself to a sort of mystical fever. The verses rush into the gaping hole left by the world of the senses, as if only the poetic word could fill this hole that is the image of the totality, this "Abyss" that is, at the same time, "Legion.")

The poem goes on to imagine a sort of alternate humanity:

> Sont-ils aussi des cœurs, des cerveaux, des entrailles?
> Cherchent-ils comme nous le mot jamais trouvé?
> Ont-ils des Spinosa qui frappent aux murailles,
> Des Lucrèce niant tout ce qu'on a rêvé… (*OP2*: 618)
>
> (Are they also hearts, brains, entrails?
> Do they seek, as we do, the word that is never found?
> Do they have Spinozas who knock at the walls,
> Lucretiuses denying all that we have dreamed…)

But this negative vision stands in stark contrast to other moments in the poem where the poet affirms that the shepherd of whom he writes does have access to a transcendent reality and truth:

> Dans le désert, l'esprit qui pense
> Subit par degrés sous les cieux
> La dilatation immense
> De l'infini mystérieux.
>
> Il plonge au fond. Calme, il savoure
> Le réel, le vrai, l'élément.
> Toute la grandeur qui l'entoure
> Le pénètre confusément. (626)
>
> (In the desert, the mind that thinks
> Undergoes by degrees under the heavens
> The immense expansion
> Of the mysterious infinity.
>
> It dives to the depths. Calm, it savors
> The real, the true, the element
> All the grandeur that surrounds it
> Penetrates it unintelligibly.)

What Hugo portrays is essentially a mystical vision devoid of linguistic content, at least as it is characterized here in the poem. The real and the true remain undescribed, and so the reader gains no insight about them other than the secondhand report that the shepherd has experienced them. Ironically, this turns poetry into the very sort of "reportage" that Mallarmé would criticize and oppose to true poetry a generation later.[3] On the view suggested by Hugo's poem, poetry is severely limited in its ability to produce, as opposed to reporting on, knowledge of the transcendent. Once again, the poet affirms that only through dying will we have access to more profound insight:

> ... —Mourir, c'est connaître;
> Nous cherchons l'issue à tâtons.
> J'étais, je suis, et je dois être.
> L'ombre est une échelle. Montons. —
>
> Il se dit: —Le vrai, c'est le centre.
> Le reste est apparence ou bruit. (627)
>
> (—To die is to know;
> We try to feel our way toward the exit.
> I was, I am, and I must be.
> The shadow is a ladder. Let's climb. —
>
> He says to himself: —The true is the center.
> The rest is appearance or noise.)

In terms of the relationship of poetry to language claims, Hugo presents a surprisingly traditional account here, suggesting that any full or complete understanding is unavailable to finite and imperfect humanity, and that therefore it is only in an afterlife of which we can have only a dim foretaste that we can hope to possess knowledge.

It would seem that a potential conclusion to draw is that poetry cannot transcend the more basic human limitations that Hugo evokes here, i.e. that it can describe but not overcome these sorts of limits, despite what Hugo's poetry might go on to claim in its more "visionary" moments. As a thoroughly human phenomenon, poetry would thus point to knowledge's limits or, at best, attempt to translate a mystical experience, with all of the attendant problems that translation brings as an imperfect medium for conveying an otherwise ineffable experience.[4]

It is indeed that kind of mystical experience that seems suggested by the shepherd's vision as portrayed in "Magnitudo parvi":

> Et, dépassant la créature,
> Montant toujours, toujours accru,
> Il regarde tant la nature,
> Que la nature a disparu !
>
> Car, des effets allant aux causes,
> L'œil perce et franchit le miroir,

Enfant; et contempler les choses,
C'est finir par ne plus les voir. (631)

(And, going beyond the creature,
Still climbing, still increased,
He looks so much at nature
That nature has disappeared!

For, going from the effects to the causes,
The eye pierces and goes through the mirror,
Child; and to contemplate things,
Is to end up no longer seeing them.)

The summit of this vision is a view of God himself, but the description of the entire vision here is in exclusively negative terms: disappearance, rather than knowledge, of earthly phenomena is the result of contemplation, and again, the role of poetry is merely to report the disappearance rather than doing the impossible task of communicating new knowledge. Children and simple figures such as the shepherd are the models, and the poet represents them, by implication, as closer to knowledge of ultimate reality than the poet could presumably hope to be, unless one were to posit the ultimate underlying unity of all people, a position that does find support in Hugo's famous claim in the preface to *Les Contemplations*, "Ah! insensé, qui crois que je ne suis pas toi" ("Oh! Insane one who thinks that I am not you!") (482). But such a systematic demolishing of the phenomenal world leaves us with only the slightest claims about what transcendent reality might be like, and furthermore, leaves open the question of what poetry might have to do with attaining access to it, given that human language is likely to be one of the phenomena that would disappear in the kind of experience described above. Whatever contemplation might be here, it is unlikely to involve speaking or writing.[5]

In that sense, there is something startlingly modern about Hugo's implied claims about poetry and knowledge here: rather than communicating a higher vision, his poetry *reports* on it via a description of an intermediate character (the shepherd), in the context of a collection that includes a poem that has advanced significant skepticism about the possibility of "reading" anything at all in the book of nature. After noting that the shepherd sees God, the poet indicates:

[Le pâtre] croit, il accepte. Il ignore
Le doute, notre escarpement;

> Le doute, qu'entourent les vides,
> Bord que nul ne peut enjamber,
> Où nous nous arrêtons stupides,
> Disant: Avancer, c'est tomber ! (632)
>
> ([The shepherd] believes, he accepts. He does not know
> Doubt, our slippery slope;
>
> Doubt, which the voids encircle,
> Shore that no one can step over,
> Where we stop, stunned,
> Saying: To move forward is to fall!)

What is canceled for this shepherd is precisely the doubts that Hugo raises about the poet's own function elsewhere in the collection. And while the placement of "Magnitudo parvi" later in the book might seem to cancel the doubts of "Je lisais …, " the fictional dating that Hugo employs in *Les Contemplations* suggests the opposite, with "Magnitudo parvi" assigned a date of 1839 and "Je lisais" a date of 1843. Poetry seems to play no role in the vision here: it is not part of the vision but rather an *ex post facto* report on the vision, and in the case of "Magnitudo parvi," of another, non-poet's, vision. Nor is poetry the source of the realization of ignorance, as it will be to some extent in the work of Philippe Jaccottet, for example. It is not via poetry that the poet comes to establish the limits of knowledge or of language. Just as in the case of knowledge, ignorance is merely reported on, rather than arrived at, in poetry or the poetic experience here.

Given the poet's conviction that humanity for the most part "plonge et rapporte le doute" ("dives and brings back doubt") (*OC2*: 762), and that it is only "par moments, perdus dans les nuits insondables," that "nous voyons s'éclairer de lueurs formidables/La vitre de l'éternité" ("we see the window of eternity lit up with terrific gleams") (763), it is hard to give credence to those moments in *Les Contemplations* that do claim that the poet, or others, have some sort of immediate access to transcendent reality. And again, in those moments, poetry seems reduced to the role of translation rather than active creation of that knowledge, a fact that maintains poetry in the role of reporting on a sometimes content-less vision. This is the case in "Les Mages," where the poet claims that these figures are capable of revelation:

> Oui, grâce aux penseurs, à ces sages,
> A ces fous qui disent: Je vois !

> Les ténèbres sont des visages,
> Le silence s'emplit de voix !…
> A leur voix, l'ombre symbolique
> Parle, le mystère s'explique. (791)

> (Yes, thanks to the thinkers, these sages,
> These crazy ones who say: I see!
> The shadows are faces,
> The silence fills up with voices!…
> At their voice, the symbolic shadow
> Speaks, the mystery is explained.)

The poet goes on to assert that from negative knowledge a positive one emerges:

> Ainsi s'accomplit la genèse
> Du grand rien d'où naît le grand tout.
> Dieu pensif dit: Je suis bien aise
> Que ce qui gisait soit debout.
> Le néant dit: J'étais souffrance;
> La douleur dit: Je suis la France !
> O formidable vision !
> Ainsi tombe le noir suaire;
> Le désert devient ossuaire
> Et l'ossuaire nation. (794–5)

> (Thus is accomplished the genesis
> Of the great nothing from which is born the great all.
> God, pensive, says: I am glad
> That everything that was lying down is now upright.
> Nothingness says: I was suffering;
> Pain says: I am France!
> Oh formidable vision!
> Thus falls the black shroud;
> The desert becomes an ossuary
> And the ossuary a nation.)

This vision of a speaking universe is reiterated in "Ce que dit la bouche d'ombre":

> Non, l'abîme est un prêtre et l'ombre est un poëte;
> Non, tout est une voix et tout est un parfum;
> Tout dit dans l'infini quelque chose à quelqu'un;
> Une pensée emplit le tumulte superbe.
> Dieu n'a pas fait un bruit sans y mêler le Verbe. (802)

(No, the abyss is a priest and the shadow is a poet;
No, everything is a voice and everything is a scent;
Everything says something to somebody in the infinite;
A thought fills the superb tumult.
God has not made a sound without mixing the Word in with it.)

Along with the poem's message of hope, there is also the implication of an invitation to trust that the Word is present in the universe to those who know how to decipher it. Such an assertion, however, does not carry us any further than earlier poems in the collection had in terms of the way such a Word can be expressed, transparently or otherwise, in poetry.[6] The poetic word here seems to serve as an affirmation that the Word exists, rather than claiming to be that word or even to translate it.[7]

What seems to be revelatory or visionary poetry in Hugo is never quite free from the danger that poetry and nature may not ultimately reveal truth. The practices of reading and interpretation are as crucial as they are hazardous in terms of the possibility that nature may prove illegible, that we may remain ignorant of truth or knowledge as it is mediated by translation. If we are not to give in to the temptation of an affirmation of mystical immediate illumination, Hugo's dependence on necessarily imperfect language risks contradicting some of his grander claims about the way poetry can reveal the world. And yet that weakness is itself a strength in that it allows poets and critics to shift the conversation about poetry and knowledge in order to take ignorance into account and to ask in what ways ignorance can be creative and productive. Ignorance is thus poised to become part and parcel of the lyric project through the tension it cultivates in its relation to knowledge.

Charles Baudelaire continues to cultivate that contradiction between knowledge and ignorance, and does so, paradoxically, by providing what looks at first glance like an affirmation of a strict division between truth and beauty, or philosophy and poetry. What may seem to be oppositions are soon revealed as far more complex interactions among poetry, knowledge, and ignorance. In those moments in his criticism and poetry where Baudelaire works through these issues, he ends up providing a highly speculative and suggestive route away from Hugo's visionary poetics, one that blurs the distinctions between knowing art and knowing the world through experience.[8]

Baudelaire's comments in "L'Art Philosophique," a text on which he worked for a decade but most especially in 1858–1860,[9] seem to establish a strict dividing line between art and philosophy, as he argues against philosophical art which he opposes, beginning in the very first sentence, to "l'art pur":

Qu'est-ce que l'art pur suivant la conception moderne ? C'est créer une magie suggestive contenant à la fois l'objet et le sujet, le monde extérieur à l'artiste et l'artiste lui-même.

Qu'est-ce que l'art philosophique suivant la conception de Chenavard et de l'école allemande ? C'est un art plastique qui a la prétention de remplacer le livre, c'est-à-dire de rivaliser avec l'imprimerie pour enseigner l'histoire, la morale et la philosophie....

Toute bonne sculpture, toute bonne peinture, toute bonne musique, suggère les sentiments et les rêveries qu'elle veut suggérer.

Mais le raisonnement, la déduction, appartiennent au livre. (*OC2*: 598)

(What is pure art according to the modern conception? It is to create a suggestive magic containing at the same time the object and the subject, the world external to the artist and the artist himself.

What is philosophical art according to the conception of Chenavard and the German school? It is a plastic art which has the pretention of replacing the book, that is, to rival printing to teach history, morality, and philosophy.

Every good sculpture, every good painting, all good music, suggests the emotions and the reveries that it wants to suggest.

But reason and deduction belong to the book.)

But these comments raise more questions than they answer. What seems clearest is that Baudelaire is opposed not so much to philosophy's presence in art as he is to an explicitly didactic function for art, as the reference to "enseigner" makes clear. To say that art should not teach is not the same as to maintain an absolute separation between art and philosophy. The question becomes all the more complicated when we attempt to extrapolate from these comments the relationship of philosophy to poetry specifically, since Baudelaire is concerned in this essay with the visual arts. Poetry, however, occupies an intermediary place between the visual arts and the "book," with which he associates philosophy here. This is something that Baudelaire himself acknowledges one page later, as he uses the word "poème" to describe a painting and immediately adds in parentheses: "nous sommes obligé de nous servir de cette expression en parlant d'une école qui assimile l'art plastique à la pensée écrite" ("we are obliged to use this expression in speaking of a school that assimilates plastic art to written thought") (2: 599). Are we simply to understand that in this context, "the book" is synonymous with philosophy and that poetry occupies some other space that would align it completely with the visual arts even though poetry is a verbal art, or is there more to this story? The "suggestive magic" with which Baudelaire opens this essay is replete with philosophical concerns in that it posits relationships of subjects and objects, art and the world.

What emerges is that Baudelaire's attack on didacticism is related to the notion of clarity, of immediate transparency: "Plus l'art voudra être philosophiquement clair, plus il se dégradera et remontera vers l'hiéroglyphe enfantin; plus au contraire l'art se détachera de l'enseignement et plus il montera vers la beauté pure et désintéressée" ("The more art wants to be philosophically clear, the more it degrades itself and heads back to childish hieroglyph; on the contrary, the more art detaches itself from instruction, the more it ascends toward pure and disinterested beauty") (2: 599). In that sense, philosophy plays a role not much different than any non-poetic use of language in that Baudelaire uses the term to stand for communicative clarity or immediate transparency, which is the kind of understanding that poetic language blocks, or at least complicates. While it might be tempting to see here nothing more than affirmation of art for art's sake, especially in light of the discourse of "purity" that Baudelaire adopts, I would argue that this refusal of transparency ultimately opens up urgent epistemological questions about poetry rather than shutting them down. Philosophy might be considered as a kind of straw man here, a key word meant to stand in for a clear or unified notion of truth. That kind of transparency might be what Hugo was aiming at in his verse, where poetry and truth seem to coincide in precisely the manner that Baudelaire is calling into question in his critique of the "hieroglyphic" model of art. Thus conceived, Baudelaire would be pointing here to a first affirmation of a fundamental reorientation of the question of poetry and knowledge, for if it does not aim at didactic truth, it does not simply dismiss philosophical content in the name of a putative artistic purity either.

Inasmuch as it is a verbal art, poetry can only with great difficulty be made to align with visual art, which in itself affirms a relationship to the world of perceptions inasmuch as it is a representational art. Baudelaire's comments signal a breakdown of the kind of unity that allowed Hugo to speak of truth revealed to the poet, and at the same time Baudelaire's approach opens wide a reconsideration of poetry where we are no longer in an either/or model as we were with Hugo: it is not that truth is communicated or not, but rather that it is reimagined in more complex negotiation between poetry and the sensual, experiential world. And in that sense, Baudelaire shifts the poetry and knowledge debate to an important reconsideration of exactly what poetry itself is. The question becomes one of poetry turning inward in a way, but that turn is not simply *away* from the experiential world. When poetry moves toward a self-definitional impulse, rather, it is precisely *because* of its relationship to the world, as Baudelaire will go on to acknowledge in ways I will enumerate below. If poetry is fundamentally about beauty, that assertion begs the question of what beauty is and how we might know it via poetry, which places us firmly back in the realm of poetry's philosophical relationship to knowledge claims.

In this light, we may reconsider and give new meaning to one of Baudelaire's more famous contentions about poetry, which appears in the "Notes nouvelles sur Edgar Poe" of 1857:

> La poésie ne peut pas, sous peine de mort ou de défaillance, s'assimiler à la science ou à la morale; elle n'a pas la Vérité pour objet, elle n'a qu'Elle-même. Les modes de démonstration de vérité sont autres et sont ailleurs. La Vérité n'a rien à faire avec les chansons. (2: 333)

> (Poetry cannot, under pain of death or breach of duty, assimilate itself to science or morality; it does not have Truth as its object, it has only Itself. The modes of demonstration of truth are other and elsewhere. Truth has nothing to do with songs.)

These lines are usually read as a proclamation of art for art's sake, the establishment of an autonomous and distinct conceptual space for art. And indeed Baudelaire's comments a few lines on confirm this sort of separation: "L'Intellect pur vise à la Vérité, le Goût nous montre la Beauté, et le Sens moral nous enseigne le Devoir" ("Pure intellect aims for Truth; Taste shows us Beauty, and the Moral Sense teaches us Duty") (2: 333). But if poetry has only itself for its object, this hardly removes us from epistemological concerns. Rather, it heightens them: if a claim is made for poetry existing on its own terms, an urgent question of definition emerges: what exactly is poetry and how may we delineate it from everything else in order to assign it its autonomous status? These definitional queries are variations on epistemological concerns: knowing poetry is itself a claim about knowledge. The very act of delineating poetry this way presupposes an epistemology whereby poetry can be known.[10] Knowledge thus does not simply disappear when we assert art's, and especially verbal art's, autonomy: rather, it emerges as an urgent question that is initially turned back onto poetry itself: what is poetry, and what is its relationship to the rest of reality from which it delineates itself but about which, presumably, it has something to say? Unless we are to abandon all claims to insight from poetry, and indeed all claims to referentiality, which would deprive the words of a poem of any semantic content whatsoever, this stance does imply knowledge about the world, and about poetry itself, that is unique to poetry. That is to say, it establishes poetry rather firmly as a mode of knowledge, in ways that poets far beyond Baudelaire's time will take up. In fact, as we shall come to see throughout this study, modern poets since Baudelaire have proposed abstract definitions of poetry that take us far beyond the metrical arrangement of words on the page into far more conceptual territory. In so doing, they demonstrate that defining poetry is at the same time attempting to characterize the kinds of knowledge claims it can make. If, then, poetry cannot, as Baudelaire points out, assimilate itself to science or morality, it does operate on terrain that we might associate with those discourses, and in so doing expands or reshapes both the potential of poetry itself and our conception of what poetry is. Knowing poetry thus becomes intimately caught up with the question of the kind of knowledge, about itself or otherwise, that poetry can or cannot generate.

One does not need to look much further in this same essay to find evidence that Baudelaire does make knowledge claims for poetry. One page on from the passage about poetry having only itself and not truth as its object, Baudelaire writes:

> C'est à la fois par la poésie et *à travers* la poésie, par et *à travers* la musique que l'âme entrevoit les splendeurs situées derrière le tombeau; et quand un poème exquis amène les larmes au bord des yeux, ces larmes ne sont pas la preuve d'un excès de jouissance, elles sont bien plutôt le témoignage d'une mélancolie irritée, d'une postulation des nerfs, d'une nature exilée dans l'imparfait et qui voudrait s'emparer immédiatement, sur cette terre même, d'un paradis révélé. (2: 334)

> (It is at the same time by poetry and *through* poetry, by and *through* music that the soul sees the splendors situated beyond the grave; and when an exquisite poem brings tears to the eyes, these tears are not the proof of an excess of pleasure, they are rather testimony of an irritated melancholy, a postulation of the nerves, a nature exiled in the imperfect and which would like to take hold immediately, on this very earth, of a revealed paradise.)

What does Baudelaire provide here if not a claim to truth as an important object of poetry? In fact, he pushes truth beyond empirical verification to metaphysical claims about eternal life known according to a model of revelation. What are we to make of these claims coexisting in the very same essay that asserts that poetry does not aim at Truth but rather at Beauty? One would have to engage in a process of redefinition of words such as "truth" in order not to see poetry as revealing it according to the model that Baudelaire presents here. This tension is not simply a result of a Romantic heritage that dies hard in Baudelaire even as he seeks something new; rather, it is a call to shape a definition of poetry that can accommodate simultaneously a truth-disclosing function and a refusal of certain kinds of truth that remain unspecified here.

The fact that "Science" can mean something akin to our contemporary use of the term, designating empirical enquiry into the material world, or more broadly something like "knowledge," already points to the fact that the kind of questioning to which poetry invites us is above all a definitional one, and a particularly modern one. Andrew Bowie has probed the ways in which "the rise of 'literature' and the rise of philosophical esthetics… are inseparable phenomena, which are vitally connected to changes in conceptions of truth in modern thought" (Bowie, *Romanticism* 1). This concomitant rise emerges in contradistinction to modern science's attempt to describe what a thing is, as opposed to how it is seen:

> What something is "seen as" is historically variable, in ways which cannot be circumscribed by a definitive scientific description of what the thing "really is." This approach begins to suggest good theoretical reasons why "literature" might continue to be a major source of the ways in which we make sense of the world…. Once one moves away from the presupposition that there is a final fact of the matter "out there," the question of interpretation, of how we understand the world through language, becomes the crucial issue. (Bowie, *Romanticism* 18)[11]

This approach does not so much cut off the world of language from the perceived world of lived experience so much as seek a model of poetry and poetic language that would be pliable enough to be negated and reconceptualized at any given time rather than eternally fixed. The fact that varying notions of "truth" could accommodate either a fixed or variable model of it suggests a certain plasticity in the idea of truth that it becomes the task of poetry in part to elucidate. This new task of poetry itself produces a kind of knowledge in turn; thus the very tension that Baudelaire sketches is one that is productive of a kind of knowledge that can be deduced from what he writes here, without his having made the claim explicitly. It might even be the case that such claims to knowledge seem, after all, to run against the grain of what he was explicitly trying to argue in this essay.

Ultimately, could one say that truth and beauty come to be made to live together via the conception of poetry that Baudelaire offers in this essay? He articulates that notion of poetry in light of what he terms "enthusiasm":

Ainsi le principe de la poésie est, strictement et simplement, l'aspiration humaine vers une beauté supérieure et la manifestation de ce principe est dans un enthousiasme, une excitation de l'âme, —enthousiasme tout à fait indépendant de la passion qui est l'ivresse du cœur, et de la vérité qui est la pâture de la raison. (*OC*2: 334)

(Thus the principle of poetry is, strictly and simply, the human aspiration toward a superior beauty and the manifestation of this principle is in an enthusiasm, an excitation of the soul, —an enthusiasm totally independent of the passion which is the intoxication of the heart, and of the truth which is the food of reason.)

Baudelaire works hard in this essay to maintain a strict distinction between poetry and truth, but as I have been suggesting, the more one attempts to articulate what poetry is or should be, the more one becomes caught up in knowledge claims. To say that enthusiasm is the manifestation of supreme beauty is to claim to know something both about beauty and about the way it manifests itself. That seems obvious, of course, but to recognize these as knowledge claims is necessarily to complicate the blanket dismissal of truth as comprising an entirely separate domain. To say as much is not to condemn Baudelaire for inconsistency or blind spots about his own arguments; rather, it is to say that he complicates the model of the relationship of poetry to truth as it was found in a poet such as Hugo. At the same time, Baudelaire prepares the way for a long line of poets for whom to engage with poetry is to attempt to delineate its borders and identify the extent to which a modern notion of poetry itself depends on its being a kind of malleable knowledge that intersects with truth in complex ways that shift and are transformed by every attempt to articulate what poetry is and does. That is to say that each time a poet writes a statement that begins, "poetry is ...," there is a new effort to empty the conception of poetry and offer a (contingent and provisional) new claim about it. Such contingency is not a defect in poetry's knowledge but rather the very heart of it according to the conception that we can see beginning to take place in Baudelaire.

This is also where we can see an important split developing between poems and poetry, with the latter becoming a discourse with a sort of life of its own, independent of a relation to poems. Characterizations and definitions of poetry begin to move further from empirical descriptions of the words on the page that collectively form a poem and toward more abstract considerations whose relations to actual poems become a problem to be addressed rather than a simple given.[12] As this happens, one important distinction to be drawn between poetry and poems is their relationship to conclusions and concluding. Poems, by necessity, no matter how open-ended they might be in form or interpretive possibilities, conclude. In that sense they are teleologically oriented, and they share this orientation toward a conclusion with philosophy, which as a process aims at the conclusions at which it will ultimately arrive. While some of Baudelaire's poems employ a kind of circular structure that weakens this drive toward conclusion, when it comes to a relationship to conclusion, poems do share more of an affinity with philosophy than the more open-ended characterization of "poetry" that I am beginning to trace. If poetry has only itself for its object, attempts to seize the nature of that object are anything but definitive and form their own types of knowledge claims in ways for which Baudelaire prepares the ground that others will travel after him.

We have seen that the claim that poetry has only itself, rather than truth, for its object does not remove us from the realm of truth claims, insofar as such a statement presupposes a truth claim about poetry and thus claims knowledge of the nature of poetry. It does, however, reorient the notion of truth involved. As Catherine Witt has noted, "Experience is Baudelaire's answer to system" (29). Baudelaire finds fault with system in his essay on the Exposition Universelle of 1855, indicating that "un système est une espèce de damnation qui nous pousse à une abjuration perpétuelle; il en faut toujours inventer un autre, et cette fatigue est un cruel châtiment" ("a system is a kind of damnation that pushes us toward a perpetual renunciation; one must always invent another one, and that fatigue is a cruel punishment") (OC2: 577). The problem he identifies with systems is their insufficiency in the face of new experiences for which they cannot account:

> Et toujours un produit spontané, inattendu, de la vitalité universelle venait donner un démenti à ma science enfantine et vieillotte, fille déplorable de l'utopie. J'avais beau déplacer ou étendre le criterium, il était toujours en retard sur l'homme universel, et courait sans cesse après le beau multiforme et versicolore, qui se meut dans les spirales infinies de la vie. (2: 577–8)

> (And always a spontaneous and unexpected product of the universal vitality came to give the lie to my childish and antiquated science, deplorable daughter of utopia. In vain I tried to displace or extend the criterium, it was always lagging beyond universal man, and endlessly ran after the many-sided and multicolored beautiful, which transformed into the infinite spirals of life.)

What Baudelaire criticizes here is not so much systems qua systems as the fact that they necessarily escape the completion to which they aspire. To say that a system is inadequate to capture "the many-sided and multicolored beautiful" is not, as his remarks in the Edgar Poe essay might have suggested, to say that poetry has nothing to do with truth, but, once again, to make a truth claim about beauty that allows, perhaps even within a system, for one of its characteristics to be that it defies efforts to capture and understand it fully. Here we glimpse an aspect of negative knowledge, an awareness of the limits of our claims to understand "poetry" as a manifestation of the beautiful. The fact that these sorts of claims can be extrapolated from what Baudelaire writes above gives the lie to what he goes on to say about a kind of modesty to be found in navïeté: "Pour échapper à l'horreur de ces apostasies philosophiques, je me suis orgueilleusement résigné à la modestie: je me suis contenté de sentir; je suis revenu chercher un asile dans l'impeccable naïveté" ("To escape the horror of these philosophical apostasies, I have pridefully resigned myself to modesty: I have become content to feel; I came back to seek shelter in impeccable naïveté") (2: 578). To identify a need for modesty in our pronouncements about poetry and its relationship to beauty (or to knowledge, or to the perceptual world) is not quite the same as evacuating all attempts at conceptualizing these relationships and rejecting them in favor of pure sensation. Modesty—or one might even say skepticism—in the face of the more grandiose claims to account for the world in terms of philosophical systems is indeed a recommendable goal, but such a thing, I hope to have suggested by now, is attainable within the act of thinking and writing about poetry, which produces a kind of knowledge, however tentative, incomplete, and open to perpetual revision.

In fact, Baudelaire's reflections on art here bring him back to the idea of wonder, that most basic of pre-philosophical categories according to Aristotle.[13]

> Tant il est vrai qu'il y a dans les productions multiples de l'art quelque chose de toujours nouveau qui échappe éternellement à la règle et aux analyses de l'école ! L'étonnement, qui est une des grandes jouissances causées par l'art et la littérature, tient à cette variété même des types et des sensations. (2: 578)
>
> (It is so true that there is in the many productions of art something always new that eternally escapes the rules and analysis of the school! Surprise, which is one of the great pleasures caused by art and literature, requires this very variety of types and sensations.)

Here Baudelaire seems to suggest wonder as an endpoint whereas for philosophy it is traditionally a beginning. Neither view excludes modesty or humility, and by coming full circle to what is for philosophers the starting point of their inquiry, Baudelaire, paradoxically perhaps, makes room for a new kind of thought that would allow us to build a relationship between poetry and knowledge rather than merely abandoning the subject to mere conceptless perception and pure sensation. Remaining at the level of pure sensation would preclude the experience of reading or writing poetry, which mediates sensation via language.

Two of Baudelaire's prose poems put these issues of experience and knowedge within situations that reinforce the kinds of skepticism and infinitely revisable approaches to knowledge that his theoretical writings have implied. "Laquelle est la vraie?" presents, under the guise of an allegory, an engagement with questions of the veracity of the ideal. The poet recounts knowing "une certaine Bénédicta, qui remplissait l'atmosphère d'idéal" ("a certain Benedicta, who filled the atmosphere with the ideal" (*OC1*: 342/*Prowler* 98). He buries her upon her death just a few days after his having met her, only to see another person who resembles the first and who says with a laugh, "C'est moi, la vraie Bénédicta ! C'est moi, une fameuse canaille! Et pour la punition de ta folie et de ton aveuglement, tu m'aimeras telle que je suis" ("it is I, the true Benedicta! It is I, a first-class riffraff! And to punish your madness and your blindness, you will love me as I am!" (342/98). The narrator refuses so violently that he buries his leg up to the knee in the freshly dug ground near the grave where he remains "attaché, pour toujours peut-être, à la fosse de l'idéal" ("fettered, perhaps forever, to the grave of the ideal") (342). The vivid imagery of the poet stubbornly refusing to give up attachment to the ideal might make readers forget that the question posed in the title of the poem remains unanswered here. The violence of the poet's gesture interrupts any sort of deliberation or appeal to evidence that would allow us to determine what is real and what is illusory, or even hallucinatory. No appeal to either system or experience can answer the question, which in this poem becomes the question of poetry itself in its relation, real or imagined, to the ideal. The unanswered and unanswerable question about identifying the "true" Benedicta leads us to a view of poetry whereby its role is not to lead to knowledge but to the unresolvable nature of the question itself. Poetry becomes both the site of questioning and the performative indication that not knowing is the state toward which modern poetry tends.[14] This is not to claim a kind of defeatism or a simple refusal of the more robust kinds of knowledge claims that Romantic poetry established for itself, but rather to be aware that neither system nor (*pace* Baudelaire's theoretical writings) experience can provide a foundation of certain knowledge.

Wonder leads to knowledge of the very limits of conventional knowledge, and Baudelaire's poetry both shows the limits of experiential knowledge and begins to suggest the ways in which poetry might serve as an exploration of a particular kind of knowledge unavailable by other means. This kind of knowledge touches on the sublime, which, as Andrew Bennett characterizes it, is "an effect of, or is itself a form of ignorance, of not knowing.... Astonishment—the experience of the sublime—is an ignorance effect" (Bennett 61). Likewise, as Kevin McLaughlin has argued, while Kant considered poets to be able to communicate "the feeling of the supersensible force of reason" (McLaughlin xii), their language expresses simultaneously the "capacity and the incapacity to communicate the feeling of the divisive finitude of reason as a force and an unforce" (xiii).[15] "Laquelle est la vraie?" gives us the means by which to ask the question while implicitly endorsing a lack of means by which to obtain the answer. And crucially, it nearly imperceptibly shifts the question from "which is the true?" to "how would we know?" Given that the poem never answers the question in the title, readers are left to wonder whether it is better to relegate the notion of "truth" to the category of the "ideal" that is called into question in the poem. Since poetry does not have truth for its object according to Baudelaire, the question necessarily becomes to some extent meaningless when posed in a poem. The fact that these questions are posed within the terrain of a poem, however, gives epistemological weight to the question of what the poem might have to say about not only how we (or the poet) would know which is the true Benedicta but also how we might pose the question of poetry's knowledge in the first place.

"La chambre double" is a prose poem which, like "Laquelle est la vraie ?," foregrounds a juxtaposition of the ideal and the real. A crucial but frequently overlooked aspect of "La chambre double" is the way it handles knowledge claims and the way it affirms not so much the ideal or illusion as a certain kind of ignorance. The poet's reaction to the idealized space of the room in the first half of the poem is often couched in terms that emphasize the presence or absence of knowledge about the room and the circumstances that bring it into being and cause it to be perceived. The pleasant space of the first half of the poem is described in negative terms: "Sur les murs, nulle abomination artistique.... Ici, tout a la suffisante clarté et la délicieuse obscurité de l'harmonie" ("No artistic abomination on the walls.... Everything here possesses the abundant light and delicious darkness of harmony") (*OC1*: 280/*Prowler* 6). The harmony of light and dark is made possible by the absence of the kind of art that would cancel it, and the perceiving subject in this space is described as an "esprit sommeillant...

bercé par des sensations de serre chaude" ("drowsy mind… lulled by hothouse sensations") (1: 280). The light and dark harmony spurs the subject not to action or lively thought or even careful attention but rather to sleep, to a state of nonconscious being in which pure sensation seems to replace mental activity. When pure perception does give way to curious wonder in the next paragraph, as the poet notes that "sur le lit est couchée l'Idole, la souveraine des rêves" ("on this bed lies the Idol, the sovereign queen of dreams") and then immediately asks: "Mais comment est-elle ici ? Qui l'a amenée ?" ("But how did she get here? Who brought her?"), he immediately answers himself: "Qu'importe ? la voilà ! je la reconnais" ("What difference does it make? Here she is! I recognize her!") (280). Questions are raised only to be dismissed rather than answered, in a gesture that finds its confirmation a bit further on in the poem when the poet inquires: "A quel démon bienveillant dois-je d'être ainsi entouré de mystère, de silence, de paix et de parfums ?" ("What benevolent demon has thus surrounded me with mystery, peace, and aromas?") (281). The ability to refuse knowledge and embrace mystery is celebrated and linked to a notion of timelessness: "Non ! Il n'est plus de minutes, il n'est plus de secondes ! Le temps a disparu; c'est l'Eternité qui règne, une éternité de délices !" ("No! There are no more minutes, there are no more seconds! Time has disappeared. Eternity now reigns, an eternity of delights") (281). Rather than associating eternity with a state of all knowingness, this release from temporality brings peace by also putting epistemological questions to rest.

The release from time is itself shown to be temporary, of course, and in fact illusory, a dreamlike state that is abruptly interrupted by a loud knock on the door. The knock announces not just a return to temporality but also the persistence of epistemological questions about conscious and actual reality as opposed to unconscious and illusory reality. Furthermore, the return to reality shows that it is impossible to affirm mystery and silence, since in the midst of that bliss the poet was indeed making knowledge claims by affirming that time had disappeared. Making even negative claims implies being anchored in knowledge, even if one claims to be beyond the realm of knowledge; the poem thus illustrates, perhaps despite itself, the impossibility of the very claims it advances about the negation of knowledge. And once again the poem itself becomes the site of questioning knowledge and its limits and proposing a situated and contextual approach to knowledge that it illustrates by only seeming to negate temporality within a poem whose very structure depends on the temporality of a before vs. after.

In contrast to the poems of Hugo where knowledge claims, however vague the content of the actual vision may be, are explicit, epistemological questions are to a large extent implicit in Baudelaire. While the title "Laquelle est la vraie?" poses an explicit question about truth or reality, we have seen that the larger epistemological question of "How would we know?" is only implied by the poem, despite its crucial importance for being able to answer the question of the title. This is a feature that the poem shares with the critical articles we analyzed above; this epistemological terrain brings Baudelaire's poetry and criticism a step closer to each other. And by doing so, I would argue, Baudelaire's writings shift the terrain of writing and thinking about poetry away from the assumption, in the wake of Romanticism, that poetry does indeed have revelatory powers that it is the task of readers and writers of poetry to decode. Baudelaire's writings move us toward a more complex epistemological ground whereby poetry's form of knowledge is affirmed but not taken for granted, being instead posed as an implicit problem embedded in the act of writing and reading poetry generally.[16]

Later modernist poets take this explicit positing of the poet's knowledge or ignorance a step further. Such is the case in "Les Fiançailles" by Guillaume Apollinaire, first published in 1908 and later included in *Alcools*. The fifth of these poems takes up the question of the poet's ignorance:

Pardonnez-moi mon ignorance
Pardonnez-moi de ne plus connaître l'ancien jeu des vers
Je ne sais plus rien et j'aime uniquement
Les fleurs à mes yeux redeviennent des flammes
Je médite divinement
Et je souris des êtres que je n'ai pas créés
Mais si le temps venait où l'ombre enfin solide
Se multipliait en réalisant la diversité formelle de mon amour
J'admirerais mon ouvrage (*OP* 132)

(Pardon me my ignorance
Pardon my not knowing the old game of verse
I don't know anything anymore and I only love
Flowers in my eyes become flames again
I meditate divinely
And I smile at the beings that I have not created
But if the time when the shadow, finally solid,
Multiplied in achieving the formal diversity of my love
I would admire my work)

At first the ignorance is related to the composition of traditional verse in meter and rhyme, and the poet ironically begs pardon for abandoning traditional forms. This abandonment of meter is visible in the narrative arc of the series of poems in "Les Fiançailles" themselves, which begin with a poem in alexandrines. It becomes clear as "Pardonnez-moi … " progresses that this forgetting of traditional forms is linked to larger questions of poetic ignorance. What is important to note is that poetic ignorance is not primal; rather, it comes after a period of knowledge, a fact highlighted by the two-fold "ne … plus" construction. Ignorance is not a primordial condition that can progress to knowledge, but is instead something more like a forgetting of what was formerly known or at least thought to be known. This point is even clearer if we consider an earlier version of this section, titled "Le Printemps" and published in 1902, which begins: "Pardonnez-moi d'avoir reconquis mon ignorance" ("Pardon for having regained my ignorance") (1068). The fruit of poetic labor, then, is this learned ignorance, a sort of emptying out of knowledge that occurs simultaneously with the emptying out of traditional form. The poem can be seen as a ground zero point for a poetry that moves beyond the questionable revelations claimed by some earlier poets; the poem seeks to reorient the poetic experience in a way that preserves part of its heritage while seeking not to replace one kind of poetic knowledge with another but rather to explore a poetics of ignorance.

The immediate result of this new poetics is a passive poet, not in the sense of one who receives some sort of mystical vision but rather one who seeks direct experience by calculated passive attentiveness. Poetic meditation still retains a place in this new schema, but not in service of any achieved vision. Creation comes in the form of non-creation, and the poem itself becomes a kind of record of a lack of revelation. The fact that the poem gives rise to questions of whether such passive revelationless poetic experience is possible testifies to poetry's impossibility of being simply synonymous with ignorance or nothingness, since once a poem has been written on the page, nothingness is necessarily canceled. This is a paradox that Stéphane Mallarmé had explored in the tercets of "Surgi de la croupe et du bond":

Le pur vase d'aucun breuvage
Que l'inexhaustible veuvage
Agonise mais ne consent,

Naïf baiser des plus funèbres !
A rien expirer annonçant
Une rose dans les ténèbres. (*OC1*: 42)[17]

(The pure vase of no drink
That the inexhaustible widowhood
Agonizes but does not consent,

Naïve kiss of the most funerary kind!
To breathe out nothing announcing
A rose in the darkness.)

The rose that is not a rose except by its presence in the poem takes on a curious ontological status and complicates the relationship of the poetic image to the world it supposedly represents at least to some extent. The poetic objects in Apollinaire's poem thus tend toward some sort of pure poetic object, but this removal from the world of lived experience does not seem to be the goal of the poet of "Les Fiançailles." Quite the opposite in fact, since the poet in his role as observer maintains a close relation to the perceived world and, if anything, resists the recasting of that world into purportedly pure poetic terms. This is evident in the following poem of "Les Fiançailles," "J'observe le repos du dimanche" (133), where the poet wonders: "Comment comment réduire/L'infiniment petite science/Que m'imposent mes sens" ("How how to reduce/The infinitely little knowledge/That my senses impose on me?") (133), but not in the name of poetic transformation of the world into a poeticized ideal. Rather, in this Sunday rest where the poet "loue la paresse" ("Praises laziness") (133), the desired end seems to be a kind of nothingness.

Returning to "Pardonnez-moi…," the last three lines announce a hypothetical scenario whereby the world would transform itself without any intervention on the part of the poet at all. If the solid shadow were to multiply and take form, the poet would admire what he deems "my work," simultaneously claiming ownership of it and taking distance from it by contemplating it as if it had not issued from himself as his creation. This is more than just a Mallarméan indication of the desire to "cede[r] l'initiative aux mots" ("cede the initiative to the words themselves") (*OC2*: 211), since the "work" in question seems to be not a poem but something with external form in the perceptual world. All of this suggests that the ignorance the poet claims to possess is as difficult to achieve as a complete elimination of perceptual sense data. The poet's difficulty in laying his senses and thus his mind to rest are evident in the development of "J'observe le repos …, " where each sense is evoked as producing frightening and monstrous results:

Monstre du mon ouïe tu rugis et tu pleures
Le tonnerre te sert de chevelure

> Et tes griffes répètent le chant des oiseaux
> Le toucher monstrueux m'a pénétré m'empoisonne (Apollinaire 133)

> (Monster of my hearing you roar and you cry
> Thunder serves as your hairdo
> And your claws repeat the song of the birds
> The monstrous touch penetrated me and poisons me.)

Taking a step back, we see that the ignorance so casually (and perhaps ironically) announced by the poet is not easily won, and may be in fact an impossible ideal rather than an achieved status. With the disappearance of the "ancient game of verses" also goes a set of assumptions about the relationship of poetry to the world from which it springs and which it is not possible simply to cast aside, an idea given formal echo in the quasi-regular lines of these poems.

What these poems of Apollinaire announce is not so much the achieved ignorance of the poet so much as a necessary tension between the desired nothingness and the poetic word which is always necessarily expressive and creative unless we are to consider it as sheer non-sense. This tension is complemented by a second one between the perceptual world and the supposedly pure poetic object. Once we begin to grapple with the problem of how a poetic word could have its origin in the perceptual world and yet come to take its distance from it, we are once again within the epistemological domain of questions about how we know the perceptual and poetic worlds and on what basis we can classify them as such. In other words, and this is crucial, there is a parallel between, on one hand, the impossible abolition of the poetic object, which remains insofar as it is inscribed in a poem on the page, and the impossibility of poetic ignorance, which remains dependent on a set of knowledge claims about what is known and unknown and therefore participates in the opposite of ignorance even while attempting to posit it. In the twentieth century, these knowledge claims turn increasingly to an interrogation of what poetry is and whether we could adequately define it in words, and it is to that question that I turn in chapter two.

2

Saying the Ineffable: Poetry Is Poetry (From the Romantics to Valéry)

As we have seen in chapter one, poetry's relationship to the real is at stake when we begin to ask epistemological questions about what poetry is and does. In this chapter, our pursuit of those questions will bring us to Novalis's tautological affirmation that "poetry is poetry" (*Schriften* 3: 685), and our attempts to come to terms with the consequences of such a definition will lead us to acknowledge that much of modern poetry's engagement both with definition and with its relationship to the real can be traced back to a set of conceptual issues first raised by the German Romantics.[1] Friedrich Schlegel identified the difficulty of providing any sort of positivistic definition of poetry and echoes the tautological definition: "A definition of poetry can only determine what poetry should be, not what it really was and is; otherwise the shortest definition would be that poetry is whatever has at any time and at any place been called poetry" (Schlegel, *Philosophical* 31). Defining poetry definitively suggests that poetry has already been achieved, and in Schlegel's conception, poetry is "still in the state of becoming; that, in fact, is its real essence: that should forever be becoming and never be perfected" (32). Twentieth-century figures continue to evoke this living heritage of Romanticism. Pierre Reverdy, for example, writes in 1927: "On a voulu tuer le romantisme. Il a la vie dure, il fallait le tuer.... Quand on s'est débarrassé du romantisme on est tombé généralement dans une désolante platitude" ("They wanted to kill Romanticism. It dies hard; it was necessary to kill it.... When we rid ourselves of Romanticism, we generally fell into an appalling platitude") (Reverdy 546). As I hope to show, of the many meanings that could be assigned to Romanticism, what is at stake for poets, at least when it comes to characterizing poetry's epistemological enterprise, is the potentially autoreflective conception of literature whereby literature comes to be synonymous in some sense with the world at large, a stance which immediately problematizes the relationship between poetry and the world (or, we could say, subject and object of knowledge) by obliterating the distinction. At the same time, the Jena Romantics also put into question the distinction between literature and theory in ways that have proven fruitful for twentieth-century writers about poetry and poetics. As Philippe Lacoue-Labarthe and Jean-Luc Nancy claim, Romanticism is "la théorie elle-même comme littérature ou, cela revient au même, la littérature se produisant en produisant sa propre théorie" (*L'absolu* 22) ("*theory itself as* literature or, in other words, literature producing itself as it produced its own theory. The literary absolute is also, and perhaps above all, this absolute *literary operation*" (*Literary* 12)).[2] All of the poets I will discuss have to some extent, sometimes implicitly and sometimes explicitly, engaged with these issues, and it is in that sense that Reverdy is right to claim that Romanticism both must be killed and cannot be killed, since "killing" it would essentially foreclose some of the most important questions that poets have addressed concerning the nature and function of their art.

Reverdy goes on immediately to link lyricism and reality in his program for what is to be done in the face of the impossibility of killing Romanticism:

> Or, ce qu'il faut faire, qui est très simple mais extrêmement difficile, c'est fixer le lyrisme de la réalité. Et là devrait se borner tout le rôle de l'art, impuissant à rivaliser avec la réalité mais réellement propre à en fixer le lyrisme, que les artistes seuls sont aptes à bien dégager. On pourrait tirer de là cette définition: l'art est l'ensemble des moyens propres à fixer le lyrisme mouvant et émouvant de la réalité. (546)

> (Now, what must be done, something very simple but extremely difficult, is to pin down the lyricism of reality. And there should be the limit of the whole role of art, unable to rival reality but really fitting for pinning its lyricism down; artists are the only ones who are well suited to bring it out. One could develop this definition from that: art is the whole of the means suitable for pinning down the moving lyricism of reality.)

Here we see reflected the uneasy relationship between art and reality whereby Reverdy is hesitant to remove the link between them while at the same time he is incapable of affirming their unproblematic and easily defined relationship. The move that results from his line of thinking is crucial: from his attempt to characterize the relationship of art to the real (that is, the epistemological question of how art allows us to know the external world beyond it and beyond ourselves), he swerves at the end of the passage just quoted to a definition of art itself. This is, no less than the other quest, an epistemological project, but this time the question of definition is turned on art itself. It is equally crucial to note that this impetus toward definition is not made in a *refusal* of the relationship of art to the real, in some kind of decadent withdrawal from the world into a hyperestheticism, but rather in an attempt to engage the complexity of that relationship. When art turns to define itself here, it does so in a way that asserts but cannot describe what exactly we might mean by "le lyrisme mouvant et émouvant de la réalité." This definitional solution, in other words, calls for further commentary in a way that keeps those who would seek to define either art or reality engaged in the epistemological complexity implied, but not always consciously recognized, by the task.

As Reverdy expands this conception of poetry in later writings, it remains clear that poetry retains its status as its own reality but one whose existence is irrevocably linked to the reality on which it depends in order to transform it:

> Le poète est un transformateur de puissances—la poésie, c'est du réel humanisé, transformé, comme la lumière électrique est la transformation d'une énergie redoutable et meurtrière à trop haute tension. Au réel vrai le poète substitue le réel imaginaire. Et c'est le pouvoir, ce sont les moyens d'élever ce réel imaginaire à la puissance de la réalité matérielle et de la dépasser en la transmuant en valeur émotive qui constitue proprement la poésie. (277–8)[3]

> (The poet is a transformer of powers—poetry is the real humanized, transformed, as electric light is the transformation of a formidable and murderous high-tension energy. The poet substitutes the imaginary real for the true real. And that is the power and the means to elevate that imaginary real to the power of material reality and to surpass it in transmuting it into emotive value that properly constitutes poetry.)

There is a tension in this extended definition of poetry between a state of being ("the humanized real") and a potential or action ("the means to elevate that imaginary real to the power of material reality"), the latter suggesting that poetry does not exist on its own terms as an object or a product but rather as a kind of catalyst, a dynamic force that does not even create the "imaginary real" but rather simply elevates it. Reverdy does not define exactly what constitutes, or differentiates, the two kinds of real he identifies here, true and imaginary, but he brings the definitional question back to the human subject by the final move toward the transformation into an "emotive value." Reverdy goes on to suggest that this operation has an important liberating potential:

Sans ce pouvoir de substituer au réel l'image qu'il s'en fait et d'établir son monde d'après cette image, et non pas seulement d'après cette image, et non pas seulement d'après les données exactes du réel, l'homme en serait resté étroitement l'esclave et sa condition ne se serait pas élevée au-dessus de celle des autres êtres qui vivent ou végètent à ses côtés. C'est pourquoi, il faut voir dans la poésie le plus haut et le plus efficace moyen de libération mis en œuvre par l'homme pour accomplir, malgré les asservissantes exigences de la nature, sa fabuleuse destinée. (1277–8)

(Without this power to substitute for the real the image that he makes of it and to establish his world according to this image, and not only according to this image, and not only according to the exact givens of the real, man would have narrowly remained its slave and his condition would not have been elevated above that of other beings who live or vegetate alongside him. That is why one must see in poetry the highest and most effective means of liberation put in place by man to accomplish, despite the subjugating demands of nature, his fabulous destiny.)

For every celebratory affirmation of the liberating and even ennobling aspects of the poetic project that Reverdy describes here, however, there is an anxiety over the possibility of achieving, as opposed to simply affirming, this potential. I turn briefly to two contemporary poets to illustrate alternative ways of sketching the relationship between the real and the definition of poetry, to show that what happens between the early and late twentieth centuries is not so much a cancellation of Reverdy's vision as, rather, a putting into tension that allows his vision to remain, but only if called into question. That questioning, in turn, becomes part and parcel of the definition of poetry itself.

Poet and critic Jean-Claude Pinson points to a contemporary retreat, among lyric poets, from the excesses of Romanticism's claims about poetry: "La poursuite du réel le plus contingent qui est aujourd'hui au cœur de mainte parole lyrique renvoie en effet à une habitation poétique où la poésie, après la mort des Muses, se délivre des excès de la spéculation et se guérit de cet asthme « ontalgique » dont se moquait Queneau" ("The pursuit of the most contingent real that is today at the heart of much lyrical language refers back to a poetic dwelling where poetry, after the death of the Muses, frees itself from the excesses of speculation and heals itself from this 'ontological' asthma that Queneau mocked" (*Habiter* 19). In a move that distances himself from the more abstract language-focused poets and aligns him with neo-lyricists, Pinson reaffirms poetry's relationship to the real:

On ne jure plus en effet aujourd'hui par le texte seul. On se souvient à nouveau qu'il y a du « hors texte », qu'un monde (à défaut d'un ciel) est « par-delà » le texte, monde que le poète a en point de mire, sans que le référent ainsi visé soit assignable à une quelconque métaphysique du sens, sans qu'il soit question pour autant de revenir à l'ancien ordre des choses et de faire à nouveau de l'œuvre un simple reflet de l'existence. (19)

(We swear only by the text nowadays. We remember once more that there is a "beyond the text," that a word (in the face of the lack of a heaven) is "beyond" the text, a world that the poet has as a target, without the referent thus aimed at being assignable to whatever metaphysics of meaning, without it being a question of returning to the former order of things and to make once more of the work a simple reflection of existence.)

This is not a mere reactionary move, however, one that would seek to act as though deconstruction had not fundamentally altered the way we think about the relationship of words to reality. What emerges above all here, rather, is a sense of humility in the face of defining the poetic task, and a hesitancy to affirm a direct link to reality (or even a transparent relationship to it) just as much as a categorical refusal of such a relationship. It is, in a word, an opening up of poetry to a multiplicity of potentials, and at the same time an acknowledgment of the unease that such an opening can generate. As Michel Deguy puts it: "Ce singulier, 'la poésie,' loin de dénoter l'unité circonscriptible d'un genre, d'un objet, d'un corpus, etc., appelle (au sens où on dit « J'ai appelé ma fille Sophie ») l'inquiétude du langage sur ses possibilités, sa destination, ses limites; langage et sujet du langage bien sûr; formes et expérience" ("This singular word, 'poetry,' far from denoting the circumscribable unity of a genre, of a corpus, etc., calls (in the sense whereby one says 'I called my daughter Sophie') for worry on the part of language about its possibilities, its destination, its limits; language and the subject of language, of course, forms and experience") (*La raison* 13). It is, furthermore, an anti-systematic stance, one that for the very reasons of the humility implied in this view refuses to take a more definitive step in terms of characterizing the precise nature of the relationship of poetry to the real, even while it affirms that such a relation must exist.

Jean-Marie Gleize, writing, like Pinson, in the early nineties, also looks back to the earlier twentieth century, identifying a continuity between René Char's poetics and the Romantic heritage he inherits. Gleize sets up an opposition between that stance and the kind of affirmation about poetry that is possible today: "René Char (ou « le poète » puisque ici il définit un rôle) croit en l'avenir, en l'inscription prophétique de l'avenir dans la poésie oraculaire, hermétiquement oraculaire; en la poésie qui dit la vérité, de la vérité; en la poésie, c'est une autre de ses formules, « connaissance productive du réel »" ("René Char (or 'the poet' since here he is defining a role) believes in the future, in the prophetic inscription of the future in oracular, hermetically oracular, poetry; in poetry that tells the truth, of truth; in poetry, and this is another of his formulations, 'productive knowledge of the real'") (101). Gleize rejects this vision of poetry as "salvatrice ou rédemptrice, réconciliatrice, bienfaisante et nécessaire" ("salvific or redemptive, reconciliatory, beneficial and necessary") (102) and goes on to indicate poetry's current non-existence or, rather, its transformation into crisis:

> « La poésie » n'existe pas, n'existe plus, ce qui ne signifie pas, bien sûr, le tarissement de la pratique poétique, mais… que la poésie vit son état de crise, sans doute *de* son état de crise, un état critique et autocritique permanent qui est certainement sa seule défintion possible aujourd'hui, qu'on s'en réjouisse et qu'on veuille porter à son maximum d'intensité dévastatrice… ou qu'on le déplore en tentant de restituer à la poésie quelque chose… de ses anciens pouvoirs. (102)
>
> ("Poetry" does not exist, no longer exists, which does not mean, of course, the drying up of poetic practice, but… that poetry lives its state of crisis, no doubt lives *on* its state of crisis, a critical and self-critical permanent state that is certainly its only possible definition today, whether we rejoice in that and want to bring it to its maximum of devastating intensity… or whether we deplore it while trying to restore to poetry something… of its former powers.)

Gleize goes on to clarify that the crisis he describes is not technical or sociological in nature but rather has to do with "la question (insoluble) du rapport au sens, au Sens, au monde, à la réalité, au Réel, et la capacité du langage à dire ce réel, à l'atteindre ou l'évoquer, etc" ("the (unsolvable) question of the relationship to meaning, to Meaning, to the world, to reality, to the Real, and the capacity of language to say this real, to attain or evoke it, etc.") (118). He thus aligns the question of crisis, in the same way as Pinson does, with the fundamental question of poetry's never-quite-defined relationship to the real that we can at best evoke in its form as crisis or questioning. It is intriguing to note that Gleize identifies crisis not just as a characteristic of the state of contemporary poetry but rather as its very definition, a move that allows us to see in this scenario, *pace* what he goes on to say here, not merely as generating an either/or where we either mourn or celebrate the passing of an excessive Romantic conception of poetry that lingered well into the modern period. One could say that these reflections invite us not to choose between celebration or mourning but to pursue a new set of options that acknowledges poetry's Romantic heritage while resisting the urge simply to replace that model with another, opposed but equally dogmatic, one. The definition of poetry emerges here as a constant state of questioning, perhaps of the inability of poetry to know. This, however, has the potential to be itself a kind of knowledge. While we may not be able to believe in poetry's more grandiose past claims in anything more than a nostalgic way, this model holds out the possibility of believing at least in the questioning, that is, believing that something is to be gained from the questioning itself, and that poetry might have something unique to contribute to that questioning.

One could say that such a stance reflects a move toward attempting to synthesize a number of developments in the relationship of poetry to the world it claims to know or to form in the modern period. This perspective continues to identify poetry as a particular practice unassimilable to other ways of thinking or creating, and yet it seeks a space that would err neither with the Romantics, in terms of transcendent potential, nor with a purely skeptical view that implicitly or explicitly questions the validity of any kind of knowledge claim on the part of poetry. Given such a position, claims about poetry as a form of knowledge necessarily involve a turn toward a definitional impulse related to poetry itself, not because poetry needs or wants to exclude the non-textual world but precisely *because* it needs somehow to account for that world. Poetry, on this view, is its own reality, but a reality that includes its own relation to another reality and, at the same time, to a redefined notion of poetic subjectivity for both readers and writers of poetry. Gleize puts it this way: "Oui, nous cherchons la poésie, nous cherchons aussi à en dire, à en communiquer quelque chose (de l'ordre d'une information, d'un savoir), mais la poésie nous, me, cherche. C'est nous, je, qui sommes en cause. « Je » lis" ("Yes, we seek poetry, we seek also to say and communicate something about it (on the order of an information, a knowledge), but poetry seeks, confronts, us, and me. It is we, and I, who are involved. 'I' read") (132). It is inevitable that this relationship of poetry to the real, or to itself *as* the real, leads to a notion of poetry not as an affirmation but a question, and to a poetic subject who is led, as an object, to that questioning by poetry itself acting as subject, as Gleize implies here. The definitional impulse that I have begun to identify, with its proliferation of definitions that attempt to be en route toward, while never achieving, the goal of precise definition, is an important indication of this new conception of poetry as question. It is a questioning that always implies an epistemological focus, given that the definitions always imply questions about how one may know poetry and how that knowledge can reflect or create a relation to the empirical world that neither simply represents it nor merely subsumes it. Each answer, in other words, will draw us back into the question, and as I will show in more detail in a later chapter on Philippe Jaccottet and Jean-Michel Maulpoix, this is the kind of knowledge to which modern poetry ultimately brings us and which it proposes.

The answers that poetry gives, then, draw us back into questions, in a model where answers are in part constituted by those questions themselves. This is as true for the issue of poetry's relationship to the world as it is for its relation to itself, a relation we have seen taking shape as an urge toward definition. Such an urge is precisely what can draw us back to the Romantic heritage that so many of the poets we have been considering are writing within or against. It is that heritage that we saw Reverdy eager to get beyond. But the ground we have traveled here can suggest an alternative: it is not so much a question of the (impossible) task of getting beyond Romanticism as it is of reinterpreting part of its heritage. In what follows I would like to suggest that the definitional impulse that we have begun to trace can itself be seen as originating in an important sense in the Romantic period, and specifically in the tautological characterization of poetry offered by Novalis, "Poetry is poetry." These questions of understanding what it would mean for poetry to be identical to itself are inseparable from the question of what it would mean for the subject who asserts this to be identical to itself, and thus questions of esthetics and subjectivity are intertwined each time we talk about what we mean when we talk about poetry. As Andrew Bowie has explored at length, this contemporary concern has its roots in Romanticism. For both Hölderlin and Novalis:

> the splitting of the I in reflection means its essential character is lost… The first and the second I in a proposition need a prior I to unite them, so that I as "content" and I as "form" can be the same, but our awareness of this is reflexive, and so is only "apparent," part of the I as "form." The I as "form" comes after the existential fact, the "content," required for the analysis to be possible in the first place. Designating myself as I by the signifier "I" means implying something external to me…. The signifier introduces a non-identity into myself in articulating my identity. As Hölderlin suggested, then, if I need to reflect on myself to know myself as myself it is already too late to know the essential ground of my self. (Bowie, *Aesthetics* 89)[4]

Attempts to break through the tautology of either the self or of poetry, and to make poetry something other than an empty signifier, constitute an essential aspect of what we mean when we start using the word. These attempts to fill the term with something other than the term itself are what ultimately constitute a series of very widely ranging non-definitions, but these attempts also, by returning us to the tautology, eternally recast poetry itself as question.

In considering the path on which Novalis's tautology can set us, my reading radically departs from the characterization of tautology that Roland Barthes gives in *Mythologies* concerning the statement "Racine est Racine" ("Racine is Racine") (96). For Barthes, tautology "signifie une rupture rageuse entre l'intelligence et son objet, la menace arrogante d'un ordre où l'on ne penserait pas" ("signifies a furious rupture between intelligence and its object, the arrogant menace of an order where we would not think") (97); he reads bourgeois anti-intellectualism in the gesture of defining by tautology. Yet this is not always the case when tautology is evoked: what I will attempt to show is that tautology can be the entry to an incredibly fecund probe into attempts at defining complex notions such as poetry. Rather than shutting down thought, tautology can encourage us to think differently, to unpack the tautology by following a plurality of paths away from it. Barthes in fact recognizes this potential in tautology when he identifies the many ways in which Racine has been viewed and concludes that "Racine est toujours quelque chose d'autre que Racine" ("Racine is always something other than Racine") (96). But to go on to add that "voilà qui rend la tautologie racinienne bien illusoire" ("that is what renders the Racinean tautology illusory") (96) is to ignore the potential in the ways we can come to grips with a Racine, or a poetry, that is always something else than itself. Asserting a tautology has the potential not necessarily to shut down further reflection (although in some cases Barthes is surely right that it can do that as well) but to open it up by highlighting the gap between our attempts to characterize or define a concept and the reality of the thing. Such a gap, while it can never be crossed, can be negotiated in different ways at different times, thus giving birth to a proliferation of discourse that is the very opposite of shutting down further reflection. Rather, the negotiation yields a kind of reflection that is provisional and always conscious of itself as tentative. This is, in other words, precisely the kind of thought that many modern poets have asserted that poetry encourages or mandates. While Barthes sees tautology as affirming laziness and providing a "petit salut éthique" ("small ethical salvation") (98) for those who employ it, a wholly more complex and much less reassuring reality can be derived from the tautology when we take it as a starting rather than an ending point.

Novalis's assertion about poetry may on first glance seem to lead to a dead-end personalized mystical approach to poetry. Here is the context in which the tautology appears: "Poetry is thoroughly personal and therefore indescribable and indefinable. Whoever does not immediately know and feel what poetry is cannot be taught what it is. Poetry is poetry. Worlds apart from rhetoric" (quoted in Trop 123–4).⁵ Here I follow Gabriel Trop in affirming that Novalis "does not assert that the ineffability of poetry can only be 'felt' or 'experienced,' and hence, can only be approached non-discursively, in some way that eludes articulation" (124). To relegate poetry to ineffability is to shut down any possibility of making meaning from the experience of it. In this sense poetry is similar to music, about which it is sometimes claimed that its meaning cannot be put into words. Critics such as Lawrence Kramer have effectively argued against such a stance in a way that breaks down the distinction between music and any other kind of experience, verbal or nonverbal. For Kramer, meaning in music is "both inchoate and immanent" (27). What he says about music here is equally true of poetry:

> Is music ineffable? Of course. What isn't? Who ever supposed that language could exhaust or replace the experiences or sensations, even the text, that it addresses? In this sense music is beyond significance in the same way that language is. Meaning is not a fixed or assignable statement; far less is it a signified. Meaning is the vanishing point of a discourse, the orienting force of a semantic performance that has always already begun and has no definite ending. (Kramer 148)⁶

For music, or poetry, or anything at all to have meaning, it must produce discourse. This is all the more true the more enigmatic the statement, as is the case with the tautological "poetry is poetry." To make headway in understanding Novalis's claim, Trop establishes a distinction, which he labels a kind of irony, between what such a statement claims and what it "intends to produce as a movement of consciousness" (124). On this view, "poetry emerges from the logical, cognitive, and creative movements implicit in the attempt to grasp a tautology" (124). In the context of the poets who interest me in this study, such an approach is a fertile one because it moves the discussion of poetry away from a Romantic interest in ineffability, manifested later in literary history as a concern for "pure" poetry. It does not simply abandon the attempt to define poetry, but instead performs a radical shift in the way we understand the notion of definition in that the definition does not simply describe the phenomenon but rather constitutes it, in a move that enlivens the task of definition by placing emphasis on the creative and processual aspect of thinking about poetry, as opposed to the product-oriented attempt to categorize and describe the result of that process. At the same time, this approach emphasizes the essential link between the poet and critic, suggesting that they are involved in aspects of the same task rather than in divergent ones.⁷

Another productive yet counterintuitive implication of Novalis's tautology is that a formula that seems to express unity of the thing with itself actually leads us to see differentiation as the key element of poetry, since poetry "must… enter the system of differences in order to appear at all" (Trop 126). The simple identity of the tautology is belied by the processual element to which it gives birth. Given that the tautology brings with it an imperative to work through the consequences of such a definition, in so doing it proposes other (variations on) definitions in what is set up as a potentially endless mental activity, what Trop refers to as "a way of life" (126). In other words, the moment we engage with the definition, we wrest it from what could only be an untenable realm of identity into the temporal and conceptual world of ever changing differences as they manifest themselves in each effort to come to terms with the definitional element of poetry. Once the tautology begins to open up in this way, it engages not just with unity and difference but also with truth and fiction:

> For Novalis, purity is a fiction, since it can only enter the world as difference, as impurity.… The tautology, far from resting in itself as a static equation, sets into motion the dynamic operation of an infinite process. It makes possible the *imagination* of absolute Being, but only by foregrounding absolute Being itself as something impossible. (Trop 128)

Once again, for such observations to lead to a productive as opposed to an eternally frustrated endeavor, we need to see fiction not as the opposite of, or hindrance to, truth, or even as a kind of regulative ideal, but rather to see it as the motor of an activity and process, one that is necessarily non-teleological, but whose meaning is to be found in the activity itself as it changes from moment to moment. This is what it means for poetry's manifestation to be differential rather than unified, and it is under these conditions, as we have seen, that poetry appears at all. For to claim that it is identical to itself is, it goes without saying, already to make a claim about it and thus to recognize its status in the differential world of manifestation rather than a purportedly pure and ineffable one. By projecting poetry beyond itself, we end up realizing that poetry is *itself* that projection, a conclusion at which we arrive only by engaging with the process of definition of poetry in ways that go beyond the arrangement of the words on the page that make up poems themselves. On this view, those poems cannot but be part of the process that is poetry, a process that involves not just the creation of the poems but the attempt to seize, via the imagination, what it is that one is doing in the process. In that sense, attempts to elaborate the tautology, to provide definitions of poetry, are no less creative, imaginative, or "poetic" than poems themselves. Rather, writing about poetry becomes not a secondary operation but an essential aspect of poeticizing, coextensive with writing poems.

With this focus on definition, we move, paradoxically, from an ontological question about poetry to an epistemological one. By moving from a static characterization to a process-oriented one, we shift to a consideration that can never separate the question of what poetry is from the question of how we know it. Trop puts it this way: "What begins as a philosophical approach to ontology ends by calling into question the terms established by ontology as such. It is not *Being* that defines poetry, but *movement*. The philosophy of movement, or of attraction, as an alternative to traditional ontology, appears as the proper domain of poetry" (142). Here we have a first suggestion of the way that poetry is not simply subject to philosophical categories but has a role in shaping the nature of those questions, transforming ontological questions into epistemological ones while also altering the teleological nature of such questions so that the goal is being perpetually relocated or redefined as a fiction. Characterized this way, poetry can never be considered a failure, as it may be if we retain a conception of poetry as necessarily doomed attempts to reach the absolute: "rather, as exercise, the poem is always achieving what it set out to do, it is always beckoning the reader to come back to its pull of attraction. Such is the fantasy of an infinite poem, a poem that never ends, something to which one always comes back, an entity that, like every mortal, moves between life and death" (Trop 178). Even this conceptual journey toward a reconsideration of the poem as identity or difference has creatively altered the way in which our imagination is able to conceive poetry, and it is thus itself a creative, and one might even say poetic, act.

Thus, thinking about poetry and producing forms of knowledge about it can be considered a creative act in itself. This notion of production that springs, paradoxically perhaps, from a knowledge of ignorance, reinforces the distinction that some poets and writers have made between poetry and mysticism. Jacques and Raïssa Maritain, for instance, in *Situation de la poésie* (1955), argue that poetry and mysticism are distinct in ways that have to do precisely with their approach to knowledge. They write in opposition to Henri Bremond, who had claimed, in *Prière et poésie* (1926), that "l'activité poétique est une ébauche naturelle et profane de l'activité mystique... le poète ne serait qu'un mystique évanescent ou qu'un mystique manqué" ("the poetic activity is natural and profane approximation of mystical activity... the poet would be only an evanescent mystic of a mystic *manqué*") (208).[8] For the Maritains, the key difference between mysticism and poetry is that mystical contemplation is its own end, whereas poetic knowledge is an instrumental kind of knowledge that leads to a work, to the production of a poem. Such knowledge is distinct both from mystical knowledge and from the everyday uses of the term:

> Son [le poète] intuition, l'intution ou émotion créarice est une obscure saisie de moi et des choses ensemble dans une connaissance par union ou par connaturalité qui ne se forme et ne fructifie, n'a son verbe, que dans l'œuvre, et qui de toute sa pesanteur vitale va à faire et à produire. Voilà une connaissance bien différente de ce qu'on appelle couramment connaissance; une connaissance qui n'est pas exprimable en idées et en jugements, mais qui est plutôt expérience que connaissance, et expérience créatrice, car elle veut s'exprimer, et elle n'est exprimable que dans une œuvre. Cette connaissance n'est pas préalable ni présupposée à l'activité créatrice, mais inviscérée dans celle-ci, consubstantielle au mouvement vers l'œuvre, et c'est là proprement ce que j'appelle *connaissance poétique*. (*Situation* 88–9)

> ([The poet's] intuition, the creative intuition or emotion, is an obscure grasping of the self and things together in knowledge by union or by connaturality which is not completed, does not fructify, does not achieve its word, except in the work and which with all its vital energy moves toward making and producing. Here is a knowledge that is different enough from what we commonly call knowledge, a knowledge which is not expressible in ideas and in judgments but which is rather experience than knowledge, and creative experience, for it wants to be expressed, and is expressible only in a work. This knowledge is neither previous to nor presupposed by the creative acivity, but inviscerated in it, consubstantial with the movement toward the work, and this is, properly speaking, what I call *poetic knowledge*. (*Situation* 51))

The Maritains go so far as to say that if poetic knowledge as they describe it here becomes divorced from the creation of a poem, it becomes a perversion:

> Bref la poésie *est* connaissance, incomparablement: connaissance-expérience et connaissance-émotion, connaissance existentielle, connaissance germe d'une œuvre (et qui ne se sait pas, et qui n'est pas *pour* connaître). En faire un *moyen de connaître*, un instrument de connaissance, la faire sortir de son être pour procurer ce qu'elle est, c'est la pervertir. (*Situation* 115–16)

> (In short, poetry *is* knowledge, incomparably: knowledge-experience and knowledge-emotion, existential knowledge, knowledge which is the germ of

a work (and which does not know itself, and which is not *for* knowing). To make of it a *means of knowledge*, an instrument of knowledge, to take it out of its proper mode of being in order to procure that which it is, is to pervert it. (*Situation* 68–9))

Although they are eager to distinguish poetry from mysticism by instrumentalizing poetic knowledge, the Maritains do suggest a certain proximity of those two kinds of knowledge by their description of "une certaine expérience qu'on peut appeler « connaissance » obscure et savoureuse" ("a certain experience which one can call an obscure and savory 'knowledge'"), which they identify as being "la source de la poésie" (*Situation* 30) ("the source of all poetry" (14)). I have been arguing that what is most productive for poetry is not knowledge but rather ignorance, the gap in expressibility that springs from the obscurity of the knowledge they evoke.

Seeing writing about poetry as springing from a productive ignorance that seeks to grasp what we talk about when we talk about poetry throws new light on poets' repeated attempts to characterize or define poetry. In this light we can reconsider what some poets might identify as a failure to define poetry satisfactorily. Such is the case of poet and essayist James Sacré, who laments in *La poésie, comment dire?* (1993) that:

> Les mots pour parler de la poésie me semblent véritablement toujours trop encombrants et dérisoirement prétentieux.... Je me rends bien compte que choisissant, pour que ce mot ait un corps sémantique, un autre vocabulaire (« pauvreté ressassée », « presque rien », « probable insignifiance » ...), je ne fais que transposer en mineur les valeurs auxquelles je m'opposais tout d'abord.... En somme, il vaudrait mieux se taire à propos de ce mot étrangement vide, semble-t-il parfois: « poésie ». (41)

(The words we have for speaking of poetry truly seem to me always too encumbering and derisively pretentious.... I do realize that in choosing, so that this word would have a semantic body, another vocabulary ("reiterated poverty," "almost nothing," "probable insignificance" ...), I only transpose into a minor key the values that I opposed at first.... In sum, it would be better to keep silent about this strangely empty word, or at least it seems so sometimes: "poetry.")

Whenever poetry is viewed in terms of the ineffable, there is a temptation to silence that returns, as we see clearly here. But given the lineage I have been tracing that sees the puzzling out of tautology as an epistemological quest, which is as much an inheritance from the Romantics as the assertion of poetry's ineffability, a reduction to silence would not simply mean either an admission of defeat in one's ability to characterize poetry nor a successful affirmation of poetry's purported mystical powers. Rather, such a silence would preclude the existence of poetry at all, since, as we have seen, to be is to be manifest, and specifically to be manifest as difference by which identity might be posited in the first place.

Sacré goes on to note the commonplace that there is no getting beyond language when it comes to attempts to capture the "thing itself," so to speak, when it comes to poetry:

> Chaque fois qu'on croit la saisir à l'œuvre, c'est toujours aussi d'autres formes de langage qu'on tire à soi. Et dans le désarroi d'écrire, persiste notre ignorance.... Errance, avec la poésie, à travers tout le langage: comme on cherche de l'ombre quand le jour est trop aveuglant, ou des lueurs, à tâtons, quand la nuit s'épaissit. Conquête et perte du langage. Conquêtes et pertes dans le langage. (49)
>
> (Each time we believe we have grasped it, we also take hold of other forms of language. And in the helplessness of writing, our ignorance persists.... Wandering, with poetry, throughout all of language: as we seek shade when the light is too blinding, or faint glimmers, by feeling around, when the night thickens. Conquest and loss of language. Conquests and losses in language.)

What I hope to have suggested by now is that ignorance in the case of knowledge of and by poetry is not to be lamented but rather to be considered as an integral part of the kind of knowing—temporary, contingent, and fragile—that poetry has to offer. Ignorance persists because it cannot be canceled, but consciousness of that fact, which is related to the elimination of a teleological end point for knowledge of poetry, is itself a crucial insight to be gained through the definitional processes I have been tracing, a necessary byproduct of the attempt to decipher the "poetry is poetry" tautology. This approach is distinct from one that would be analogous to a negative theology whereby poetry is defined as a series of "not this, not that"-type negations. The endless deferral of definition that might be the endpoint of a deconstructive approach here becomes the point of departure for an epistemological approach attuned to the way poetry's knowledge is inextricably linked to what it is. Sacré ultimately establishes a parallel between the obscurity of words and the experience of living itself and places poetry at that point of intersection: "Peut-être que la poésie c'est l'expérience faite du langage, de la même façon qu'on fait toute autre expérience: l'obscurité de vivre se mêlant à celle des mots. Le poème ne s'avive-t-il pas entre tension désespérée pour dire (désir d'immédiateté, d'authenticité) et abandon à l'écriture silencieuse ?" ("Perhaps poetry is the experience made of language, in the same way that we make any other experience: the obscurity of living mixing with that of words. Does the poem not intensify between desperate tension for saying (desire of immediacy and authenticity) and abandonment to silent writing?") (50).

Sacré thus harks back to Baudelaire in the emphasis on experience, but what is notable here is that he does not see poetry as any kind of corrective to experience or to ignorance but rather itself an original kind of experience that unites two different but related kinds of obscurity, that of lived experience and of language. Poetry thus exists as a kind of middle ground between language and experience, but one that unites the two or provides the space or ground for their encounter. In the remainder of this chapter I consider Paul Valéry who, at a temporal midpoint between mid-nineteenth-century reflections on poetry and the late twentieth century, takes up questions of poetry in terms of its relation to ignorance, and the possibility or impossibility of defining it and indicating precisely the nature of its relationship to the world from which it springs.

At times, Valéry privileges ignorance as a primary experience:

Avec une précision extrême, en parfaite connaissance de cause, au point le plus net entre les points nets, à la limite de la lucidité habitable, sentir et prononcer le: *Je ne sais pas—J'ignore*; et connaître ce moment comme véritablement le plus difficile, le plus parfait, le but par excellence, le centre où l'esprit de l'humain ne peut que de toutes ses forces tendre, et d'où il est furieusement repoussé ... (2: 587)

(With an extreme precision, in full awareness, at the clearest point among the clear points, at the limit of habitable lucidity, to feel and pronounce the *I don't know; I am ignorant*; and to know this moment as truly the most difficult, the most perfect, the goal par excellence, the center where the human mind cannot help but incline with all its might, and from where it is furiously pushed back.)

He makes of ignorance a sort of dwelling: "On se réfugie dans ce qu'on ignore. On s'y cache de ce qu'on sait" ("We take refuge in what we do not know. We hide there from what we know") (2: 612), and makes of that ignorance the fount of hope for thought, given that thought can only be stimulated into motion by what is not already known. And since ignorance is crucial to thought, it is also thereby crucial to language and discourse: "On parle bien plus volontiers de ce qu'on ignore. Car c'est à quoi l'on pense. Le travail de l'esprit se porte là, et ne peut se porter que là" ("We speak much more willingly of what we do not know. Because that is what we think about. The work of the mind heads toward that, and can only head toward that") (2: 643). While Valéry does not make an explicit link to poetry here, this observation is crucial in terms of the relation we have been tracing between ignorance and the definitional impulse in modern poetry, the attempt both to attempt to articulate what it is and to speculate on the possibility of doing so effectively. If ignorance is the motor of both thought and discourse, it will have a crucial role to play in any consideration of what poetry is. The discussion springs from ignorance and, as we saw with Sacré, need not proceed linearly from ignorance to knowledge. Rather, ignorance or obscurity may become part and parcel of the definitional model we adopt when considering poetry. It is this that saves us from simply affirming the ineffability of poetry, even as we acknowledge that attempts to define poetry will fail. To take Valéry's notion that we are much more willing to speak of what we do not know than what we know as fundamental for thinking about poetry is to identify that it is always within the context of ignorance that the work of defining poetry happens. It is within that frame that we most effectively articulate attempts to disentangle the tautology "poetry is poetry," an assertion which, following Valéry's model, itself says nearly nothing but gives birth to an endless definitional discourse when we consider the implications of not quite understanding what we mean by the tautology when we utter it.

This form of knowledge that not only incorporates ignorance but also depends on it in order for it to proliferate is different from a more everyday approach to knowledge that would see it as simply overcoming ignorance rather than being imbricated with, and to that extent dependent, on it. This difference in terms of the kind of thinking one should expect in and from poetry is signaled by Valéry in comments on Stéphane Mallarmé where Valéry reveals that this difference in thought is just as crucial to the poetry/prose distinction as are the more usual markers of that distinction such as attention to the sound of the words themselves:

> On aurait dit que [Mallarmé] voulait que la poésie, qui doit essentiellement se distinguer de la prose par la forme phonétique et la musique, s'en distinguât aussi par *la forme du sens*. Pour lui, *le contenu du poème devait être aussi différent de la pensée ordinaire que la parole ordinaire est différente de la parole versifiée.* C'était là un point capital. (1: 668)

> (One would have said that [Mallarmé] wanted poetry, which must distinguish itself essentially from prose by its phonetic and musical form, to distinguish

itself also by *the form of meaning*. For him *the content of the poem should be as different from ordinary thoughts as ordinary language is different from versified language.* That was a crucial point.)

At other times, Valéry claims that poetry's aim is not for a merely different kind of meaning but rather *more* meaning than ordinary discourse: "La poésie est l'ambition d'un discours qui soit chargé de plus de sens, et mêlé de plus de musique, que le langage ordinaire n'en porte et n'en peut porter" ("Poetry is the hope for a discourse that would be charged with more meaning, and mixed with more music, than ordinary language carries or could carry") (1: 712). With this reference to music Valéry may well mean a heightened attention to the sonority of words in a poem, but this implicit link to music also reminds us that poetry has in common with music that it depends on discourse external to it in order for it to have any meaning at all. The struggle to articulate exactly what and how poetry might mean implicates critical discussion of poetry into our understanding of poetic experience and makes it impossible to speak of an immediacy of ineffability of experience. Our attempts to understand how poetry and critical discourse work together in order to create poetic meaning is a crucial aspect of the epistemological task of defining poetry and thus of moving beyond the tautology.

In Valéry's use of the term *poésie* we can see an ambiguity between the two habitual uses of the term. Does it refer to poems or to the larger, more abstract sense that we have been considering? Or is it the case that the term *poésie* itself generates a discourse that performs what it describes to an even greater extent than the texts that we label "poems" do? The ambiguity of the term itself is an initial step in this direction, and the definitional impulse that we have been tracing leads both to a conception of "poetry" that is removed from texts we typically call poems and to an approach to thought that is perhaps best played out in writings about poetry rather than in poems themselves. This is not to say there is an opposition between poems and writings about poetry, but rather that there is a complementarity there that is lost if we label writings about poetry as, for instance, "criticism."[9] This is so because the implications of "poetry" are played out in the discourse it produces. And it is this discourse that leads us away from silence in the face of the purportedly ineffable and towards an infinite task. We see this conception even in Valéry, who at first glance might seem to affirm the unchanging nature of the Beautiful and our inability to give expression to the purported "purity" of poetry. But inasmuch as he implicitly aligns thinking with poetry, there is a sense of movement and instability built into Valéry's conception of poetry. Note how he returns to the definitional impulse when characterizing the Beautiful:

> Le Beau implique des effets d'indicibilité, d'indescriptibilité, d'ineffabilité. Et ce terme lui-même ne dit RIEN. Il n'a pas de définition, car il n'y a de vraie définition que par construction.
>
> Or, si l'on veut produire un tel effet *au moyen de* CE QUI DIT,—du langage,—ou si l'on ressent, causé par le langage, un tel effet, il faut que le langage s'emploie à produire ce qui rend muet, exprime un mutisme. (1: 374)

> (The Beautiful implies effects of unsayability, undescribability, ineffability. And this term itself says NOTHING. It has no definition, since there is no true definition except by construction.
>
> Now, if one wants to produce a given effect *by means of* WHAT SAYS,—of language,—or if one feels, caused by language, a certain effect, language must be employed to produce what renders mute and expresses a muteness.)

Paradoxically, muteness that is unexpressed would not be muteness because it could not be named or identified as such. Such a conception forces us to alter our sense of ineffability in that it calls for ineffability itself to be given voice and for discourse to be produced. Unless we are to deny any link between beauty and thought, we need to affirm that "thought" as Valéry conceives it and notions of beauty or poetry operate according to similar kinds of structures, both of which involve a conceptual restlessness that produces ever more discourse in an effort that is recognized beforehand as contingent and temporary:

> *Penseurs* sont gens qui re-pensent, et qui pensent que ce qui fut pensé ne fut jamais assez pensé. Revenir sur une question, sur un mot,—y revenir indéfiniment; y revenir presque comme on revient à son bureau,—à un café … Ne pouvoir se passer de n'être satisfait d'aucune solution,—cela existe: il y a des hommes dont c'est la vie et le bonheur. Ils ont donc *instinctivement* créé toutes les questions insolubles,—les questions pour penseurs seuls … (2: 767)

> (*Thinkers* are people who re-think, and who think that what was thought was never thought enough. To come back to a question, a word,—to return indefinitely to it; to return to it almost as one came back to one's office, or a café … To not be able to do without not being satisfied with any solution,—that exists: there are men whose lives and happiness are made of that. They have thus *instinctively* created all the unanswerable questions,—questions for thinkers only …)

Notable here is the lack of emphasis on originality: to think is to engage in a relationship with the past history of thought consciously in order to reject it or call it into question. By this definition, metaphysicians seeking stable truth would not be thinkers. In fact, for Valéry it is the very act of stabilizing an insight or thought that renders it in need of further elaboration and revision: "Ce qui était clair au passage, et si vivement *compris*, se fait obscur quand on le fixe" ("What was clear in passing, and so vividly *understood*, becomes obscure when one pins it down") (1: 1041). More than an activity, the characterization of thinking as rethinking suggests that thinking is more a way of life, a habit of mind and a way of seeing the world that involves a level of comfort with the restlessness and uncertainty of any answers generated through the process of thought. Here there are obvious links to poetry as a way of life as we saw it characterized in the context of Novalis's challenge: committing oneself to the unending task of identifying the differences generated by the tautological unity of "poetry" goes far beyond the act of poetic creation conceived as the writing of poems, and toward an epistemological quest that meets thought on this common ground that poetry shares with thinking as conceived here by Valéry. He goes on to include poetry in a list of common words whose meaning is destabilized as soon as one begins to reflect on their meaning:

> Insistez, par exemple, le moins du monde, sur des noms comme *temps, univers, race, forme, nature, poésie*, etc., et vous les verrez se diviser à l'infini, devenir infranchissables. Tout à l'heure, ils nous servaient à nous entendre; ils se changent à présent en occasions de nous confondre. (1: 1041)
>
> (Insist, even a little bit, for example, on nouns such as *time, universe, race, form, nature, poetry*, etc., and you will see them divide infinitely and become insuperable. Just a while ago, they were useful for understanding each other; now they change into occasions to confuse ourselves.)

On one hand, this gesture lumps poetry together with any other phenomenon presented to the mind for reflection, but when considered together with the definitional impulse we have been considering, and of which Valéry offers many examples throughout his writings, poetry emerges from Valéry's list as uniquely given to the kind of de-familiarization that he characterizes here, since attempts to move past that defamiliarization are elsewhere considered to be part of poetry's task, a fact which moves poetry closer to thought than to the other items on this list.[10]

For Valéry, such defamiliarization and the resulting engagement with ignorance go hand in hand with the plurality of expression that we have been associating with the task of deciphering the tautology "poetry is poetry." As we have noted, to make sense of such a proposition requires a fall from unity to difference, a move without which poetry would have no meaning whatsoever. The difference, then, is built into the understanding of the unity as soon as we seek to say to something about it. For Valéry, poetic expression is valuable because it allows us to say what cannot be otherwise said, but this requires a plurality of expressions via metaphor, none of which is reducible to a single formulation:

> La métaphore, par exemple, marque dans son principe naïf, un tâtonnement, une hésitation entre plusieurs expressions d'une pensée, une impuissance explosive et dépassant la puissance nécessaire et suffisante. Lorsqu'on aura repris et précisé la pensée jusqu'à sa rigueur, jusqu'à un seul objet, alors la métaphore sera effacée, la prose reparaîtra. Ces démarches, observées et cultivées pour elles-mêmes, sont devenues l'objet d'une étude et d'un emploi: c'est la poésie. (1: 1450)

> (Metaphor, for example, marks in its naïve principle, a groping in the dark, a hesitation among several expressions of a thought, an explosive impotence that goes beyond the necessary and sufficient power. When we will have taken back thought and rendered it precise in all its rigor and identified it with only one object, then metaphor will be erased and prose will reappear. These approaches, observed and cultivated for themselves, have become the object of a study and a use: this is poetry.)

It is important to note that Valéry is not implying here that poetic metaphor is simply a poor substitute for the more precise and unified language of prose. Rather, the plurality of metaphorical expression, and the tentativeness implied by a *tâtonnement*, a feeling around, is the only vehicle by which the phenomena that Valéry is considering here may be expressed. From these considerations, Valéry concludes that

> la poésie a pour objet spécial, pour domaine véritablement propre, l'expression de ce qui est inexprimable en fonctions finies de mots. L'objet propre de la poésie est ce qui n'a pas un seul nom, ce qui en soi provoque et demande plus d'une expression. Ce qui suscite pour son unité devant être exprimée, une pluralité d'expressions. (1: 1450)

> (poetry has for its special object, for its truly proper domain, the expression of what is inexpressible in the finite functions of words. The proper object of poetry

is that which does not have one single name, that which in itself provokes and asks for more than one expression, what creates a plurality of expressions for its unity that must be expressed.)

Poetry takes over, then, where a singular and prosaic expression of thought would fail. Its unity and its definition thereby spring from the plurality which defines its particular mode of expression. This is a conception that introduces a divide into the characterization of poetry itself. Poetry thus risks self-cancelation if a unified or definitive form of thought is achieved through it. Looking more closely at Valéry's own formulation here, we note the ambiguity in the phrase "the expression of what is inexpressible in the finite functions of words." Is this to say that poetic language allows the expression of what it is impossible for more definitive kinds of expression to express, i.e. that ineffability is canceled by poetic language, or is this to claim merely that poetic language expresses the inexpressibility of certain kinds of phenomena, a situation whereby ineffability would in fact be preserved and only expressed *as* ineffability? Valéry seems to suggest that the plurality of expression that poetry involves does indeed cancel ineffability by substituting plurality for unity. But for this to be the case, those metaphorical formulations would need to be immune from generating further discourse, a situation where the metaphors would become indistinguishable from the definitive singular expression to which he opposes them. For poetry to remain poetry by this definition, it needs to remain potentially capable of generating difference from itself, and so this definitive-seeming characterization of the difference between poetic and prosaic language is itself susceptible to being called into question to the point of cancelation, not in order merely to invalidate the claims but rather to push further on them, a move perfectly in keeping with poetic thought as Valéry defines it here as "a hesitation."

This emphasis on movement is itself in tension with Valéry's emphasis on *la poésie pure*, a concept which he acknowledges has garnered criticism but which he defends on the grounds that it functions as a kind of impossible but regulatory ideal:

> Ceux qui m'en ont fait le reproche ont oublié que j'avais écrit que la poésie pure n'était qu'une limite située à l'infini, un idéal de la puissance de beauté du langage ... Mais c'est la direction qui importe, la tendance vers l'œuvre pure. Il est important de savoir que toute poésie s'oriente vers quelque *poésie absolue* ... C'est celle-ci dont Mallarmé a médité l'existence et de laquelle il a essayé, à tout prix, de se rapprocher par les développements de son art. (1: 676-7)

(Those who have reproached me about this have forgotten that I had written that pure poetry was only a limit situated in infinity, an ideal of the beautiful power of language ... But it is the direction that matters, the tendency toward the pure work. It is important to know that all poetry orients itself toward some *absolute poetry*. ... It is that absolute poetry whose existence Mallarmé meditated and of which he tried, at all costs, to approach by the developments of his art.)

If by pure poetry Valéry means an aspiration toward a poetry of pure "musicality," devoid of any relationship to meaning and the inevitable plurality it provokes, then pure poetry is an odd regulatory ideal indeed, given that attaining it would mean the abolition of poetry itself because all of what animates poetry would be canceled. Poetry thrives not only on the impossibility of achieving such an ideal but also on the impossibility of conceiving such an ideal as a goal to be aimed at, as Valéry's mentor Mallarmé knew well, when he wrote, in a passage I have already cited in my discussion of Hugo, that if languages were perfectly transparent, "*n'existerait pas le vers*: lui, philosophiquement rémunère le défaut des langues, complément supérieur" ("*verse would not exist*, verse which philosophically makes up for what is missing in languages, superior complement") (*OC2*: 208). Intriguingly, pure poetry would lead to the same kind of result as the philosophically definitive thought to which Valéry opposes poetic thinking, in that both would propose a definitive endpoint beyond which one could not, and would not want to, continue.

Valéry speaks elsewhere of an *état poétique* that is more in keeping with his notion of poetry as tentative plurality of expression. This poetic state is not static or contemplative in the usual sense but rather animated by the perpetual restlessness of the impossibility of satisfaction, a state that Valéry explicitly characterizes as *jouissance* and which he opposes to a notion of "philosophical poetry" as it is commonly conceived:

> Parler aujourd'hui de poésie philosophique (fût-ce en invoquant Alfred de Vigny, Leconte de Lisle, et quelques autres), c'est naïvement confondre des conditions et des applications de l'esprit incompatibles entre elles. N'est-ce pas oublier que le but de celui que spécule est de fixer ou de créer une notion—c'est-à-dire un *pouvoir* et un *instrument de pouvoir*, cependant que le poète moderne essaye de produire en nous en *état*, et de porter cet état exceptionnel au point d'une jouissance parfaite ? (1: 1274)

> (To speak today of philosophical poetry (whether it be to invoke Alfred de Vigny, Leconte de Lisle, and a few others), is to naïvely confuse conditions and

applications of the mind which are incompatible with each other. Is it not to forget that the goal of he who speculates is to pin down or to create a notion—that is a *power* and an *instrument of power*, whereas the modern poet tries to produce in us a *state*, and to bring this exceptional state to the point of a perfect pleasure?)

And yet, while the poetic state seems characterized here by a certain restlessness, at other times Valéry seems to be suggesting something more tranquil and more stable when he speaks of a poetic state. Take, for instance, this elaboration of two different meanings of the word "poetry":

> Il désigne d'abord un certain genre d'émotions, un état émotif particulier, qui peut être provoqué par des objets ou des circonstances très diverses. Nous disons d'un paysage qu'il est poétique; nous le disons d'une circonstance de la vie; nous le disons parfois d'une personne. Mais il existe une seconde acception de ce terme, un second sens plus étroit. *Poésie*, en ce sens, nous fait songer à un art, à une étrange industrie dont l'objet est de constituer cette émotion que désigne le premier sens du mot. Resituer l'émotion poétique à volonté, en dehors des conditions naturelles où elle se produit spontanément et au moyen des artifices du langage, tel est le dessein du poète, et telle est l'idée attachée au nom de *poésie*, pris dans le second sens. Entre ces deux notions existent les mêmes relations et les mêmes différences que celles qui se trouvent entre le parfum d'une fleur et l'opération du chimiste qui s'applique à le reconstruire de toutes pièces. Toutefois, on confond à chaque instant les deux idées, et il en résulte qu'une quantité de jugements, de théories et même d'ouvrages sont viciés dans leur principe par l'emploi d'un seul mot pour deux choses bien différentes, quoique liées. (1: 1362)
>
> (It designates first a certain kind of emotions, a particular emotive state, that can be provoked by objects or very diverse circumstances. We say of a landscape that it is poetic; we say it of a certain life circumstance; we sometimes say it of a person. But there exists a second, narrower, meaning of the term. *Poetry*, in this sense, makes us dream of an art, a strange industry whose object is to constitute that emotion that the first meaning of the word designates. To resituate poetic emotion at will, beyond the natural conditions where it occurs spontaneously and by means of the artifices of language, thus is the design of the poet, and thus is the idea attached to the name of *poetry*, taken in the second sense. Between these two notions the same relations and the same differences exist as those that are found between the scent of a flower and the operation of the chemist who works to reconstruct it. Nevertheless, at every moment we confuse the two ideas, and there results from that a number of judgments, theories, and works which are invalidated in their principle by the use of just one word for two very different, although linked, things.)

By opposing the active, creative second definition to the first one, which he describes as an "emotive state," Valéry seems to encourage us to read that state as a calm or unified one, an almost stereotypical notion of the "poetic" as pretty or perhaps calming. He suggests at the end of the passage that these two uses result in confusion where one would be taken for the other. In light, however, of the theory of plurality he develops in the passages I have cited above, we can apply a "poetic" approach to the distinction he makes in this passage here by claiming that it is not a matter simply of sorting out which meaning is operative at which time, but rather of seeing the two meanings in productive tension, as not only existing simultaneously but constituting, together, the kind of difference-to-oneself that we have been identifying as characteristic of the poetic. That is what it would presumably mean to think "poetically" about poetry itself, as opposed to attempting to find definitional clarity. On this reading, the tranquility implied by certain uses of the term "poetry" is itself part of a larger and irreducible restlessness that stems from our inability to remain within that experience or conception of tranquility.

On this model, even arrival points are not a source of stability, as philosophical truth would presumably be, and an important part of the reason why this is so is because of poetry's division from itself, not only in the sense of interpreting the tautology of "poetry is poetry," but also because of the two different common uses of the term. Valéry acknowledges this division within the term itself:

> Vous savez qu'on comprend sous le nom de poésie deux choses très différentes qui, cependant, se lient en un certain point. Poésie, c'est le premier sens du mot, c'est un art particulier fondé sur le langage. Poésie porte aussi un sens plus général, plus répandu, difficile à définir, parce qu'il est plus vague; il désigne un certain état, état qui est à la fois réceptif et productif. (1: 1387)

> (You know that we understand under the name of poetry two different things which, nevertheless, are linked at a certain point. Poetry, and this is the first meaning of the word, is a particular art founded on language. Poetry also carries a more general and widespread meaning, difficult to define, because it is more vague. It designates a certain state which is at the same time receptive and productive.)

Valéry then makes a crucial move that, unexpectedly perhaps, links poetry directly to lived experience by claiming that it is the motor of the fictions that constitute what we call our lives:

> Il est productif de fictions, et remarquez que la fiction c'est notre vie. Nous vivons continuellement en production de fictions ... Vous pensez à présent au moment désirable où j'aurai fini de parler ... C'est une fiction ! Nous ne vivons que de fictions, qui sont nos projets, nos espoirs, nos souvenirs, nos regrets, etc., et nous ne sommes qu'une invention perpétuelle. Remarquez bien (j'y insiste) que toutes ces fictions se rapportent nécessairement *à ce qui est*; en outre, chose curieuse, c'est *ce qui est* qui engendre *ce qui n'est pas*, et c'est *ce qui n'est pas* qui répond constamment *à ce qui est* ... (1: 1387)
>
> (It is productive of fictions, and notice that fiction is our life. We live continually in the production of fictions ... You think now of that desirable moment when I will have finished speaking ... That is a fiction! We live only on fictions, which are our plans, our hopes, our memories, our regrets, etc., and we are only a perpetual invention. Notice, I insist on it, that all these fictions refer back necessarily to *what is*; beyond that, the curious thing is that *what is* engenders *what is not*, and *what is not* answers back to *what is* ...)

Valéry provides such an expansive definition here that poetry becomes assimilable to all imaginative mental faculties by which we project ourselves into the past and future and which makes our own lives a work of art, given that we are "a perpetual invention." Poetry as a verbal construction on the page thus becomes continuous with mental constructions by which we constitute our lives; a poem is thus both distinct from and completely assimilable to larger acts of self creation and world creation. While Valéry proposes at the end of this passage a dialectical relationship between the real world and our imaginative response to it (and crafting of it), he significantly alters the terms of the discussion we have been tracing about the relationship of poetry to the real when he introduces the category of fiction and relates it directly to life. It is no longer a question of attempting to establish the relationship of poetry to the real, but rather shifting the terrain of the discussion to our internal mental life, not in order to close out the external world but to posit our minds as the site where we make sense of the world and give it shape and meaning.

Elsewhere Valéry returns to this question of poetry's role in the creation of something beyond poems that relates to the way we interpret lived experience, this time underscoring the essential role of language in that process of understanding:

> Donc, tout différent du musicien et moins heureux, le poète est contraint de créer, à chaque création, *l'univers de la poésie*,—c'est-à-dire: l'état psychique et

affectif dans lequel le langage peut remplir un rôle tout autre que celui de signifier ce qui est ou fut ou va être. Et tandis que le langage pratique est détruit, résorbé, une fois le but atteint (la compréhension), le langage poétique doit tendre à la conservation de la forme. (1: 1414)

(So, completely different from the musician and less happy, the poet is restricted to creating, with each creation, *the universe of poetry*—that is, the psychic and affective state in which language can fill a role totally different than that of signifying what is or was or will be. And whereas practical language is destroyed, reabsorbed, once the goal is attained (understanding), poetic language must tend toward the conservation of form.)

This complicates, and even may contradict, the stance Valéry announced in the passage we have been considering. He returns to the notion of past and future in their relation to meaning here, but seems now to be making a distinction between factual and imaginative reality. His earlier statement was in fact the more radical one, suggesting as it did that our mental constructions of meaning take priority over, and may even replace, any supposedly factual account of what "happened." Now he maintains the notion of signifying, but seems to be using it here more in the sense of "delineating" rather than "meaning" in the sense of giving importance and value to an experience in the context of a lived life. And he draws a distinction between poetic and non-poetic language that seems to refer more to the limited definition of poetry as "un art particulier fondé sur le langage," given his emphasis on language's remaining as form. But how does this relate to the more expansive definition that he seemed to be invoking at first in the reference to the creation of the "universe of poetry"? There is a productive tension between the static conservation of form and the creation of the mental space by which language can accomplish its work of world making. For the conservation of form to be itself meaningful, it needs the productive counterpart by which language creates knowledge of the world rather than merely reflecting it. What remains unarticulated here is the precise relation of the static form of the poem on the page, i.e. poetry in the narrower sense, and the creative use of language in the mind to create the world of understanding, which is a process that seems to go beyond, and maybe be independent of, those words on the page.

The distinction that Valéry originally drew between the two understandings of the word "poetry" is now less than clear, given that the nature of the interaction, or lack of interaction, between the two understandings remains unspecified. The further we go in Valéry's writings on poetry and philosophy, the less clear his distinctions become. What results is a kind of performative example of the ideas about definition that we have been elucidating, namely, that poetry calls us to the task of definition while also showing how that task unravels at every step, at which point we are called upon to continue the task, in a definitional activity that intersects with lived experience and that itself constitutes what we mean by "poetry." Consider, for instance, this definition of philosophy:

> On pourrait se représenter la philosophie comme l'attitude, l'attente, la contrainte, moyennant lesquelles quelqu'un, parfois, pense sa vie ou vit sa pensée, dans une sorte d'équivalence, ou d'état réversible, entre l'*être* et *le connaître*, essayant de suspendre toute expression conventionnelle pendant qu'il pressent que s'ordonne et va s'éclairer une combinaison, beaucoup plus précieuse que les autres, du réel qu'il se sent offrir et de celui qu'il peut recevoir. (1: 1264)
>
> (We could represent philosophy as the attitude, the expectation, the constraint, by which someone, sometimes, thinks about his life or lives his thought, in a sort of equivalence, or reversible state, between *being* and *knowing*, trying to suspend all conventional expression while he senses that a combination is falling into place and will become clear, one that is much more precious than the others, of the real that he feels offering itself and the one that he can receive.)

It would hardly be inconsistent with other writings by Valéry to substitute the word "poet" for "philosopher" in this characterization. While he sometimes characterizes philosophy as oriented toward definitive truth and unquestionable answers, here his remarks establish continuity with the passages we have been considering about poetry's role in mediating knowledge and lived experience, even extending to his comments on the suspension of conventional expression in favor of more insightful formulations of experience and its relation to the world from which it springs. In that sense, the philosopher and the poet are more united than divided if their tasks meet at this middle ground of establishing knowledge as a way of being and, by extension, a way of understanding and acting in the world. This intersection of philosophy and poetry, as Valéry understands it, demonstrates once again that if poetry is not to risk becoming a meaningless category, synonymous even with terms that are sometimes construed as its opposite, it needs to maintain itself in an infinitely revisable definitional space where that impulse to define is as essential to poetry's existence as a category as it is impossible to accomplish definitively.

This productive blurring of distinctions between certain characterizations of philosophy and poetry is in tension with Valéry's own occasional attempts to craft a self-referential poetics by which poetry would be unassimilable to other ways of knowing and acting in the world. This is often accomplished in the context of a discussion of poetry's purity or perfection:

> On voit enfin, vers le milieu du XIXe siècle, se prononcer dans notre littérature une volonté remarquable d'isoler définitivement la Poésie, de toute autre essence qu'elle-même. Une telle préparation de la poésie à l'état pur avait été prédite et recommandée avec la plus grande précision par Edgar Poe. Il n'est donc pas étonnant de voir commencer dans Baudelaire cet essai d'une perfection qui ne se préoccupe plus que d'elle-même. (1: 1270)[11]

> (We see, in our literature toward the middle of the nineteenth century, a remarkable will definitively to isolate Poetry from all other essence except itself. Such a preparation of poetry for the pure state had been predicted and recommended with the greatest precision by Edgar Allen Poe. It is thus not surprising to see in Baudelaire the beginning of this attempt at a perfection that is no longer concerned with anything but itself.)

And here lies the paradox inherent not just in Valéry but in the general movement of defining poetry in the modern era that we have been tracing: as poetry isolates itself and focuses intensely and exclusively on itself, a move epitomized in the tautological definition, it necessarily by the very same gesture, opens itself up once again because of the impulse to plumb the implications of the tautology, a move that requires moving into language, without which poetry itself would not exist. That move into language is thus itself "poetic," which means that the fall away from tautology is just as poetic as the impulse for poetry to isolate itself had been. An ineffable phenomenon accessible only to itself is simply not meaningful, and part of poetry's way of knowing the world is to require the movement beyond the tautology that the move into the tautology itself generates.

Having established that the quest for knowledge about and through poetry is not to be seen as resulting in definitive answers—he even goes so far as to say that "croire comprendre" ("to believe one understands") is "un état bien dangereux" ("a very dangerous state") (2: 497)—Valéry comes back to a characterization of poetry in relation to ignorance:

> N'est-il pas admirable que l'on cherche et que l'on trouve tant de manières de traiter d'un sujet sans même en effleurer le principe, et en démontrant par les méthodes que l'on emploie, par les modes de l'attention qu'on y applique, et jusque par le labeur que l'on s'inflige, une méconnaissance pleine et parfaite de la véritable *question* ? Davantage: dans la quantité de savants travaux qui, depuis

des siècles, ont été consacrés à la Poésie, on en voit merveilleusement peu (et je dis « peu » pour ne pas être absolu), qui n'impliquent pas une négation de son existence. Les caractères les plus sensibles, les problèmes les plus réels de cet art si composé sont comme exactement offusqués par le genre des regards qui se fixent sur lui. (1: 1284)

(Is it not admirable that we seek and find so many ways to speak of a subject without even scratching the surface, and in demonstrating by the methods that we employ, the modes of attention that we apply, and even the labor that we impose on ourselves, a full and perfect misunderstanding of the true *question*? More: in the number of learned works which, for centuries, have been dedicated to Poetry, we see marvelously few (and I say "few" in order not to be absolute), which do not imply a negation of its existence. The most sensitive characters, the most real problems of this complex art are as if exactly obfuscated by the kind of glances fixed on it.)

Perhaps we can take Valéry's observations a step further in light of the line of development we have been following. For he seems to imply here a kind of quasi-positivist knowledge of what poetry is; his criticism falls on those who have misunderstood the question of what poetry is and claims that their misguided answers to the question end up negating its existence. But if poetry is conceived as *itself* a kind of question, as we have seen Valéry himself imply, then it is a misunderstanding of the question to consider it as a standard one in the sense of a question for which an answer can be provided. While seeming to imply that he holds the key to the question, Valéry could also be implying that it is those who have sought definitive answers about what poetry is who have gotten the question wrong.

What is important to retain here is that issues of questioning and of the potential negation of poetry's existence are not to be addressed as tangential to the question of what poetry is, but rather as important elements of the attempt to articulate what it is. That is why the process of questioning and negating, which is frequently carried out not in poems but in writing about poetry, must be kept at the forefront of efforts to think through what poetry is. And it is that sort of take on the question of what poetry is that allows us to stave off the frustration that Valéry confesses to feeling in the wake of so many contradictory conceptions of what the elements of poetry are:

Cependant que j'écoute de ces dissertations auxquelles ni les « documents », ni les subtilités ne manquent, je ne puis m'empêcher de penser que je ne sais même pas ce que c'est qu'une *Phrase* … Je varie sur ce que j'entends par un *Vers*. J'ai lu ou j'ai forgé vingt « définitions » du *Rythme*, dont je n'adopte aucune …

Que dis-je ! ... Si je m'attarde seulement à me demander ce que c'est qu'une *Consonne*, je m'interroge; je consulte; et je ne recueille que des semblants de connaissance nette, distribuée en vingt avis contradictoires ... (1: 1289)

(While I listen to these discourses where neither "documents" nor subtleties are missing, I cannot help thinking that I do not even know what a *Sentence* is ... I vary in terms of what I understand by a *line of poetry*. I have read or forged twenty "definitions" of *Rhythm*, of which I do not adopt a single one ... What am I saying! ... If I linger over the question of what a *Consonant* is, I ask myself questions, I consult, and I gather only semblances of this clear knowledge, dispersed among twenty contradictory opinions ...)

While Valéry resists a model of ignorance about poetry rather than embracing it, he is nonetheless led to acknowledge that esthetics is indeed guided by negation:

Je n'ose pas dire que l'Esthétique est l'étude d'un système de négations, quoiqu'il y ait quelque grain de vérité dans ce dire. Si l'on prend les problèmes de face, et comme corps à corps, problèmes qui sont celui de la jouissance et celui de la puissance de produire la jouissance, les solutions positives, et même les seuls énoncés nous défient. (1: 1312)

(I do not dare say that Esthetics is the study of a system of negations, even though there be some grain of truth in that. If we take the problems head on, and hand-to-hand, problems of pleasure and of the power to produce pleasure, positive solutions and even just the expressions challenge us.)

He does not go on to flesh out the implications of this view of esthetics as a system of negation, which is understandable given his reluctance to embrace it in the first place. It will be left to others after Valéry, as I will show, to plumb further the relationship of poetry to a productive kind of negation or ignorance. For now let us retain that Valéry once again has recourse to the notion of *jouissance*, which sets us on the path of the infinitely unsatisfiable nature of the desire to know.

Even in his hesitation to affirm negation here, he adopts a method of negation in that he affirms the negation by admitting that he does not dare admit it, in what amounts to a negation of the affirmation of negation. There is even a certain nihilist tendency in the way Valéry talks about the regulatory ideal or useful fiction of definitive answers in esthetic answers. He evokes Flaubert, who could arguably be seen as one of the founding thinkers of "pure" art or style, only to reject his view completely:

Flaubert était convaincu qu'il n'existe pour une idée qu'une seule forme, qu'il s'agit de la trouver ou de la construire, et qu'il faut peiner jusque-là. Cette belle doctrine n'a malheureusement aucun sens. Mais il n'est pas mauvais de la suivre. Un effort n'est jamais perdu. Sisyphe se faisait des muscles. (1: 1476)

(Flaubert was convinced that there exists only one form for an idea, that it is a question of finding or constructing it, and that one must suffer until that point. This lovely doctrine, unfortunately, is meaningless. But it is not bad to follow it. An effort is never lost. Sisyphus developed big muscles.)

The search for a unified esthetics takes on absurd dimensions here in a kind of act of defiance of what Valéry knows to be the case about poetry and esthetic creation generally. It is here that the split between poetry as the composition of poems and poetry in the larger sense re-emerges, with theorizing about poetry actually negating the possibility of what the creator of poems might wish to accomplish. While the poet might, like Sisyphus, end up with stronger muscles, perhaps it is a more tenable position to abandon the regulative ideal of unity in favor of the conception of poetry that we have seen forming in Valéry by implication, one that acknowledges the tension between the unity of poetry and the division implied by the discourse that is born from any attempt to characterize that unity. As we have seen, "pure" poetry yields, paradoxically, and like music itself to which it was often compared, not ineffability but, rather, more discourse. Something important about poetic "knowing" emerges not so much from what is said about poetry as from the process, or experience, of what is said, or negated, or affirmed as sayable or unsayable. In that sense we return to a model of experiential knowledge, not in the sense of acting in the world beyond poetry but rather in the experience of attempting to seize what we mean when we speak of poetry to begin with. It is not a question of opposing textual experience to experience "in the world," but rather of seeing engagement with poetry as itself an experience in the world. The difference-to-itself that emerges once we attempt to unpack the statement "poetry is poetry" also yields the split between poetry as poems and poetry as a more abstract notion. Given that any attempt to speak of poems necessarily belongs to the domain of the more abstract notion of "poetry," at least if it is going to be more than descriptive technical analysis of the words on the page, discourse about poetry emerges as a full partner with poems as an integral part of talking about poetry, one that produces an open-ended kind of poetic "knowing" that emerges from an ignorance but also remains tied to ignorance as an essential motor of the discourse. This is not to say that we should embrace a total lack of knowing or lament such a state, but rather allow it to generate the next, always tentative, step toward the articulation of "poetry."

3

Non-knowledge, Limit, and Productive Impossibility (Bataille and Blanchot)

We have seen in the previous chapter how the tautological definition of poetry yields not the cancelation of reflection on poetry but its proliferation as a series of attempts to say what risks being unsayable. Along the way, our approach to knowledge of or by poetry is affected by awareness of the limitations of any answer poets could provide to the question of what poetry is, and the tentativeness and incompleteness of any knowledge that poetry can provide about the world, in stark contrast to those in the nineteenth century who might have claimed revelatory power, of perhaps even a divine sort, for poetry. This repositioning of knowledge of and by poetry implies an important dynamic between knowledge and ignorance, the latter characterized not negatively but as a neutral state of unknowing that serves as a kind of check on overconfident knowledge claims and an invitation to revise knowledge in the face of new experience and new kinds of discourse about poetry and the relation to the world from which it springs and which it forms.[1]

This chapter and the next consider poets and thinkers who explicitly or implicitly have defined poetry as a question about itself or about the world, not in order to put in doubt poetry's ability to serve as a source of knowledge but rather to animate the dynamic tension between knowledge and ignorance. I examine Georges Bataille's idiosyncratic account of poetry whereby both words and meaning become poetry's victims in a sacrifice that can never be fully carried out. On Bataille's view, poetry can never coincide with itself; it occurs, paradoxically, at those moments when it posits its own impossibility. Blanchot operates on similar ground by affirming the impossibility of seizing and describing the ever-changing relationship of poetry to the world of other experience. In that sense, he leads us away from the question of knowledge or non-knowledge about poetry and towards the question, inspired by reflection on poetry, of what it might mean to live in such a way that we become nothing but question and what kind of response that might evoke in subjects living in the world.

Not content to settle into the non-knowing, non-saying state of the mystic, poets such as Philippe Jaccottet and Jean-Michel Maulpoix, the subjects of chapter four, who write extensively about poetry in addition to writing poetry, repeatedly renew the attempt to capture what kind of knowing poetry might provide while always using that same discourse to unsettle definitive claims. The distinction between unsettling and canceling is an important one, because for none of the poets and thinkers I am considering is it a question of debunking poetry's knowledge claims altogether or dismantling a now-outdated poetic tradition. Rather, former claims are tempered by a new awareness of the ignorance that they open up in their wake, so that poetry's truth claims are resituated within the realm of fiction, which is not to say that they are cast into the domain of the false. Rather, these kinds of fictions can generate a way of living that resonates with this new approach to the balance between knowledge and ignorance, so that our truth claims are made in a more lucid way. Maulpoix, for instance, will not speak of presence but of the fiction of presence that poetry provides. To say that we organize our knowledge of the world as a series of fictions is to acknowledge the crucial role that literature can play in mapping and also in establishing our relation to the world we inhabit, and in that sense the epistemological questions that poets raise about poetry are also directly about the world from which poetry springs and which it helps us to understand. Because modern poets are not seeking to resolve ignorance or simply to dwell there, their exploration of the relationship among poetry, ignorance, and knowledge is not anxiety-ridden or quietist but, rather, productive of discourse. As Andrew Bennett argues, ignorance is "specifically articulated within the definitions of literature that we have largely inherited from the Romantics, and is intrinsic to what we think we know about literature and what, even now, we tend to think literature allows us to know" (Bennett 5–6). The unknowability of poetry and of the world moves toward the knowability of both in tandem, in a way that allows for perpetual revision in light of new thought and new experience. Poetry is, in Bennett's formulation, "the place where ignorance can be entertained, explored, enacted" (22).

While the process of working with and within ignorance is not anxiety-ridden, it is nonetheless unsettling, lending itself to a perpetual dissatisfaction and restlessness. Poet Lionel Ray has underscored this aspect of a knowability that seems always just out of reach: "« L'insaisissable est proche » dit Marie-

Claire Bancquart. Il est toujours si proche qu'on croirait à chaque instant pouvoir l'atteindre. D'où notre fièvre, notre perpétuelle insatisfaction. Le poète par nature est condamné à l'attente insatisfaite" ("'The unseizable is near,' says Marie-Claire Bancquart. It is always so near that at each instant we would think we were able to attain it. From that comes our fever, our perpetual dissatisfaction. The poet by nature is condemned to unsatisfied waiting") (213). The inaccessibility or unknowability is in this sense similar to the imperfection of language and its inability perfectly to represent its object. On one hand, this could be a source of regret, but on the other hand, just as language's imperfection is precisely what gives birth to poetry, which depends on language's impossible transparency, the inaccessibility of the world is what gives rise to and feeds poetry, giving it both its task and a sense of urgency. Bernard Desportes has made this point:

> L'inaccessibilité du monde par quelque bout qu'on le prenne est le fondement de la création poétique. Quelles que soient la profondeur ou la violence de ses lumières, le chaos de ses ombres, le souffle de ses vents, le monde nous demeure insaisissable—et nous restons pareillement inaccessibles à nous-mêmes, fragmentaires, parcellisés, dans la douleur infinie d'un éclatement toujours multiplié du sens. C'est notre incapacité à lier l'accord de l'éphémère et du temps, à résoudre l'équivalence de notre origine et de notre fin, à embrasser simultanément cette infinité de sens et de sensations qui nous traversent et nous révèlent à une unité toujours plus inaccessible qui, dans le même mouvement qu'elle est dévoilement de la mort et révélation de notre tragédie, est naissance de notre élan poétique.... Le poème naît d'un manque. Il naît de la conscience d'une inaptitude et de la perception lucide d'un *échec*.... Cette accession parcellaire que nous avons de la réalité du monde aussi bien que de nous-mêmes nous est inacceptable qui nous réduit en fragments; elle fait ainsi du poème, d'abord, un acte de refus. (quoted in Stout 73)

(The inaccessibility of the world by whatever end one takes it is the foundation of poetic creation. Whatever the depth or violence of its insights, the chaos of its shadows, the way its winds blow, the world remains ungraspable—and we, likewise, remain inaccessible to ourselves, fragmentary, broken up, in the infinite pain of an ever multiplied explosion of meaning. It is our incapacity to link the ephemeral and time, to resolve the equivalence of our origin and our end, to embrace simultaneously that infinity of meaning and sensations that cross through us and reveal to us a unity that is more and more inaccessible, which in the same movement whereby it is the unveiling of death and revelation of our tragedy, is also the birth of our poetic inclination.... The poem is born of a lack. It is born of the awareness of an inaptitude and of the lucid perception of a *failure*…. That fragmentary attainment that we have of the reality of the world as well as of ourselves, which reduces us to fragments, is unacceptable to us. It makes of the poem, first of all, an act of refusal.)

Desportes brings together several crucial conceptual strands here. To the relation between poetry and the world, he adds the human subject itself, which holds in common with the world a fundamental inaccessibility. Poetry is founded on this foreign relation we have both to ourselves and to the world. While Desportes does not indicate explicitly the extent to which poetry may or may not serve as a corrective to this inaccessibility or simply give voice to it, the kinds of tensions he sketches between the unity we would like to perceive and the fragmentation which we often perceive in its stead are precisely the sort of tension that poetry as we have been conceiving it is well suited to reveal and develop. Poetry, and here I would understand the term to include writing about poetry just as much as actual verse if not more so, is thus the vehicle of the revelation of a positive ignorance about both the subject and the world (and their relation).[2] What remains impossible to categorize precisely here is the status of poetry as negation or refusal: does the "act of refusal" get us all the way to overcoming the inaccessibility of the world, or does poetry simply protest against that inaccessibility by inviting us to attempt, ultimately unsuccessfully, to negate it? If a throw of the dice will never abolish chance, and if revolt will not change that against which one revolts, poetry takes on an existential urgency that allows us to address our ignorance of the world without mitigating it. The "infinite pain of an ever multiplied explosion of meaning" is at the same time productive of new forms of meaning unavailable to us without such reflection on poetry and the poetic task. What Desportes outlines here is an excellent summary of the set of concerns to which modern lyric poets turn when they consider the relationship among poetry, knowledge, the world, and the self that situates itself, as it situates poetry, at the site of an endlessly changing multiplicity that both produces meaning and complicates the relationship of the subject to that meaning.

Contemporary poet Claude Royet-Journoud has linked poetry and thought by identifying both as a pause or empty space imposed on experience.

> La pensée aussi n'existe que par rapport à un arrêt qui est un blanc…. Ecrire, c'est faire ce trou dans l'espace. Tout part de l'immobilité, de ce travail d'attention qui est également un travail corporel. Le funambule a le même problème, il tente de réunir le mouvement et l'arrêt, de trouver le juste équilibre entre eux. La table de l'écrivain est mentale, c'est une façon de savoir s'arrêter, de commencer en sachant qu'il n'y a aucune origine. (9)

(Thought, as well, exists only with regard to a stop which is a blank.... To write is to carve that whole in space. Everything takes off from immobility, from the effort of attention that is also a corporeal effort. The tightrope walker has the same problem; he tries to bring together movement and rest, to find perfect equilibrium. The writer's desk is in the mind, a matter of knowing when to stop, of starting out aware that there is no beginning. (11, translation modified))

While at first glance this could be construed as the rather evident claim that to think and write involve suspending daily activities for a time, Royet-Journoud goes on to include immediately thereafter that "Ecrire est un *métier d'ignorance*" (9) ("Writing is a *craft of ignorance*" (11)). This phrase, which Royet-Journoud uses as a chapter title as well, has become well known, but we should proceed cautiously when considering the implications of such an assertion. It is tempting to see here an anti-theory stance that affirms the poet as the vehicle of some kind of direct unmediated experience that can only be sullied by intellectual reflection. This seems to be the way poet Fabienne Courtade understands the assertion when she states: "Je suis absolument d'accord avec cette phrase. La théorie n'a *aucun* droit sur moi. Je la tiens à distance, et je reste dans un questionnement, dans l'intranquillité" ("I absolutely agree with that sentence. Theory has *no claim* over me. I keep it at a distance, and I remain in a questioning and in a non-tranquility") (in Stout 247–8). While much hinges on what exactly one understands by "theory" here, it is a dubious move to oppose theory to questioning as if they were mutually exclusive. As we have seen, those who associate poetry both with a kind of knowing and an intense questioning could be said to be theorizing otherwise. While they would certainly oppose systematic and/or closed approaches to thought and knowledge, their position could not be characterized as antitheoretical in most senses of the term. Ignorance as Royet-Journoud evokes it here performs the work of clearing away received ideas and preconceived notions of the world in order to build them anew, rather than simply to dwell in ignorance.

In that sense, ignorance is not an originary state to be overcome. Courtade's emphasis on questioning does align with other views we have been considering, but in order to question, one needs a basis of prior knowledge on which the questioning depends, and theory can of course lead to questioning and restlessness even more than it can resolve it. The poet, by the act of writing, engages the tension between writing and ignorance rather than eternally describing that ignorance; if that were not so, poetry would risk ceasing to be a creative act at all and would simply mirror the kind of questioning and restlessness that Courtade evokes. Royet-Journoud goes on in fact to speak of thought, making it clear that ignorance is not, on his view, a place where the poet dwells indefinitely: "Pour que la pensée se fasse acte, il faut qu'il y ait arrêt" (10) ("For thought to become act, it must stand still" (12)). Once thought passes into action, it will ultimately not build an unshakeable foundation, but that is not to say that meaning is evacuated from the poet's task. Quite the contrary: "L'unique question est celle du sens et elle demeure insoluble. On voudrait saisir un sens au moment où il se met en marche, où il reste indécidable" (10) ("The only question is the one of sense, and that is insoluble. Sense has to be caught the moment it develops, while it remains still undetermined" (12)). So what poetry captures is not just questioning but also meaning, in order to give form to a meaning that would otherwise disappear. It thus cannot be a question of keeping theory at a distance, but rather of theorizing poetically by being open both to the meanings that poetic creation can capture and the doubt that they can inspire about those very creations. It is that simultaneous act of theoretical building and destruction that the poets and thinkers I examine in this chapter and the next engage with in their prose writings, which become simultaneously poetic and theoretical in that sense.

Without that sense of doubt or questioning, we get the optimism of an Yves Bonnefoy, who constantly affirms poetry's relation to presence and its anti-conceptual stance,[3] or of those who would align poetry and science as differing but equally effective sources of knowledge. That distinction between scientific and poetic knowledge is at the base of Aimé Césaire's considerations in his 1945 essay "Poésie et connaissance": "La connaissance poétique naît dans le grand silence de la connaissance scientifique.... La physique classe et explique, mais l'essence des choses lui échappe" ("Poetic knowledge is born in the great silence of scientific knowledge.... Physics classifies and explains, but the essence of things escapes it") (157). Likewise, Saint-John Perse indicates, in his 1960 Nobel Prize acceptance speech:

> La grande aventure de l'esprit poétique ne le cède en rien aux ouvertures dramatiques de la science moderne.... Aussi loin que la science recule ses frontières,... on entendra courir encore la meute chasseresse du poète. Car si la poésie n'est pas, comme on l'a dit, « le réel absolu », elle en est bien la plus proche convoitise et la plus proche appréhension, à cette limite extrême de complicité où le réel dans le poème semble s'informer lui-même.
>
> (The great adventure of the poetic mind cedes nothing to the dramatic overtures of modern science.... However far science rolls back its border... we

will still hear the poet's hunting pack. For if poetry is not, as they have said, "the absolute real," it is its closest desire and its closest apprehension, at that extreme limit of complicity where the real in the poem seems to inform itself.)

Such approaches seem to avoid acknowledging the role of ignorance, and they are open to what Jean-Marie Gleize has called an "optimisme conquérant" ("conquering optimism") (101).[4] For Saint-John Perse and others who establish parallels between poetry and science,[5] according to Gleize, "la poésie se justifie pour eux d'être une arme, ou en tout cas un instrument aux immenses capacités virtuelles, une valeur, une des formes les plus achevées (et les plus sacrées) que puisse prendre l' « honneur des hommes », salvatrice ou rédemptrice, réconciliatrice, bienfaisante et nécessaire" ("poetry justifies itself for them by being a weapon, or at any rate an instrument with immense virtual capacities, a value, one of the most accomplished (and most sacred) forms that 'men's honor' can take, saving or redemptive, reconciliatory, beneficent and necessary") (102). Gleize rightly critiques a poetry that aligns itself with nineteenth-century-style positivism while seeming to neglect poetry's relation to negation, ignorance, and doubt; he is quick to denounce any kind of nostalgic approach to poetry and claims that poetry can only exist nowadays as a sense of crisis:

> « La poésie » n'existe pas, n'existe plus, ce qui ne signifie pas, bien sûr, le tarissement de la pratique poétique, mais seulement que la poésie vit son état de crise, sans doute *de* son état de crise, un état critique et autocritique permanent qui est certainement sa seule définition possible aujourd'hui, qu'on s'en réjouisse et qu'on veuille le porter à son maximum d'intensité dévastatrice… ou qu'on le déplore en tentant de restituer à la poésie quelque chose de son intégrité ancienne, de ses anciens pouvoirs. (102)

> ("Poetry" does not exist, no longer exists, which does not mean, of course, the drying up of poetic practice, but only that poetry is living its state of crisis, without a doubt living *on* its state of crisis, a critical and self-critical permanent state that is certainly its only possible definition today, whether one rejoices at that or wants to bring it to its maximum devastating energy… or whether one deplores it and attempts to give back to poetry something of its former integrity and its former powers.)

Such a position rightly identifies modern poetry's turn toward self-interrogation as a key component of the way it identifies itself, but the two polar alternatives Gleize provides here, either celebrating or nostalgically lamenting such a turn, discard a more nuanced approach that will be the position of so many poets.

For Jaccottet and Maulpoix, whom we'll explore in the next chapter, and many others, the question of poetry is not a matter of choosing to embrace or reject its modern crisis but to negotiate new self-reflective directions for the lyric that retain a space—a tentative, undogmatic space—for the possibilities that poetry held before the moment of modern crisis. It may even be that the nostalgia Gleize evokes here for poetry's "former powers" were never in fact divorced from doubts about those very powers, if we think back to the Romantic period or to Mallarmé's time, when poets laid the groundwork for the kind of intense self-interrogation that Gleize evokes while also making unprecedentedly expansive claims about poetry's powers. Advancing the doubt *as well as* the statement of powers is the position that many poets will adopt, and it is one that sees a certain continuity with earlier forms of poetic theorizing while also seeking lucidity about the limits of those claims. To say that poetry "lives… on its state of crisis" is not necessarily to advocate destruction of a poetic ideal but rather to negotiate constantly the space of affirmation and rejection of poetry's powers in a critical move that makes of that very negotiation a central task of poetry and, at the same time, to make thinking about poetry and writing about it in prose a crucial, and not a secondary, poetic act. It is by that move that we can, for instance, engage Gleize's contention that a state of crisis is "certainly its only possible definition today." As we have seen, this definitional impulse might be, even more than a sense of crisis, a central poetico-critical concern among those eager to name or shape the relation of poetry to the world it claims to know. This dissatisfaction or restlessness with the tautological "poetry is poetry" has arguably marked reflection on poetry just as much as a sense of crisis, and the fact that Gleize's remarks have brought us to considering this definitional point is evidence of the way conversations about poetry more broadly necessarily circle back to questions of its definition.

Gleize also brings the discussion of crisis back to the question of meaning, and in this he highlights the relation I have been tracing between the way poetry defines itself and the interrelated way in which it establishes a relationship to the world in terms of knowing or making sense of it. This necessary turn back out toward the world prevents such considerations of poetry from becoming insular; poetry's particular kind of autoreflexivity is one that includes rather than rejects the world to which it stands in relation:

> Ce que nous nommons « crise » de la poésie ne saurait être simplement pensé en termes sociologiques ou « techniques », elle concerne, antérieurement

pourrait-on dire, la question (insoluble) du rapport au sens, au Sens, au monde, à la réalité, au Réel, et la capacité du langage à dire ce réel, à l'atteindre ou l'évoquer, etc. La « crise » que désigne Mallarmé n'est pas seulement la crise *du vers*, c'est celle dont il fait état dans *Igitur*, cette « illumination négative » dont il a fait *réellement* l'expérience et qui n'est pas d'abord une question formelle. (118)

(That which we name "crisis" of poetry cannot simply be thought in sociological or "technical" terms; it concerns, previously, we might say, the (unsolvable) question of the relationship to sense, to Meaning, to the world, to reality, to the Real, and the capacity of language to put this real into words, to attain or evoke it, etc. The "crisis" that Mallarmé identifies is not only the crisis *of verse*, it is the one he deals with in *Igitur*, that "negative illumination" that he *truly* experienced and which is not first of all a formal question.)

Gleize even goes so far, as we saw in the last chapter, as to assign poetry a kind of subjectivity, with which the reader enters into relation in order to be defined by that relation: "Oui, nous cherchons la poésie, nous cherchons aussi à en dire, à en communiquer quelque chose (de l'ordre d'une information, d'un savoir), mais la poésie nous, me, cherche. C'est nous, je, qui sommes en cause. « Je » lis" ("Yes, we seek poetry, we seek also to say and communicate something about it (on the order of an information, a knowledge), but poetry seeks, confronts, us, and me. It is we, and I, who are involved. 'I' read") (132). Here Gleize puts in play all of the strands we have been considering thus far, including poetry's relation to the subject and to knowledge, and more specifically, if implicitly here, to ignorance, since Gleize positions the subject as seeker of knowledge who then sees that quest frustrated by poetry, which does not provide it. But the ignorance that poetry provides in knowledge's stead is portrayed here as constitutive of the subject, as subject-as-not-knowing.

What begins to emerge here is that perhaps poetry's function lines up neatly neither with knowledge nor with ignorance: perhaps the role of poetry, in the larger sense of the term that we have been employing, is to call into question typical meanings of terms such as knowledge or ignorance so as to avoid creating a simple but false dichotomy between them. If ignorance could be said to be itself a kind of knowledge, we will have emptied those terms of their conventional meaning in order to leave them open to new potential meanings. And in that sense, we may perform the same operation on terms such as knowledge and ignorance that we have been performing on the term poetry itself. In other words, we will have acted on those terms poetically. When words get emptied of their typical content, we risk meaninglessness when we attempt to use the terms or, perhaps, tautology. But what we have seen as true for poetry is also true for categories such as knowledge and ignorance: by emptying them of received meaning, we can begin to unravel tautological approaches to meaning and, in so doing, resituate that meaning. This may very well be the "question (insoluble) du rapport au sens [… et] au monde" ("(unsolvable) question of the relationship to sense [… and] to the world") that Gleize describes, but while it may be irresolvable, we have gained ground by realizing the unresolvability, and we have generated a kind of knowledge of and from ignorance, in a process that "poetic" writing helps put into motion.

Angela Leighton has argued that, in contrast to philosophers for whom ignorance is a problem and knowledge the solution, "knowing and not knowing are not absolute opposites for the poet" (168). She goes on to note that:

> the one can be layered over the other, and both remembered at once. The poet might come to know what he doesn't know, or not know what he knows. The contradiction catches something of the surprise and familiarity that poetry can bring, both to writer and reader. It is not an exchange of knowledge-content, passed through the pleasurable medium of rhythmic language; it is, instead, a constant, mutual rediscovery of "something I didn't know I knew." (168)

Leighton's description aptly captures the element of unknowing inherent in the poetic enterprise; I would disagree, however, that what occurs is a "rediscovery of something I didn't know I knew." Such a description seems to put us solidly back on Platonic grounds of pre-existent knowledge that need only be brought to the surface by the right stimulus. This conception risks negating poetry's creative function by overemphasizing its revelatory one. Still, Leighton is right to note that poets such as W. S. Graham, who suggests that "the poet does not write what he knows but what he doesn't know" (quoted in Leighton 169), "make not knowing the condition of writing at all" (169). Once again we see that ignorance, rather than shutting down discourse, gives rise to it, not in order merely to reveal or describe the ignorance, nor simply to cancel it, but to renegotiate the space of knowledge and ignorance itself. This process shapes the subjectivity of both poet and reader; when Leighton claims that "what we want from a poem is not ultimately… a graspable or paraphraseable message" but rather "an invitation to listen" (176), she brings us quite close to the notion of the subject constituted in listening as theorized by Jean-Luc Nancy.[6]

To know in this way is, as Leighton acknowledges, "to know *differently*" (178). Intriguingly, she suggests a kind of intransitive knowledge, "like a verb without an object, or like a suspended participle, something to be found only in the finding, discovered in the discovering, heard and listened for as if in the hearing and listening" (180). While highly unsatisfying according to philosophical criteria for knowledge, this object-less knowledge returns us once again to experience, not in the sense of a direct or unmediated experience but rather one created by the words we use not only to describe but also to create it. While writing about experience, and the experience that is poetry, confirms and highlights the absence of direct experience, or what we could label our ignorance of it, that act of writing simultaneously reorients our knowledge toward the words on the page as we write, which is what the best writing about poetry does as well. Not content merely to refer back to poems, prose writing on poetry itself participates in that reorientation of knowledge. If as Leighton suggests, for philosophers, what matters is "'what' might be known" whereas "in poetry, the burden falls on the ongoing 'how' of it" (180), we also need to acknowledge that there is, so to speak, a "what" in the "how," that objectless knowledge nonetheless yields a kind of knowledge that is not simply all process, even if the product is destined to change with each new intervention in the thinking and writing of and about poetry. In that sense, ignorance itself becomes dynamic: an acknowledged ignorance, one seen as a vehicle for knowledge or even as itself a kind of knowledge, is differentiated from a simple state of unknowing. As Barbara Johnson has suggested:

> perhaps rather than simply questioning the nature of knowledge, we should today reevaluate the static, inert concept we have always had of ignorance. Ignorance, far more than knowledge, is what can never be taken for granted. If I perceive my ignorance as a gap in knowledge instead of an imperative that changes the very nature of what I think I know, then I do not truly experience my ignorance. (332)

By following Johnson's lead in the way we have been talking about ignorance, we have begun to unravel the tautology "ignorance is (simply) ignorance" and have pursued, via exploration in language, the ways in which ignorance may be differentiated from itself. This process will by now look familiar, as it is exactly the process I have outlined in the quest to know and say something about poetry, which is a series of attempts to unravel its tautological definition. Rather than seeing experience as a corrective to ignorance, we can see ignorance *as* a kind of experience which, like the experience of poetry or any other, needs to be transformed into language in order to be interpreted and thereby made meaningful in ways that can be articulated.

With this conceptual framework established, and in light of the fact that for poetry or ignorance to mean anything at all it has to be elaborated in discourse, how can we keep the issues of poetry, knowledge, and ignorance in play simultaneously without resorting either to claims of immediate knowledge or to the risk of a kind of meaningless babble or affirmations of mere ineffability? Both lyric poets and thinkers continued to grapple with these questions throughout the twentieth century; much of what I have been tracing in terms of the relations among poetry, knowledge, and ignorance was first explicitly brought together and explicitly theorized by Georges Bataille and Maurice Blanchot. They offer important insight into the question of poetry's relation to knowledge by claiming, as Elisabeth Arnould has pointed out, that poetry "n'est pas nouveau savoir, sa forme subjective ou souveraine" ("is not a new knowledge, its sovereign or subjective form"). It is "non-savoir" ("non-knowledge") which, "échappant à l'absolu, échappe aussi à toute tâche, comme à toute pensée" ("in escaping the absolute, also escape all tasks and all thought") ("La poésie" 790, n.23).[7] Bataille's remarks on poetry are integrated into the more general lines of his thought. In particular, he aligns poetry with sacrifice:

> De la poésie, je dirai maintenant qu'elle est, je crois, le sacrifice où les mots sont victimes. Les mots, nous les utilisons, nous faisons d'eux les instruments d'actes utiles. Nous n'aurions rien d'humain si le langage en nous devait être en entier servile. Nous ne pouvons non plus nous passer des rapports efficaces qu'introduisent les mots entre les hommes et les choses. Mais nous les arrachons à ces rapports dans un délire. (*OC5*: 156)[8]

> (Of poetry, I will now say that it is, I believe, the sacrifice in which words are victims. Words—we use them, we make of them the instruments of useful acts. We would in no way have anything of the human about us if language had to be entirely servile within us. Neither can we do without the efficacious relations which words introduce between men and things. But we tear words from these links in a delirium. (*Inner* 135))

In its broadest outlines, Bataille's thought is concerned with the notion of limits and transgression. As Stuart Kendall summarizes: "Beginning with the suicide of language, his famous holocaust of words, Bataille effects the annihilation of consciousness, the death of thought, a prelude to the final shattering. On the one hand, thought, consciousness, discourse, knowledge and, on the other, transgression, impossibility, inner experience, nonknowledge, silence" ("Introduction" xli). By a voluntary estrangement and removal from the realm of ordinary experience ("Aucun jugement de valeur: je ne peux pas arriver à la moindre condamnation de ceux qui savent, qui vivent dans le monde où je vis moi-même, dans lesquels je ne peux plus vivre" (*OC8*: 196)) ("No value judgment: I am unable to arrive at the least condemnation of those that know, that live in the world wherein I myself live, in the world in which I can no longer live" (*Unfinished* 117)), Bataille pursues non-knowledge as the inevitable conclusion of this estrangement:

> J'ai tout fait pour savoir ce qui est connaissable et ce que j'ai cherché est ce qui est informulable au fond de moi. Je suis moi dans un monde dont je reconnais qu'il m'est profondément inaccessible puisque dans tous les liens que j'ai cherché à nouer avec lui, il reste je ne sais quoi que je ne peux vaincre, ce qui fait que je reste dans une sorte de désespoir. Je me suis rendu compte que ce sentiment est assez rarement éprouvé....
>
> Position de celui qui ne sait pas ce qu'il y a dans une malle cadenassée qu'il n'a pas la possibilité d'ouvrir. C'est à ce moment qu'on emploie un langage littéraire où il y a plus que ce qu'il est nécessaire de dire. Seul, le silence peut exprimer ce qu'on a à dire, donc dans un langage trouble, dans un état d'esprit de parfait désespoir, dans un sens au moins, non comparable à celui qui cherche quelque chose et qui ne l'a pas; c'est un désespoir beaucoup plus profond, que nous avons toujours connu, qui tient à ceci que l'on a un projet en tête qui ne peut aboutir, que l'on est sur le point d'être frustré alors que l'on tient essentiellement à ce qui en est l'objet. Ce désespoir est équivalent à celui que peut être la mort. Aussi étranger à la mort qu'ignorant du contenu de ce coffre dont je parlais tout à l'heure. (*OC8*: 192–3)

(I have done everything to know what is knowable and I have looked for that which is unformulatable in my depths. I myself am in a world I recognize as profoundly inaccessible to me: in all the ties that I sought to bind it with, I still don't know what I can conquer, and I remain in a kind of despair. I recognize that this feeling is rarely experienced....

This is the position of someone who doesn't know what is in the locked trunk, the trunk there is no possibility of opening. At this moment one typically uses literary language, wherein there is no longer anything that one must say. Only silence is able to express what we have to say. Therefore, in a troubled language, in a perfect state of despair, in a sense at least, incomparable to that of those people who look for something and don't have it; this is a much more profound despair, that we have always known, that is linked to the fact that we have a project in mind, a project that cannot be completed, that we are on the point of being frustrated such that we are essentially attached to our object. This despair is equivalent to despair over death. As foreign to death as ignoring the contents of the trunk I was talking about earlier. (*Unfinished* 113, translation modified))

It is, however, impossible to dwell in the state of nonknowledge that Bataille describes here. The limit, once it is reached, is unlivable. Bataille is tracing a path, and identifying a dilemma, similar to those we have seen poets arrive at whenever they are tempted to affirm poetry as an immediate experience or an incommunicable phenomenon or a site of absolute ignorance: as soon as one attempts to give voice to that kind of experience, one is necessarily released from it, given that nonknowledge is aligned with a silence that is broken once words are used to describe or evoke it.

Bataille extends this impossibility of dwelling in ignorance to the even more fundamental, pre-discursive level of "the suffering owed to the impossibility of knowledge": "Je ne sais rien mais la douleur que j'ai de ne rien savoir, devenant un objet de connaissance, me donne justement la réponse à l'instant même où je désespérais de la trouver" ("I know nothing, but the suffering that I have from knowing nothing, becoming an object of knowledge, gives me the response at the very instant that I despaired of finding it") (*OC*8: 571/*Unfinished* 164). While non-knowledge is the goal, then, it is simply an unfulfillable one because the realization of the non-knowledge is self-negating once suffering is taken into account. This experience is parallel to what we have been saying about poetry, in that the inability to define it, the indication of our non-knowledge of it, is precisely what creates an interesting and varied poetic discourse of attempts to seize what has been classified as unseizable, and in that sense becomes a new object of creation, a poetic attempt to seize the notion of poetry which, in so doing, becomes a new poetic object. As Christopher Gemerchak puts it: "If, therefore, Hegel—our paradigm of meaning—relates discourse to a horizon of knowledge, Bataille will relate discourse, and the subject who cannot but fail to master it, to one of non-knowledge. The method by which he does so goes by the name of poetry" (126).

What is essential according to Bataille's characterization of poetry is what he calls "effusion," at which we arrive when we move beyond (or, as he would say, sacrifice) themes, rhythms, and other components of poetry. We could say that in this move, Bataille turns "poems" into "poetry." The experience of poetry is, for him, "l'effusion la plus proche d'une méditation" ("the effusion that is closest to a meditation") (*OC5*: 220). If poems, in Bataille's view, sacrifice words, they also sacrifice meaning: "Le moment où la poésie brise avec le *thème* et le sens est du point de vue de la méditation l'arrachement résolu, qui la peut séparer des balbutiements (des agenouillements de l'ascèse)" ("the moment where poetry breaks with the *theme* and the meaning is, from the point of view of meditation, the resolute breaking away that can separate it from stammering (from the kneelings of asceticism")) (*Méthode* 77). But, as we shall see, this brings us full circle to a moment of non-differentiation between poetry and the mystic state, since what they would both have in common is a lack of meaning, a full moment of presence that is uncommunicable in words. What separates poetry from the mystic experience, as we have seen in earlier chapters, is that drive to articulate in what poetry consists, a move that puts us back in the realm of language and thus, on Bataille's view, an incomplete or even failed sacrifice. Bataille's notion of poetry projects onto it a total negation of limits: "limitée, la poésie ne pouvait affirmer la pleine souveraineté qui n'est qu'une négation de toutes les limites" ("limited, poetry could not affirm full sovereignty which is only a negation of all limits") (*Méthode* 79). Such an unlimited condition is hardly different from the absolute claims made for it in the nineteenth century, and as we have already seen, Bataille is conscious of the impossibility of remaining within such an unlimited state. Such ideals of nonknowledge thus remain mere projections of an impossibility, whereas what becomes truly generative of productive discourse is the mining of the consequences of that impossibility, the move toward maintaining discourse in the face of the known impossibility of the project. As Arnould has argued, "Bataille, in fact, is not even interested in the 'unknown.' Rather, he is interested in the mystery of its mechanism, in what persists as witness to its withdrawal" ("Impossible" 90). Poetry, as Bataille and others will go on to characterize it, is an important player in this "mechanism" of the unknown, as opposed to the mere indicator of it. In an important sense, Bataille's engagement with poetry and knowledge mirrors the much longer and larger history of modern engagement with poetry, which does not abandon poetry completely so much as attempt to give voice to the ways in which we may reshape our conception of it, and indeed making that shaping the main object of the subject we label "poetry."

Bataille's prototype for the ultimate abandonment of poetry and the poetic project is Arthur Rimbaud's renunciation of poetry.[9] But, as in the case of Rimbaud himself, what is most intriguing and productive for our thinking about poetry is not the renunciation itself but the meaning we can or cannot assign to it, and what happens in its wake, given that poetry does not in fact simply pass over into silence.[10] Bataille himself provides much that is of great interest not when he veers, like Rimbaud or the mystic, into silence but rather when he attempts to give voice to the experience of wanting and not being able to attain silence, renunciation, and non-knowledge. By that move, he shifts the terrain of the question itself so that we are no longer asked to choose between, say, knowledge and nonknowledge, but rather to see poetry as the working ground on which to ask different kinds of questions. Let us consider, for instance, one of his opening moves in *L'expérience intérieure*:

> Si la poésie introduit l'étrange, elle le fait par la voie du familier. Le poétique est du familier se dissolvant dans l'étrange et nous-mêmes avec lui. Il ne nous dépossède jamais de tout en tout, car les mots, les images dissoutes, sont chargés d'émotions déjà éprouvées, fixées à des objets qui le lient au connu. ... Nous ne sommes totalement mis à nu qu'en allant sans tricher à l'inconnu. C'est la part d'inconnu qui donne à l'expérience de Dieu—ou du poétique—leur grande autorité. Mais l'inconnu exige à la fin l'empire sans partage. (*OC*5: 17)
>
> (If poetry introduces the strange, it does so by means of the familiar. The poetic is the familiar dissolving into the strange, and ourselves with it. It never dispossesses us entirely, for the words, the images (once dissolved) are charged with emotions already experienced, attached to objects which link them to the known.... We are only totally laid bare by proceeding without trickery to the unknown. It is the measure of the unknown which lends to the experience of God—or of the poetic—their great authority. But the unknown demands in the end sovereignty without partition. (*Inner* 5))

What begins as a rather standard account of art as defamiliarization of the familiar moves quickly on to implicate the reading subject: "and ourselves with it." Bataille soon turns, however, to the consequences of a defamiliarization that does not, and cannot, go far enough to accomplish what he would ask of poetry: the remains of the sacrifice, that which cannot be negated or forgotten, persist in order to keep ourselves anchored to some extent in our subjectivity, which can be transformed but never abolished in poetic experience. Poetry's "demand" of sovereignty must remain unfulfilled in an experience that risks canceling the meaning or even the existence of poetry altogether. In this regard it is significant that Bataille almost casually suggests a substitutability between God and the poetic. As we shall see is the case with Blanchot as well, part of understanding Bataille's thought is determining to what extent terms such as "poetry" and "God"—or nonknowledge, or sacrifice, or effusion, and so on—are interchangeable. Such would be one consequence of the breakdown of meaning of the terms in the kind of sacrifice Bataille endorses.[11] But an important distinction to be made here, even if making it moves us further away from mystical nonknowledge, is that poetry, even in its most metaphysical conceptions, cannot be divorced from expression in language the way that God can be conceived, *pace* the indication in the Gospel of John that "the Word was God," as extra-linguistic. In other words, poetry's unknown cannot be assimilable to a divine unknown unless we were to assign to poetry a transcendent existence independent of the words we use to conceive it.

Bataille is of course well aware of the impossibility of our reducing ourselves to silence, given that we ourselves would then cease to exist as linguistic and temporal beings. That realization gives rise to a battle:

> Mais la difficulté est qu'on n'arrive pas facilement ni tout à fait à se taire, qu'il faut lutter contre soi-même…: nous cherchons à saisir en nous ce qui subsiste à l'abri des servilités verbales et, ce que nous saisissons, c'est nous-mêmes battant la campagne, enfilant des phrases, peut-être au sujet de notre effort (puis de son échec). Mais des phrases et dans l'impuissance à saisir autre chose. Il faut nous obstiner—nous faisant familiers, cruellement, avec une impuissante sottise, d'habitude dérobée, mais tombant sous la pleine lumière: assez vite augmente l'intensité des états et dès lors ils absorbent, même ils ravissent. Le moment vient où nous pouvons réfléchir, à nouveau ne plus nous taire, enchaîner des mots: cette fois, c'est à la cantonade (à l'arrière-plan) et, sans plus nous soucier, nous laissons leur bruit se perdre. (*OC5*: 27–8)
>
> (But the difficulty is that one manages neither easily nor completely to silence oneself, that one must fight against oneself…: we seek to grasp within us what subsists safe from verbal servilities and what we grasp is ourselves fighting the battle, stringing sentences together—perhaps about our effort (then about its failure)—but sentences all the same, powerless to grasp anything else. It is necessary to persist—making ourselves familiar, cruelly so, with a helpless foolishness, usually concealed, but falling under full light: the intensity of the states builds quite quickly and from that moment they absorb—they even enrapture. The moment comes when we can reflect, link words together, once again no longer silence ourselves: this time it is off in the wings (in the background) and, without worrying any longer, we let their sound fade away. (*Inner* 15))

What Bataille ends up describing, as many writers might attest, is a rather typical cycle whereby one fights against silence with a sense of desperation and lack of faith in the words one manages to assemble, in order to produce words that will fade away until one next takes up the battle and continues to write. While there is certainly a dose of the absurd in the Beckett-like proliferation of potentially meaningless words that this description suggests, it is also, again in microcosm, a portrait of what happens when we try to know poetry, and only a remnant of nineteenth-century nostalgia about our necessary failure to attain the absolute could see in this description an unflinchingly negative or consistently anguished process.[12] It is because of our inability to define poetry precisely that Bataille's characterizations of poetry are so varied; he has identified poetry as "le désordre des mots" ("the disorder of words") (6: 22), "la renonciation à la connaissance" ("the renunciation of knowledge") (2: 518), and "ce qui... peut être chanté" ("that which... can be sung") (11: 88). While such a variety of definitions might signal a failure to account successfully for what poetry is, seen from another angle, such a process of attempted definition is what we call thought, or poetry, itself, given that poetry is caught up in questions of its own definition in a way that makes that definitional attempt a part of the nature of poetry itself.

It is not, however, what Bataille calls poetry, which on Bataille's account would need to be wordless:

> On ne peut rien savoir de l'homme qui n'ait pris forme de phrase et l'engouement pour la poésie d'autre part fait d'intraduisibles suites de mots le sommet. L'extrême est ailleurs. Il n'est entièrement atteint que communiqué (l'homme est plusieurs, la solitude est le vide, la nullité, le mensonge). Qu'une expression quelconque en témoigne: l'extrême en est distinct. Il n'est jamais littérature. Si la poésie l'exprime, il en est distinct: au point de n'être pas poétique, car si la poésie l'a pour objet, elle ne l'atteint pas. Quand l'extrême est là, les moyens qui servent à l'atteindre n'y sont plus. (*OC5*: 63–4)

> (One can know nothing of man which has not taken the form of a sentence, and the infatuation for poetry, on the other hand, makes of untranslatable strings of words a summit. The extreme limit is elsewhere. It is only completely reached if communicated (man is several—solitude is the void, nothingness, lies). Should some sort of expression give evidence of it: the extreme limit is distinct from it. It is never literature. If poetry expresses it, the extreme limit is distinct from it: to the point of not being poetic, for if poetry has an object, it doesn't reach it. When the extreme limit is there, the means which serve to attain it are no longer there. (*Inner* 50))

Poetry can only be coterminous with the extreme limit by not consisting of words. Poetry is by this characterization a term that can never coincide with itself, since wordless poetry would be an impossible or at least an empty term. By existing in words, the poem denies what Bataille claims of it, and in that sense becomes other to itself in an operation similar to what we have observed in the attempt to elaborate the tautological definition of poetry. So by not being able to correspond to Bataille's criteria for it, poetry opens up another space of differentiation from itself, which is the kind of writing about poetry that we have identified as the central aspect of what poetry is, apart from any manifestations of poetry as particular poems. Poetry becomes, on this account and perhaps despite Bataille's own efforts to show otherwise, what occurs when its own impossibility is posited. The process does not end in wordlessness because, quite simply, it cannot do so.

One cannot remain in the realm of the ineffable and simultaneously ascribe a meaning to it, since that very ascription is in the form of (poetic) language. Nor can one completely align poetry on the side of madness or silence, precisely because of the way discourse functions as an ordering principle, even if it is not an explicitly rational, systematically oriented discourse:

> Poétique, à nouveau le langage m'ouvre à l'abîme.
>
> Mais la poésie ne peut effectivement nier l'affirmation du discours cohérent, elle ne peut longuement dissiper le mensonge du discours. Jamais la poésie n'établit ce qu'elle donne à voir. Niant l'ordre où m'enferme un discours cohérent, c'est encore en moi la cohérence du discours qui le nie. Un instant, le discours ordonne en moi ce qui défait l'ordre où il m'enferme, il ordonne ce qui—tragiquement—me rend jusqu'à la mort au délire de la poésie.
>
> Accédant au possible, au repos sans fin, la certitude me serait-elle donnée de vivre *éternellement* devant la vérité, je gémirais. Ce que je veux et que veut en moi l'être humain: je veux, un instant, excéder ma limite, et je veux, un instant, n'être tenu par rien. (*OC*12: 476–7)

> (Poetic language once again opens me to the abyss.
>
> But poetry cannot effectively deny the affirmation of coherent discourse, it cannot dissipate the lie of this discourse for long. Poetry never establishes what it makes visible. Denying the order in which I am enclosed by a coherent discourse, the coherence of the discourse that denies it is still within me. In an instant, discourse orders within me that which undoes the order wherein I am enclosed, it orders that which—tragically—brings me to death, to the delirium of poetry. Attaining the possible, endless repose, I would be granted the certainty of living before the truth, *eternally*, I would groan. What I want and what human being wants in me: one moment, I want to exceed my limit, and, another moment, I want to be gripped by nothing. (*Unfinished* 222–3))

Even denouncing poetry's inability to live up to its own standards requires language, and so poetry, on Bataille's account, is necessary by its impossibility. But that impossibility is itself fertile ground for reflection on what we call poetry and its relation to thought and experience, a fact which generates another discourse. This new discourse about poetry, while it can never come to settle in the silence that Bataille seems to long for as an antidote to suffering and the abyss, is itself removed from the imperative of reduction to silence and thus has the potential to fall outside the demands we place on poetry as Bataille conceives it here. Sketching a poetics of impossibility, in other words, is a process generated from engaging with notions of what "poetry" is but takes a step beyond "poetry" by accounting for and, to some extent, coping with poetry's incapacity to deliver on its own demands. Generating this new poetics does not simply cancel earlier poetic aspirations but rather sees them as in dialogue with the exploration of their own impossibility, a discourse that depends on, but is not reducible to, former claims about poetry's powers.

Bataille's conception of poetry is non-systematic and complex. In that sense, it is faithful to the multifaceted nature of what we understand "poetry" to be generally because it mirrors that shifting of meanings present in the uses of the word "poetry" in its many different contexts and in the multiplicity of understandings of what we mean when we use the word. Bataille's discourse on poetry thus becomes parallel to poetry itself when it considers the relation between poetry and knowledge. Shortly after claiming, in *L'expérience intérieure*, that poetry is sacrifice, he makes the following epistemological claim about it:

> *La poésie mène du connu à l'inconnu.* Elle peut ce que ne peuvent pas le garçon ou la fille, introduire un cheval de beurre. Elle place, de cette façon, devant l'inconnaissable. Sans doute ai-je à peine énoncé les mots que les images familières des chevaux et des beurres se présentent, mais elles ne sont sollicitées que pour mourir. En quoi la poésie est sacrifice, mais le plus accessible. Car si l'usage ou l'abus des mots, auxquels les opérations du travail nous obligent, a lieu sur le plan idéal, irréel du langage, il en est de même du sacrifice de mots qu'est la poésie. (*OC5*: 137)

> (*Poetry leads from the known to the unknown.* It can do what neither the boy nor the girl can do: introduce the idea of a butter horse (as opposed to mentioning butter, or horse, and knowing what we mean). It places one, in this way, before the unknowable. No doubt I have barely enunciated the words when the familiar images of horses and of butter present themselves, but they are solicited only in order to die. In which sense poetry is sacrifice, but of the most accessible sort.

For if the use or abuse of words, to which the operations of words oblige us, takes place on the ideal, unreal level of language, the same is true of the sacrifice of words which is poetry. (*Inner* 136))

It is important to note that Bataille is not claiming that poetry makes the unknown known here by some kind of revelatory power. Rather, poetry *places us* before the unknowable, pointing toward a limit but not itself engaging with that limit. One could say that poetry, by leading us to that limit, *defines* it, and produces knowledge about precisely what it cannot provide knowledge about. On the surface, Bataille's example bears some resemblance to David Hume's notion of ideas, by which we combine perceptions originally acquired by the senses into new and as yet unperceived ideas.[13] But rather than affirming the knowability of such a thing as a "butter horse," or affirming poetry's ability to lead our imagination to representing what is not visible in the "real" world, Bataille maintains the unknowability of the example, which ends not in knowledge but in sacrifice. Bataille's own writing about poetry here travels the same arc that he claims that poetry does, bringing us from the known to the unknown and leaving us to dwell there.

Discourse about poetry no longer reveals what poetry is but rather points to the limit of our knowledge and brings poetry and epistemology together to attempt to articulate the limits of the known and thereby define both. And this is where Bataille points the way toward a conception of poetry that does not need to come to rest in silence in the wake of the failure of transcendence. By assimilating discourse about poetry to poetry itself, Bataille helps forge a space, which will come to be occupied by poets and non-poets alike, where attempts to define poetry themselves constitute an important form of poetic writing, if poetry is understood as engagement with the unknown. Maurice Blanchot will go on to develop these ideas further, but it is Bataille who provides important evidence of the emergence of a new relationship among poetry, knowledge, and ignorance in the mid-twentieth century. The discourse can never come to rest, and silence thereby can only serve as a temporary moment, a springboard to further discourse, rather than a necessary or desired ending point. What Bataille construes as a failure or as the impetus for a hatred of poetry is in fact the moment of renewed possibility, as Gemerchak has suggested: "The meaning of Bataille's construction *as* a completed project, *as* a goal reached which retroactively confers meaning on the activity of building, is that which is annulled. What it affirms, on the contrary, is continual incompletion, unending disagreement with itself" (122).[14] Likewise, Sylvain Santi has noted that supposedly failed attempts to define poetry are meaningful precisely because they demonstrate the inadequacy of discourse in terms of providing a stable characterization of what it seeks to define: "Plus les « définitions » de la poésie manquent ce qu'exige le discours, et plus elles montrent ce que le discours manque: ce que ce dernier ne voulait et ne pouvait pas dire commence à se formuler" ("The more that 'definitions' of poetry are missing what discourse demands, the more they show what discourse lacks: what discourse didn't want to and couldn't say begins to formulate itself") (43). Once poetry, by Bataille's characterization, arrives at its extreme limit by no longer being words, we reach a turning point in our understanding of the term "poetry" and are able to see it as a term that cannot coincide with itself, which is a first step toward a kind of definition. Santi identifies a problematic but paradoxical aspect of Bataille's engagement with poetry. Poetry is:

> poétique dans l'exacte mesure où elle saura rompre avec les opérations qui se lient à une production mais, dans le même temps, elle devra pourtant donner lieu à une œuvre; le faire poétique sera un faire qui devra faire œuvre sans faire œuvre, telle est l'absence d'œuvre. Une œuvre ? Peut-on encore solliciter ce vocable ? (Santi 168)

> (poetic in the exact measure where it would be able to break with the operations that are linked to a production but, at the same time, it will need to give rise to a work; poetic making will be a making that will need to make a work without making a work; such is the absence of a work. A work? Can we still call on that word?)

Poetry thus "perverts" categories such as the "work" by inviting us to see the work of poetry as a rendering impossible of the poetic "work" as typically understood, that is, as a poetic product.[15] The impossibility of the work, or of "poetry" broadly understood, becomes fertile ground for reflection on what poetry might mean in the face of its potential annihilation or reduction to silence.

While Bataille may be said to be announcing a critique of poetry, that critique is folded into itself and reveals the assumptions about notions such as "poetry" and "work" that a new understanding of poetry *as* critique can go on to transform. Discourse on poetry can never remain shut down in silence so long as poetry remains, as it does on Bataille's reading, a necessarily incomplete sacrifice. Insofar as there is something to be said about the silence to which poetry reduces itself, poetry is renewed in the reinstantiation of discourse about it, in an eternally changing present which, in its most extreme form, is unseizable as an instant in time: "Il faut appréhender une poésie qui n'est qu'à la condition de mourir immédiatement, une écriture dont la manifestation coïncide avec sa disparition simultanée" ("It is necessary to understand a poetry that only exists on condition of dying immediately, a writing whose manifestation coincides with its simultaneous disappearance") (Santi 184). Bataille sets us up for the necessary reimagining of poetry: if it is not to be silence, if it in fact cannot be silence, how to account for poetry in a way that necessarily includes attempts at defining poetry as themselves a key aspect of the poetic enterprise? The fissure in silence whereby discourse resumes is the place where poetry is made to continue by other means.

In this operation in, and on, poetry, both the "work" and knowledge vanish. Poetry, on Bataille's account, points the way beyond reason and thus beyond knowledge. He writes in "De l'âge de pierre à Jacques Prévert":

> La poésie est *aussi* pour nous *la littérature qui n'est plus littéraire*, qui échappe à l'ornière où généralement la littérature est enlisée. Est pour nous « poétique » ce qu'on ne peut estimer paisiblement, comme on peut faire du vin d'Anjou, du drap anglais; « poétique » ce qui coupe en nous le désir de réduire aux mesures de la raison. (OC11: 88)[16]

> (Poetry is *also* for us *literature that is no longer literature*, which escapes the rut where literature is generally trapped. What is "poetic" for us is what we cannot esteem peacefully, as we can Anjou wine or English fabric. What is poetic is what cuts off in us the desire to reduce to the limits of reason.)

Poetry is thus what moves us outside the domain of understanding through reason; in this conception, the epistemological question of the kind of knowledge poetry produces becomes linked to the ontological question of what poetry is. Bataille often speaks of the ontological question of what poetry is in relation to the epistemological question of its (negative) relationship to knowledge: "La poésie ou le ravissement suppose la déchéance et la suppression de la connaissance, qui ne sont pas données dans l'angoisse. *C'est la souveraineté de la poésie.* En même temps la haine de la poésie—*puisqu'elle n'est pas inaccessible*" ("Poetry or rapture supposes the decline and suppression of knowledge, which are not given in anguish. *It is the sovereignty of poetry.* At the same time the hatred of poetry—*since it is not inaccessible*" (11: 306)). And the link between the ontological and the epistemological occurs at the point at which poetry necessarily takes itself as its object of knowledge, in an effort at self definition that must, for the reasons we have seen, necessarily fail. As Santi notes: "Quand Bataille affirme que la poésie est le langage de l'impossible, il ne songe pas à une poésie qui serait une fuite hors du langage, mais désigne plutôt une manière de mettre le langage à la merci des forces qui le commandent et qu'il veut ignorer" ("When Bataille affirms that poetry is the language of the impossible, he is not thinking of a poetry that would be an escape out of language, but rather one that designates a way of putting language at the mercy of the forces that command it and that it wants to ignore") (Santi 251). And this is not to say that poetry retreats into a self-reflexive space that denies all connection to the world of lived experience. Rather, it becomes the space where knowledge dissolves into question, where Bataille's "inner experience" guides the eternal questioning that living in accord with this characterization of poetry suggests. It is a refusal of the quietism of silence and an affirmation that the phenomenon and our experience of it and resultant discourse about it come together. While this operation happens in and through poetry as Bataille understands it, the same operation necessarily extends to lived experience in the world in a way that the poets we shall examine in the next chapter are keen to attempt to seize.

Like Bataille's, Maurice Blanchot's remarks on poetry, scattered throughout most of his major works, often characterize it as posing questions rather than offering answers. In fact, he aligns poetry with thought rather than philosophy, if the latter is considered as seeking definitive solutions and irrefutable conclusions. Blanchot, like Bataille, reshapes the questions of what poetry or, in the case of Blanchot, writing more generally, is and can do. By seeking to define poetry, he participates in a similar kind of destruction of received ideas in a way that generates poetic discourse rather than shutting it down. As he writes in *L'écriture du désastre*: "Le philosophe qui écrirait en poète viserait sa propre destruction. Et même la visant, il ne peut l'atteindre. La poésie est question pour la philosophie qui prétend lui donner une réponse, et ainsi la comprendre (la savoir). La philosophie qui met tout en question, achoppe à la poésie qui est la question qui lui échappe" ("A philosopher who would write as a poet would be aiming for his own destruction. And even so, he could not reach it. Poetry is a question for philosophy which claims to provide it with an answer, and thus to comprehend it (know it). Philosophy which puts everything into question, is tripped up by poetry, which is the question that eludes it") (*L'écriture* 104/ *Writing* 63). As Gerald Bruns remarks, by understanding poetry in this sense, Blanchot expands its meaning far beyond the concerns of poetics, which Bruns identifies as "the word for keeping poetry in its place" (*Blanchot* 3) by controlling it, categorizing it, and establishing norms for it. By freeing it, as all of the poets and thinkers I have been addressing in this study do, from a narrow set of definitional limits, Blanchot encourages us to think about how poetry engages the larger domain of thought and to ask about the extent to which it could be considered synonymous with it. He returns it as well to the domain of lived experience, since to engage these questions involves more generalized commitments to what we might say is both a style of life and a style of thought. Blanchot writes in *Faux pas* that poetry "suppose dans celui qui la reçoit un homme capable, dans l'exercice même de ses dons, de se mettre tout à fait en jeu, de se considérer sans cesse comme problème et, chaque fois qu'il touche le port, de se rejeter en pleine mer" ("supposes the one who receives it to be able, in the very exercise of his gifts, to put himself completely into play, to consider himself endlessly as a problem and, each time he arrives at port, to throw himself back into the open sea") (152/130). While this approach risks expanding poetry's reach beyond the scope of anything one might recognize as specifically related to poetry, that weakness is also the strength of the approach, as it reorients thought along the lines of question.

To philosophize would mean, on this view, to break from poetry. As Bruns has noted, Blanchot's work puts into question the very possibility of this break: "The question is whether the break with poetry can ever be clean or complete" and thus "whether the passage into philosophy is ever possible" (*Blanchot* 61). To remain in poetry is in some sense to dwell, but it is to dwell in perpetual question rather than in certainty. For Bruns, this situates Blanchot as if he were "a philosopher for whom philosophy is never a possibility, a philosopher who remains within the space of poetry or writing, as if refusing philosophy" (61). The move is a negation and an affirmation at once: it denies the move into philosophy, but by denying at the same time the full validity of the poetry/philosophy opposition, it opens new possibilities for poetry in ways that have everything to do with its definition, which can only be established in dialectical relation with the world from which it springs and which it in turn forms. If poetry turns out, like philosophy, to be an impossibility according to some of its own definitional terms, poetry can and must, unlike philosophy, give voice to its own impossibility. That giving voice is an important part of the project of poetry, conceived broadly as both poems and as discourse about poetry. If philosophy were to attempt to articulate failure, the result would presumably be either the breakdown of philosophy or its poeticization. And yet Blanchot takes this saying of poetry's own impossibility a step further by claiming that it cannot in fact say it, but only respond, and the response itself thereby becomes a kind of saying:

Arrêtons ce chemin de réflexions: que, par la poésie, nous soyons orientés vers un autre rapport qui ne serait pas de puissance, ni de compréhension, ni même de révélation, rapport avec l'obscur et l'inconnu, il ne faut pas compter sur une simple confrontation de mots pour en recevoir la preuve. Nous pressentons même que le langage, fût-il littéraire, la poésie, fût-elle véritable, n'ont pas pour rôle d'amener à la clarté, à la fermeté d'un nom, ce qui s'affirmerait, informulé, dans ce rapport sans rapport. La poésie n'est pas là pour dire l'impossibilité: elle lui répond seulement, elle dit en répondant. Tel est le partage secret de toute parole essentielle en nous: *nommant* le possible, *répondant* à l'impossible. (*Faux pas* [French edn] 68)

(Let us leave this path of reflection. We ought not count on a simple confrontation of words to prove that poetry might orient us toward another relation—a relation with the obscure and the unknown that would be a relation neither of force [*puissance*], nor of comprehension, nor even of revelation. We sense even that it is not the role of language, be it literary or that of poetry, even true poetry, to bring to light or to the firmness of a name what would affirm itself, unformulated, in this relation without relation. Poetry is not there in order to say impossibility: it simply answers to it, saying in responding. Such is the secret lot, the secret decision of every essential speech in us: *naming* the possible, *responding* to the impossible. (*Faux pas* [English edn] 48))

It is in this act of attempting to name the possible and respond to the impossible that Blanchot's thought moves from consideration of poems to a conception of poetry more broadly defined and potentially synonymous with terms such as writing.

Blanchot, as is well known, made important contributions to the interpretation of Mallarmé's poetry and his poetic project. Indeed some of Blanchot's statements about Mallarmé now are so familiar to us as a way of looking at poetry as to seem to be commonplaces. Reacting against the exegetical tendency to affirm a definitive meaning hidden somehow within the complexities of Mallarmé's syntax, Blanchot notes that "les esprits qui prétendent que tout poème a un sens et en attendent la révélation ont une attitude parfaitement correcte; leur erreur commence dès qu'ils entendent le mot sens comme ils chercheraient à l'entendre à propos d'un texte qui relèverait de la pensée définie" ("those who claim that every poem has a sense and who await its revelation have a perfectly correct attitude; their mistake begins as soon as they understand the word *sense* as they would try to understand it in reference to a text concerned with the exposition of rational thought" (*Faux pas* 127/*Faux pas* 108). Echoing Mallarmé's famous remark to Edgar Degas that it is not with ideas but with words that one makes a poem,[17] Blanchot affirms that "la signification poétique est ce qui ne peut être séparé des mots, ce qui rend chaque mot important et qui se dénonce dans ce fait ou cette illusion que le langage a une réalité essentielle, une mission fondamentale: fonder les choses par et dans la parole" ("poetic signification is that which cannot be separated from words, that which makes each word important and that reveals itself in the fact or the illusion that language has an essential reality, a fundamental mission: to establish things by and in the word") (*Faux pas* 129/*Faux pas* 109–10). In both instances Blanchot foregrounds the question of meaning and challenges the reader to reconsider what meaning might be and where it might be found. In that sense, he extends the spatial approach that we first identified in terms of the territory of philosophy and poetry, but now he puts into question the relationship of the poem's words to the world they either create or reflect. And here he necessarily enters into contradiction. On one hand, he extends the Mallarméan insight whereby poetic language embarks on an essentially destructive operation at first, removing words from the world of what Blanchot calls "la parole brute" ("crude speech") (*L'espace* 31/*Space* 39) in order to form a more abstract space that evokes pure ideality: "On est donc tenté de dire que le langage de la pensée est, par excellence, le langage poétique et que le sens, la notion pure, l'idée doivent devenir le souci du poète, étant cela seul qui nous délivre du poids des choses, de l'informe plénitude naturelle" ("One is thus tempted to say that the language of thought is poetic language par excellence, and that sense—the pure notion, the idea—must become the poet's concern, since it alone frees us from the weight of things, the amorphous natural plentitude") (*L'espace* 31/*Space* 39). And yet further on he affirms that, far from removing us from the "weight of things," the poetic word always sends us back to the world:

> Mais cette parole de la pensée est tout de même aussi la parole « courante »: elle nous renvoie toujours au monde, elle nous montre le monde tantôt comme l'infini d'une tâche et le risque d'un travail, tantôt comme une position ferme où il nous est loisible de nous croire en lieu sûr.
>
> La parole poétique ne s'oppose plus alors seulement au langage ordinaire, mais aussi bien au langage de la pensée. (*L'espace* 33–4)
>
> (But this language of thought is, all the same, "ordinary" language as well. It always refers us back to the world, sometimes showing it to us in the infinite qualities of a task and the risk of an undertaking, sometimes as a stable position where we are allowed to believe ourselves secure.
>
> The poetic word, then, is no longer opposed only to ordinary language, but also to the language of thought. (*Space* 41))

It is impossible to pin down the relations of poetic language, ordinary language, and the material world, and this is precisely the point. To discuss poetry in the larger sense is to give voice to the contradictions whereby these precise relations are unknowable because they are in dynamic relation, a fact to which poetic language can respond and, in responding, indicate the impossibility of going further. This is thus the limit point at which the passage to philosophy becomes impossible, and also the point where knowing becomes a kind of unknowing.

Poetic language is thus de-situated in Blanchot's thought: neither pure language nor pure world, it becomes a kind of experience that participates in both language and world without being reducible to either one. If poetic language speaks without a speaker, it thereby calls for interpretation. As experience, poetic language needs to be understood retrospectively and via the medium of language itself, a move that allows us to stay within the domain of poetic language even as we try to make sense of it; this is the point at which discourse about poetry joins poetry itself. Without an interpretive move, a speakerless poetic language would remain a meaningless experience, given that there is nothing that could be said about it. If that were the case, then poetic language would necessarily be inherently meaningless. If poetry could potentially exist without the subject, it cannot exist without being talked about. We can read Blanchot's discourse on poetry as a response to that situation, and as the creation of a (verbal) experience that seeks to make sense of poetic language while affirming all the while that the meaning is undefinable. It is at the point where we seek to reply to poetic language by making meaning of it that the question of poetry's relation to the world and to knowledge about it is necessarily reopened, not as an auxiliary concern but as an essential one, entirely wrapped up in the notion of poetic language to begin with and able to be abandoned only at the cost of meaninglessness. While poetry may emerge from silence and create silence around ordinary chatter, it cannot dwell there, even though it may continue to have an affinity with silence. Poetry makes sense of itself only through language, and through a language that needs to some extent be considered as vital as the words of the poems themselves.[18]

Writing is, for Blanchot, the act that silences speech understood as chatter, but this is not to say that it is the source of poetic or critical revelation:

> Ecrire commence seulement quand écrire est l'approche de ce point où rien ne se révèle, où, au sein de la dissimulation, parler n'est encore que l'ombre de la parole, langage qui n'est encore que son image, langage imaginaire et le langage

de l'imaginaire, celui que personne ne parle, murmure de l'incessant et de l'interminable auquel il faut imposer *silence*, si l'on veut, enfin, de faire entendre. (*L'espace* 41)

(Writing begins only when it is the approach to that point where nothing reveals itself, where, at the heart of dissimulation, speaking is still but the shadow of speech, a language which is still only its image, an imaginary language and a language of the imaginary, the one nobody speaks, the murmur of the incessant and interminable which one has to *silence* if one wants, at last, to be heard. (*Space* 48))

Nor is it, however, a mere nothing, because silence, Blanchot affirms in *L'écriture du désastre*, is impossible:

Le « mysticisme » de Wittgenstein, en dehors de sa confiance dans l'unité viendrait de ce qu'il croit que l'on peut *montrer* là où l'on ne pourrait *parler*. Mais, sans langage, rien ne se montre. Et se taire, c'est encore parler. Le silence est impossible. C'est pourquoi nous le désirons. Ecriture (ou Dire) précédant tout phénomène, toute manifestation ou monstration: tout apparaître. (*L'écriture* 23)

(Wittgenstein's "mysticism," aside from his faith in unity, must come from his believing that one can *show* when one cannot *speak*. But without language, nothing can be shown. And to be silent is still to speak. Silence is impossible. That is why we desire it. Writing (or Telling, as distinct from anything written or told) precedes every phenomenon, every manifestation or showing: all appearing. (*Writing* 10–11))

In the same work, Blanchot proposes silence as a way of escaping not only the commonplace, the already said, but also Knowledge (le Savoir) (*L'écriture* 154). But again, if this silence is itself a form of discourse, then poetry opposes itself not only to the total absence of discourse but to any claims to knowledge, understood as Blanchot consistently characterizes it as something fixed and stable. The moment we articulate silence, even in naming it, the silence disappears, and hence an immediate knowledge is also impossible. Poetry is what remains from this impossibility that cannot be a simple absence of discourse, giving name to its own impossibility of defining itself. Blanchot brings the threads of philosophy, poetry, and knowledge together.

The question that is inaccessible to questioning is here named poetry, the absolutely inaccessible domain for philosophy, and thus poetry is subsumed under the identity of the question. In place of the tautology "poetry is poetry,"

Blanchot implies an eternal question whereby poetry can only be poetry by being question, a question that can come to rest neither in the poetic text nor in the silence of the end of the poem.

This active nature of the question that is poetry precludes any coming to rest in the stillness of a tautology as typically understood and prescribes a particularly active role for the poet, which once again affirms the intimate rapport between poetry and (and as) lived experience:

> La poésie n'est pas donnée au poète comme une vérité et une certitude dont il pourrait se rapprocher; il ne sait pas s'il est poète, mais il ne sait non plus ce qu'est la poésie, ni même si elle est; elle dépend de lui, de sa recherche, dépendance qui toutefois ne le rend pas maître de ce qu'il cherche, mais le rend incertain de lui-même et comme inexistant. (*L'espace* 85–6)
>
> (Poetry is not granted the poet as a truth and a certainty against which he could measure himself. He does not know whether he is a poet, but neither does he know what poetry is, or even whether it is. It depends on him, on his search. And this dependence does not make him master of what he seeks; rather, it makes him uncertain of himself and as if nonexistent. (*Space* 87))[19]

This uncertainty stems precisely from poetry's instability, which in turn engenders a more far-reaching non-identity. As Gerald Bruns puts it, "The poem... is not a sealed-off artifact...; rather, it is porous, exposed to the world, subjected to it, and vice versa: poetry is an event in which the world and its discourses are themselves exposed to the nonidentical, or in which they experience a failure of self-identity" (*Blanchot* xvi). Poetry, as question, enables this destabilizing of tautology with reference both to itself and to the world of discourse and the actors within it more broadly. This is a characteristic that poetry shares, in Blanchot's terminology, with literature or art more broadly; perhaps, when all is said and done, these words correspond, by virtue of their questioning, to nothing at all: "Il n'est même jamais sûr que le mot littérature ou le mot art réponde à rien de réel, rien de possible ou rien d'important. Cela a été dit: être artiste, c'est ne jamais savoir qu'il y a déjà un art, ni non plus qu'il y a déjà un monde" ("It is not even certain that the word *literature* or the word *art* corresponds to anything real, anything possible or anything important. It has been said that to be an artist is not to know that art already exists, or that the world already is there") (*Le livre* 244/*Book* 201). The experience of asking the question of poetry, when poetry is itself that question or perhaps nothing at all, brings a subject to the transformation that is effected by "inner experience" by which the subject him or herself ceases to be anything but question, a move that invites an assimilation of poetry now not just to question but also to the reader or writer of poetry as well. And here it is important to note that neither the poet, nor the reader, nor poetry disappears in this transformation. In all cases, the experience calls for a response: "Il se peut que tout écrivain se sente comme appelé à répondre seul à travers sa propre ignorance, de la littérature" ("It is possible that every writer feels called to answer alone, through his own ignorance, for literature") (*Le livre* 244/*Book* 201). From ignorance springs response that exists alongside the question and that constantly transforms itself anew into that question; poetry thus avoids coming to rest in ignorance just as much as it resists coming to rest in knowledge. Given that we cannot grasp poetry, we can only respond to it.

Blanchot thus articulates the space of poetry in terms that ask us to rethink the relationship of poetry to knowledge: poetry presents neither something that will eventually be known, or is known in some alternative way to other kinds of knowing, nor the absolutely, radically unknowable. The unknowable occupies the space of what Blanchot calls the neutral:

> L'inconnu est un neutre. L'inconnu n'est ni objet ni sujet. Cela veut dire que penser l'inconnu, ce n'est nullement se proposer « le pas encore connu », objet de tout savoir encore à venir, mais ce n'est pas davantage le dépasser en « l'absolument inconnaissable », sujet de pure transcendance, se refusant à toute manière de connaître et de s'exprimer. Au contraire, posons (peut-être arbitrairement) que la recherche—celle où la poésie et la pensée, dans leur espace propre, s'affirment, séparées, inséparables—a pour enjeu l'inconnu, à condition toutefois de préciser: la recherche se rapporte à l'inconnu comme inconnu. (*Faux pas* 442)

> (The unknown is neutral, a neuter. The unknown is neither object nor subject. This means that to think the unknown is in no way to propose it as "the not yet known," the object of a knowledge still to come, any more than it would be to go beyond it as "the absolutely unknowable," a subject of pure transcendence, refusing itself to all manner of knowledge and expression. On the contrary, let us (perhaps arbitrarily) propose that in research—where poetry and thought affirm themselves in the space that is proper to them, separate, inseparable—the unknown is at stake; on condition, however, that it be explicitly stated that this research relates to the unknown as unknown. (*Faux pas* 300))

There is a knowledge of the unknown, which Blanchot distinguishes from the absolutely unknown and which can be disclosed in poetry:

nous supposons une relation où l'inconnu serait affirmé, manifesté, voire exhibé: découvert—et sous quel aspect? précisément en cela qui le retient inconnu. L'inconnu, dans ce rapport, se découvrirait donc en cela qui le laisse à couvert. C'est une contradiction? En effet.... La recherche—la poésie, la pensée—se rapporte à l'inconnu comme inconnu. Ce rapport découvre l'inconnu, mais d'une découverte qui le laisse à couvert; par ce rapport, il y a « présence » de l'inconnu; l'inconnu, en cette « présence », est rendu présent, mais toujours comme inconnu. Ce rapport doit laisser intact—non touché—ce qu'il porte et non dévoilé ce qu'il découvre. Ce ne sera pas un rapport de dévoilement. L'inconnu ne sera pas révélé, mais indiqué. (*Faux pas* 442)

(we are supposing a relation in which the unknown would be affirmed, made manifest, even exhibited: disclosed—and under what aspect?—precisely in that which keeps it unknown. In this relation, then, the unknown would be disclosed in that which leaves it under cover. Is this a contradiction? In effect... Research—poetry, thought—relates to the unknown as unknown. This relation discloses the unknown, but by an uncovering that leaves it under cover; through this relation there is a "presence" of the unknown; in this "presence" the unknown is rendered present, but always as unknown. This relation must leave intact—untouched—what it conveys and not unveil what it discloses. This relation will not consist in an unveiling. The unknown will not be revealed, but indicated. (*Faux pas* 300))

Poetry, then, neither discloses nor creates knowledge, but rather stands in a relation to its absence by signaling it and replying to it. This is the "ignorance" of the poet in the positive, productive sense, not an absence of knowledge but the signaling of the knowledge of ignorance, the awareness of poetry's inability to produce or disclose knowledge, and in that sense, and that sense only, to be a form of knowledge in its very ignorance. That ignorance, far from disabling poetic production, serves as its motor.[20] Such a reconception of knowledge forces a rethinking of the metaphors associated with it, as it is no longer a question of seeking, through knowledge, to get a grasp on something: "Parler l'inconnu, l'accueillir dans la parole en le laissant inconnu, c'est précisément ne pas le prendre, ne pas le com-prendre, c'est se refuser à l'identifier, fût-ce par cette saisie "objective" qu'est la vue, laquelle saisit, quoique à distance" (*Faux pas* 445) ("To speak the unknown, to receive it through speech while leaving it unknown, is precisely not to take hold of it, not to comprehend it; it is rather to refuse to identify it even by sight, that 'objective' hold that seizes, albeit at a distance" (*Faux pas* 302)). This is a position that, as we shall see, Philippe Jaccottet takes up from the standpoint of the poet.

Far from a conception of poetry that seeks to cut off its relation to the world from which it springs, Blanchot's notion of the neuter and of the unknown has immediate consequences for lived experience: "vivre 'authentiquement,' 'poétiquement,' c'est avoir rapport à l'inconnu comme inconnu et ainsi mettre au centre de sa vie cela-l'inconnu qui ne laisse pas vivre en avant de soi et qui, en outre, retire à la vie tout centre" ("to live 'authentically,' 'poetically,' is to have a relation with the unknown as such, and thus to put at the center of one's life *this-the-unknown* that does not allow one to live ahead of oneself and, moreover, withdraws every center from life") (*Faux pas* 444/*Faux pas* 302). Conceiving poetry in this way necessarily entails an approach to life that privileges the unknown, and thus retains an important place for poetry as that which gives voice to the unknown as a central guiding principle. Poetry thus allows an articulation of the way in which we confront ignorance and make it a productive source of engagement with the world. As we engage with poetry, we renegotiate what it means to be a subject and object in a world devoid of those relations of knowledge as they are usually construed in a model of knowledge that leads from the unknown object to the known object via the engagement of the subject. Here, by contrast, what is at stake is a deeper understanding of what it means not to know, to remove oneself from that schema of subject and object. Crucially, there are political implications in this reformulation of knowledge and ignorance:

> vivre devant l'inconnu et devant soi comme inconnu, c'est entrer dans cette responsabilité de la parole qui parle sans exercer aucune forme de pouvoir, même ce pouvoir qui s'accomplit lorsque nous regardons, puisque, regardant, nous maintenons sous notre horizon et dans notre cercle de vue—dans la dimension du visible-invisible—cela et celui qui se tient devant nous. (*Faux pas* 445)
>
> (to live before the unknown, and before oneself as unknown is to enter into the responsibility of a speech that speaks without exercising any form of power; even the power that accrues to us when we look, since, in looking, we keep whatever and whomever stands before us within our horizon and within our circle of sight—thus within the dimension of the visible-invisible. (*Faux pas* 302))

If knowledge of an object implies control or domination over it, Blanchot's approach to poetic ignorance, by putting that subject/object relationship into question both as an epistemological category and as a relation of power, forces us to reject that power dynamic in favor of a neutral relation of ourselves to that which we encounter. Abuses of power are, by definition, excluded from the poetic as a lived practice.

Blanchot's understanding of poetry creates a paradoxical situation whereby poetry has to destroy itself for poetry itself to emerge: "qu'il y a un en-deça et un au-delà de la poésie qui est la poésie même et que sans cette capacité de se détruire et de se trouver en se détruisant, celle-ci ne serait presque rien" ("there is a 'here-and-there' of poetry that is poetry itself and that, without this capacity to destroy itself and find itself in its destruction, poetry would be almost nothing") (*Faux pas* 167/*Faux pas* 145). Arthur Rimbaud plays a key role in Blanchot's articulation of this paradox. We return once again to the notion that poetry, defined as pure or essential language, would in fact be undifferentiated from silence:

> Qu'annonce la poésie au monde ? Elle affirme qu'elle est le langage essentiel, qu'elle comprend toute l'étendue de l'expression, qu'elle est aussi bien l'absence de mots que la parole, enfin qu'être fidèle à la poésie c'est concilier la volonté de parler et le silence. La poésie est silence parce qu'elle est langage pur, voilà le fondement de la certitude poétique. (*Faux pas* 166)
>
> (What does poetry announce to the world? It asserts that it is the essential language, that it includes the entire range of expression, that it is the absence of words as well as speech, finally that to be faithful to poetry is to reconcile the will to speak with silence. Poetry is silence because it is pure language; that is the foundation of poetic certainty. (*Faux pas* 144))

Poetry then must think against itself in order to articulate the notion of "pure language"; this move would then cancel the purity by a fall into discourse. That fall into question, into infinitely revisable attempts to give voice to what poetry is, is precisely what constitutes poetry on the model of poetry as ignorance that Blanchot develops. And Blanchot goes on to say that Rimbaud is the one who dismantles that poetic certainty by falling into a silence that is precisely not the silence of poetry as pure language but rather the silence of everyday life, what Blanchot calls "l'incognito du vacarme quotidien" ("the incognito of everyday noise") (*Faux pas* 166/*Faux pas* 144). For Blanchot, there is a kind of death and resurrection narrative in this rebirth of poetry from its own destruction: "La poésie n'existe que par ce qui la menace. Elle a besoin de pouvoir succomber pour survivre. Elle ne renaît que détruite" ("Poetry exists only through what threatens it. It needs to be able to succumb in order to survive. It is reborn only when destroyed") (*Faux pas* 166/*Faux pas* 144).

Blanchot's quasi-metaphysical drama of death and rebirth is also, as I hope to have shown, an epistemological one whereby poetry is to be found in the defining and redefining of poetry itself, a definitional process that affirms the necessity and impossibility of silence and the unknown and that reorients poetry's knowledge as a productive giving of voice to that ignorance that affirms it, responds to it, and also rescues poetic language from the trap of the silence that it would become if it were to be "pure" language. Blanchot once again has recourse to spatial metaphors to describe the status of meaning as returning itself to a space where it would be deprived of that acquired meaning. This would be a "passage du monde où tout a plus ou moins de sens, où il y a obscurité et clarté, à un espace où, à proprement parler, rien n'a encore de sens, vers quoi cependant tout ce qui a sens remonte comme vers son origine" ("passage, that is, from the world where everything has more or less meaning, where there is obscurity and clarity, into a space where, properly speaking, nothing has meaning yet, toward which nevertheless everything which does have meaning returns as toward its origin") (*Faux pas* 204/*Faux pas* 196).

Blanchot identifies, in the context of a discussion of Robert Musil, the difference between literature and philosophy, when it comes to expressing thought, in the idea that literature expresses what are "not yet" thoughts:

> dans une œuvre littéraire, on puisse exprimer des pensées aussi difficiles et d'une forme aussi abstraite que dans un ouvrage philosophique, mais à condition qu'elles ne soient *pas encore* pensées. Ce « pas encore » est la littérature même, un « pas encore » qui, comme tel, est accomplissement et perfection. (*Le livre* 182-3)

> (in a literary work, one can express thoughts as difficult and of as abstract a form as in a philosophical essay, but only on the condition that they are *not yet* thoughts. This "not yet" is literature itself, a "not yet" that, just as it is, is accomplishment and perfection. (*Book* 148))

Blanchot's discussion of literature generally here echoes much of what he says about poetry specifically; a thought fully realized at the conceptual level passes over into philosophy, and literature or poetry thus remains perpetually in the space of the not yet, which is not the Derridean *à venir* but rather a thought on the other side of the concept, as opposed to one infinitely deferred. For to be transferred into the realm of the philosophical or conceptual is to become fixed or hardened in a way that a literary thought never can be, defined as it is by its transience and by the potentially infinite commentary to which it gives rise and which becomes itself part of the thought. Poetry is thus what is and is not yet experienced; working out that paradox is part of poetry's epistemological project as it defines itself in Blanchot's thought. That thought can identify and respond to the paradox, but never resolve it, and it is the task of response that ultimately defines poetry for Blanchot.

And this task also leads us to the way in which poetry becomes lived experience. Blanchot describes this in terms of the transformation of the poet: "C'est l'essence de la poésie de prétendre transformer celui qu'elle inspire. Le poète est invité à être ce qu'il écrit. En écrivant, il fait quelque chose, et il ne peut le faire sans chercher à devenir ce qu'il fait" ("It is the essence of poetry to aim to transform the one it inspires. The poet is invited to be what he writes. By writing he makes something, and he cannot make it without seeking to become what he makes") (*Faux pas* 157/*Faux pas* 135). If poetry is the space where subject and object cease to operate as vehicles of knowing the world, the poet (and the reader responding to poetry) him or herself becomes question and reorients him or herself in the world according to a consciousness of productive ignorance. Living and thinking come together with reading and writing here in an approach to poetry that is transformative only in the sense that there is no object of the transformation; lived poetic experience becomes, itself, that transformation that ceases only at risk of ceasing to be that experience at all. Responding to that creative ignorance, and entering it more fully, is the task that poet Philippe Jaccottet sets for himself, and it is to his engagement with this emergent conception of poetry as ignorance that I now turn.

4

"Moving Forth from Uncertainty All the Same" (Jaccottet and Maulpoix)

The two poets I will examine in this chapter, Philippe Jaccottet and Jean-Michel Maulpoix, write in full acknowledgment of the ways that a long-standing view of poetry as possessing transcendent powers is no longer tenable in the twentieth century. Both write with what, from the perspective of the avant-garde, could be labeled a nostalgic approach. But neither Jaccottet nor Maulpoix could be said to mourn the passing of a transcendent lyric poetry. Rather they, like so many poets in the twentieth century and beyond, seek to extend the lyric tradition in light of, and not despite, the dismantling of some of its most important assumptions about what poetry can do and be.[1] A new esthetics and epistemology of doubt emerge from these poets' writings as they seek to preserve a role for lyricism that is faithful to a new vision of it, one that makes room for uncertainty and doubt and catastrophe and actually generates a poetics from them.[2] In that sense, we can read this passage from Jaccottet's *La Semaison* as a kind of poetic program:

> A partir de l'incertitude avancer tout de même. Rien d'acquis, car tout acquis ne serait-il pas paralysie ? L'incertitude est le moteur, l'ombre est la source. Je marche faute de lieu, je parle faute de savoir, preuve que je ne suis pas encore mort.... Comment recommencer pourtant ? Tout est là. Par quel chemin détourné, indirect ? Par quelle absence de chemins ? A partir du dénuement, de la faiblesse, du doute. (*Œuvres* 434)[3]

> (Moving forth from uncertainty all the same. Nothing for granted, for anything taken for granted, would that not be paralysis? Uncertainty is the motor, darkness is the source. I walk without a place, I speak without knowledge, proof that I am not yet dead.... How to begin again though? That's the question. By what roundabout, indirect path? By what absence of paths? Starting out from destitution, weakness, doubt.)

Giving voice to incertitude thus becomes a new poetic program, a new way for poetry to craft a form of knowledge, and in this, poetry may continue to play the role that I have been suggesting that it plays, not as a reflection of ways of knowing or unknowing but as an active creation of them. What this would mean is, necessarily, irreducible to a series of propositions, which is always the case when claiming that poetry yields a kind of knowledge. Jaccottet moreover continues down the path whereby prose reflections on poetry play a key role in what we might call poetry's way of knowing. Explicit acknowledgment of uncertainty and tentative assertion brings with it a potentially endless set of contradictions, the risk of nostalgia, and the possibility that the process of thinking about poetry may end up being of greater import than any product or result of that process. Both Jaccottet and Maulpoix have explored what it might mean for poetry and reflection on poetry to give form to these doubts and these contradictions and yet not be foreclosed by them. Their writing becomes a prolonged meditation on the relationship of poetry to ignorance and on the way in which the lyric subject can or should persist in an age where the very notion of the lyric or the lyric subject is called into question. In that sense, they both offer a version of poetry that is just as much a way of life and of understanding experience as it is of writing per se.

There is occasionally, to be sure, a sense of nostalgia for Romanticism in Jaccottet. He quotes Novalis's Fragment 32, for instance, and reflects on order and chaos: "« nous sommes chargés de mission: appelés à former la terre ». Au moins, à mettre un peu d'ordre dans notre chaos intérieur. Que les paroles éclairent cette route confuse, qu'elles n'ajoutent pas à son obscurité, mais fassent la lumière. Qu'un poème se lève, comme le jour" ("'We are charged with a mission: called to form the earth.' At least, to create a little order in our interior chaos. May words light up our unclear route, may they not add to its obscurity, but create light instead. May a poem arise, like the day") (37). But Jaccottet is not limited by that nostalgia and in fact comes to change the terms of what it might mean, for instance, for words to illuminate darkness. Beneath a fairly traditional vocabulary lies the potential for rethinking poetry's possibilities when it comes to personal or collective enlightenment. In that sense, Jaccottet takes up, and increasingly so in the years beyond the very early work I have just quoted, and transforms the tradition of thinking about the relation of poetry and knowledge, rather than simply harking back to older conceptions of that relation. One way that a poet can be opened up to new possibilities is to abandon an active search for revelation in favor of a passive model of availability, an attention to what is given:

> Parfois, il me semble être là seulement pour écouter. Dans une certaine qualité de silence et de repos intérieur, dans une certaine inactivité éveillée, il me semble que des voix peuvent être perçues, étrangement touchantes et vivantes. Il y faut,

plutôt que de l'attention (toujours trop volontaire), un état d' « accueillement », quelque chose de tranquille et de détendu que favoriseraient peut-être des métiers manuels... (58)

(Sometimes it seems to me that I'm only there in order to listen. In a certain quality of silence and interior repose, in a certain awakened inactivity, it seems to me that voices can be perceived, strangely touching and alive. What is necessary is, rather than attention (always too voluntary), a state of "welcoming," something tranquil and relaxed that manual labor would maybe help along...)

We could read this state of openness as a renewed commitment to the possibilities of poetry and the attempt to keep alive the spirit of Romantic questions about its capabilities while rethinking the answers, or even the possibility of answers. Still, poetry, inasmuch as it is active creation, would be lost if the poetic subject were simply a passive receptive vehicle. If poetic vocation is defined only as listening, as the first sentence quoted seems to imply, then poetry becomes a kind of broken promise to give oneself over to listening. Already we are in the realm of paradox and potential impossibility that will define poetry in Jaccottet's textual world any time we try to give it a fixed definition. Coming to terms with the consequences of such a conception of poetry becomes a crucial task in his texts.

Jaccottet works through these questions in many of his prose texts, and especially in *La Promenade sous les arbres* (1957), to which I now turn. In that text, presented as a dialogue, Jaccottet staunchly refuses a return to a purportedly clear and reasonable world, opposing such a thing to what he calls the real:

On doit bien voir, maintenant, qu'il ne s'agit absolument pas dans mon esprit d'un retour à un monde raisonnable, explicable, même pas à l'acceptation de certaines limites; que je rêverais plutôt d'un enfoncement du regard dans l'épaisseur de l'incompréhensible et contradictoire réel; d'une observation à la fois acharnée et distraite du monde, et jamais, au grand jamais, d'une évasion hors du monde. (91)

(We should see now that in my mind it is absolutely not a question of a return to a reasonable and explainable world, not even to the acceptance of certain limits; that I would dream rather of a penetration of the eye into the thickness of the incomprehensible and contradictory real; of an observation of the world that is both relentless and distracted, and never, never ever, of an escape from the world.)

Such a turn to the real is not without its risks: "J'en vins même à me dire que la considération simplement honnête et attentive du réel devait fatalement conduire à la folie; que seule quelque habileté, quelque tricherie nous en préservait. Et cette pensée ne me fut pas agréable" ("I even came to tell myself that simply honest and attentive consideration of the real would inevitably lead to insanity; that only some cleverness, some cheating could keep us from it. And that thought was not pleasant") (134). Transparency of meaning is relegated to the status of a dream in this text, a kind of poetic utopia, a place one can think about but where one cannot dwell:

> Le rêve qui nous saisit à ce moment-là est celui d'une transparence absolue du poème, dans lequel les choses seraient simplement situées, mises en ordre, avec les tensions que créent les distances, les accents particuliers que donne l'éclairage, la sérénité aussi que suscite une diction régulière, un discours dépouillé de tout souci de convaincre l'auditeur, de faire briller celui qui discourt, ou, à plus forte raison, de lui valoir une victoire de quelque espèce que ce soit. (126)

> (The dream that takes hold of us at that moment is one of an absolute transparency of the poem, in which things would be simply situated, put in order, with the tensions created by distances, the particular accents that lighting gives, and the serenity that a regular diction gives rise to, a speech stripped of all concern about convincing the hearer, to make the one speaking shine or, even more so, to earn for him a victory of whatever kind.)

What is important to note, and what is emphasized via the dialogic structure of the text, is that this "dream" is temporary, even as dream: it is not proposed as an unchanging ideal in the light of which we need to mourn the impossibility of its realization. Rather, Jaccottet makes room for loving the contradictions inherent in making and appreciating modern beauty in a way that makes that conceptual restlessness coexist, at least at certain moments, with the nostalgic unified vision:

> Il ne faut pas louer les choses comme si elles faisaient partie d'un paradis bienheureux que nos seules faiblesses empêcheraient de se dévoiler entièrement, car aussitôt, une oreille sensible à la justesse percevra dans les mots l'altération de la vérité: et pourtant, la plus grande part de la poésie est de cet ordre, doucereuse peinture de nuées bien faite pour la disqualifier aux yeux des serviteurs fatigués du quotidien. Non. Si ce que j'ai cru comprendre des sources de la beauté n'est pas illusoire, il faudrait, non point que nous acceptions la contradiction qui règne sur notre vie, mais que nous entrions en elle, que nous nous portions à son extrême pointe, c'est-à-dire que nous vivions en adorant la beauté d'autant

plus ardemment qu'elle est plus fragile, en ce lieu où il y a le plus de joie parce qu'il y a aussi le plus de menaces. (131)

(We shouldn't praise things as if they were part of a happy paradise that only our weaknesses would prevent from revealing themselves completely, for then, an ear sensitive to accuracy will perceive in the words the alteration of the truth: and yet, the biggest share of poetry is of this kind, sweet painting of clouds well made to disqualify it in the eyes of the tired servants of the everyday. No. If what I thought I understood about the sources of beauty is not illusory, we would not at all need to accept the contradiction that reigns over our lives, but enter into it and bring ourselves to its extremity, that is, that we live while adoring beauty all the more ardently because it is more fragile, in this place where there is the most joy because there are also the most threats.)

What is fragile is all the more precious, and it is in light of this conception of poetry's power as real but temporary and always subject to disappearance that Jaccottet formulates what I would argue is his most important characterization of poetry:

La poésie est donc ce chant que l'on ne saisit pas, cet espace où l'on ne peut demeurer, cette clef qu'il faut toujours reperdre. Cessant d'être insaisissable, cessant d'être douteuse, cessant d'être ailleurs (faut-il dire: cessant de n'être pas?), elle s'abîme, elle n'est plus. Cette pensée me soutient dans les difficultés. (139)

(Poetry is thus that song that you cannot grab, that space where you cannot dwell, that key that you must always keep on losing. Ceasing to be ungraspable, ceasing to be doubtful, ceasing to be elsewhere (should one say: ceasing not to be?), it spoils, it is no longer. This thought sustains me in difficult moments.)

Poetry is defined here not despite the doubt that it inspires but precisely in terms of that doubt; poetry on this view contains within itself the fragility and temporality of its existence and the constant questioning and reformulating to which it gives rise. The restless pursuit of definition that we have been tracing throughout this study is here identified not as a threat to poetry but at the very heart of that definition itself. Failing to lose the key is, by this definition, to leave the realm of poetry itself by advancing a definition that is too static and too sure of itself to count as poetry. Seeing poetry this way leads not to despair or to rejection of poetry but to consolation for the poet, as it inscribes doubt as necessary to thinking about poetry and not as a threat to its existence.

In *La promenade sous les arbres*, Jaccottet associates poetry with questions of knowing but also of living in a full and fulfilling way. He speaks of his "sentiment d'avoir vécu, certains jours, mieux, c'est-à-dire plus pleinement, plus intensément, plus *réellement* que d'autres" ("feeling of having lived, certain days, better, that is, more fully, more intensely, in a more *real* way than others") and indicates that he gradually discovered that "ces jours, ou ces instants, chez moi, étaient liés, d'un lien qui restait évidemment à définir, à la poésie" ("those days, or those instants, in my case, were linked, by a link that remained obviously to be defined, to poetry") (179). Here again, that personal sense of wholeness is generated not despite the doubtfulness of poetic experience and an inability to define it precisely but rather because of that doubt and inability. The non-immediate legibility of the world lends fullness to lived experience because it orients it toward a search for knowledge about poetry, in an experience that is self-reflective to the extent that it defines that experience in the process of defining poetry itself. This autoreferentiality accomplishes the very opposite of what some might claim about poetry closing itself off from the referential world. In the schema that Jaccottet traces here, the process of defining poetry is entirely and necessarily bound up with lived experience, and attempting to articulate that very relation becomes a crucial component both of the lived experience and of the definition. Jaccottet reclaims lived experience, in other words, not through a quasi-mystical affirmation of directly perceived lived experience but rather in the vein of ignorance and impermanence. Jaccottet notes that pre-modern poetry evokes a plenitude from which we now feel our distance, reduced as we are to speaking "de la nostalgie, de la recherche, ou de la brusque et éphémère redecouverte, de cette plénitude" ("nostalgia, searching, or the brusk and ephemeral rediscovery of this fullness") (120). For Jaccottet, modern poetry is marked by its "infériorité" but also by modern poems' "caractère plus tragique, plus frêle et plus poignant" ("more tragic, fragile, and poignant character") (121). He argues for resisting the temptation to nostalgia for this earlier time and its poetry, rejecting a desire for "le retour des dieux" ("the return of the gods") (121) and states his preference for remaining "attentive à ces quelques lueurs douteuses, mais pures, qui viennent parfois éclairer mon travail" ("attentive to those few doubtful, but pure, glimmers that sometimes come to illuminate my work") (121).

What we might call the "in-betweenness" of Jaccottet's position, whereby he recognizes both an intermittent flicker of poetry's power as well as a more permanent sense of doubt about that power, is a middle ground between two positions that he critiques at various points in his early works. In *L'Obscurité* he dismisses "ces hommes presque assurés du néant, et qui n'en étaient que plus désireux d'agir, d'aimer, de conquérir" ("those men who are almost assured of nothingness, and who only all the more wanted to act, love, and conquer") (247) even though he admits to having admired them and the "amer bonheur" ("bitter happiness") that comes with such a position of sustained negation. While he sees such a position as justified, he adds: "je n'avais jamais eu sincèrement le désir de me joindre à eux" ("I've never sincerely had the desire to join them") (247). In light of Jaccottet's comments about the intermittent moments of temporary clarity that poetry can still provide, we can see his dismissal of absolute negativity as a refusal of easy answers; those who dismiss all but the abyss risk the accusation of facile oversimplification. This is essentially the same kind of critique he addresses, in *La Promenade sous les arbres*, toward the poet A.E. (pseudonym of Irish poet George William Russell): "A.E., ayant pris conscience de l'intelligibilité du monde visible, ne songerait plus dès lors qu'à l'interroger comme on déchiffre un texte;… cette perfection oubliée ou cachée, il s'acharnerait à nous la faire découvrir dans les choses" ("A.E., having become aware of the intelligibility of the visible world, would only think, from then on, of questioning it as one would decipher a text;… he would persist in making us discover that forgotten or hidden perfection in things") (86). To give up on the task of interpretation by affirming either the intelligibility of the world or its total lack thereof is to give up on poetry itself. Poetry thus takes us beyond the question both of affirmation and negation; it changes the game and the terms completely such that, while ideas such as the absolute or purity disappear from modern characterizations of poetry, certain structures related to that way of thinking remain, not as ghostly traces but as vehicles by which we define poetry in a way that comes to terms with ignorance and uncertainty and makes them part of what we still might call a "poetic" way of life.[4]

Poetry, rather than serving as a source of knowledge or connection, stands in question in Jaccottet just as nature does; the two are united by being unseizable, or seizable only provisionally and in a way that is immediately subjected to doubt.[5] When either poetry or nature is present, it is unknowable, since its very presence cancels the ability to see it as the object of knowledge. The process of knowing, whether applied to poetry or nature, is always undergone retroactively, in an effort to perceive what has already passed. This becomes apparent in the following apostrophe to mountains:

Qu'êtes-vous donc en effet, mes montagnes? Le souvenir (qui s'effacera bientôt) de grandes colères, une pause apparente dans l'affaiblissement d'une planète, un geste qui retombe ... Mais cela concerne votre histoire, quand c'est votre présence qui me touche. Tous les jours je vous revois; j'ai beau me dire: qu'ai-je à faire de ces montagnes, mille soucis sont plus urgents, mille présences plus proches, je vous regarde encore, et vous n'avez pas fini de m'étonner. (99–100)

(What are you then, in fact, my mountains? The memory (which will soon be erased) of great anger, an apparent pause in the weakening of a planet, a gesture that falls ... But that's about your past, when what moves me is your presence. Every day I see you again. Even though I tell myself: what do I have to do with these mountains, a thousand worries are more urgent, a thousand presences are closer, I still look at you even so, and still you continue to surprise me.)

Thought necessarily mediates the poet's relationship to the presence of the mountains, and complicates that relationship, or renders it impossible in its usual form, by that mediation. But as with poetry, such mediation is not a source of regret or mourning, but rather of possibility, as thought and writing can only begin where presence ends. Sometimes the poet claims to want to retreat into passive contemplation as opposed to active poetic creation: "Ah ! sûrement, j'adopterai un jour un langage plus vif et plus chantant pour m'y élever [dans l'air] comme l'alouette et le conquérir dans l'allégresse de la poésie ! On ne résiste pas à ces trouées ! Mais aujourd'hui je vais rester assis à ma fenêtre et me contenter de regarder, de rêver, de réfléchir" ("Ah ! Surely I will one day adopt a livelier and more melodious language to raise myself up [in the air] like the lark and conquer it in the joy of poetry! You cannot resist these gaps! But today I will remain seated at my window and be content to look, to dream, to reflect") (100). But, unlike those more permanently drawn to this kind of contemplation, he finds that such silence brings horror rather than peace.

Le silence presque absolu qui se fait parfois au dehors, même dans une grande ville, à la fin de la nuit, ne m'est jamais apparu comme un bonheur, j'en étais effrayé plutôt, et je reprendrai un jour l'examen de ces moments parfois curieusement difficiles: il semble que dans l'espèce de mur qui nous protège se soit ouverte brusquement une faille derrière laquelle s'amassent, mais sans entrer, les troupes du vide, de gros fantômes cotonneux. Tout au contraire, en cette nuit de lune dont je veux parler, le silence semblait être un autre nom pour l'espace, c'est-à-dire que les bruits très rares, ou plutôt les notes qui étaient perçues dans la fosse nocturne, et en particulier le cri intermittent d'une chouette, ne s'élevaient que pour laisser entendre des distances, des intervalles. (104)

(The almost absolute silence that sometimes occurs outside, even in a big city, at the end of night, has never appeared to me as a happy thing; rather, I was afraid of it, and one day I will once again take up an examination of those sometimes curiously difficult moments: it seems that in the sort of wall that protects us a fault has opened all of a sudden, behind which are piling up, but without going in, the troops of the void, fat cottony ghosts. In total contrast, in this moonlit night that I would like to talk about, the silence seemed to be another name for space, I mean that the very occasional noises, or rather the notes that were perceived in the nocturnal pit, and in particular the intermittent cry of an owl, only emerge in order to let me hear the distances and the spaces.)

Peace is thus an intermediary step, and not the telos of the process; poetry separates itself from contemplation rather than uniting with it. A "poetic" way of life would be one that is restless and unsettled rather than peaceful and centered. The role of nature is to inspire the disagreeable feelings that push us away from nature and back toward poetry.

I turn now to *Éléments d'un songe*, which extends Jaccottet's reflections on nature, poetry, and ignorance, in the sense I have been using it here, as a state of unknowing. Here too, while Jaccottet seems at times to lament a lost harmony or unity ("On rêve d'un ordre souverain, d'un murmure soutenu, et l'on n'en sauve que de vagues fragments" ("We dream of a sovereign order, of a sustained murmur, and we can only recover vague fragments of it") (257)), he develops sustained reflections on the status of willed ignorance and its benefits as, perhaps, a replacement, and not simply a consolation prize, for that impossible order. Replacing peace of mind with ignorance allows the poet to fill that void, affirming the attempt to do so even as the affirmation of ignorance serves as a reminder of the always only temporary way in which that filling can occur. A sense of the advantage of this approach is visible in this remark:

> Je crois vraiment pouvoir affronter maintenant sans faiblir les mille opinions divergentes qui ont cours sur la poésie, même sachant que des esprits infiniment plus subtils et mieux informés que le mien sont là pour les défendre. Car je ne me soucie pas tant de connaissance que de ne pas être enterré vivant comme beaucoup d'autres. (309)

(I truly think I can now confront without weakening the thousand divergent opinions that people have about poetry, even while knowing that infinitely subtler and better informed minds than mine are there to defend them. For I am not concerned so much with knowledge as with not being buried alive like so many others.)

Willed ignorance is a defense against a kind of certainty that brings enclosure rather than liberation:

> Souvent, comme tout le monde, j'ai été près de désespérer, mais en dessous, en deçà plutôt qu'au-delà des brumes et des lueurs alternées, si j'avais réussi à me défaire des théories, du savoir, de l'assurance qu'ils nous prêtent, enfin de tout ce qui nous protège, nous enferme et nous ferme. (309–10)

> (Often, like everyone else, I was near despair, but beneath that, falling short rather than being beyond the alternating fogs and glimmers, if I had succeeded in getting rid of theories, of knowledge, of the assurance that they lend us, of everything that protects, encloses, and closes us.)

On one hand, knowledge protects, but on the other hand it encloses and closes off. An awareness of the danger of such knowledge, and of the way it can harden the knowing subject so that further growth is impossible, is itself a kind of knowledge that springs, paradoxically, from an affirmation of ignorance. It is such an affirmation that makes knowledge suspicious of itself and of the solidity of its claims; it is the same kind of awakening to movement that we saw Jaccottet characterize above as the shift from contemplation to poetic creation. The poet represents speech as a countermeasure to despair: "J'ai envie de parler, peut-être sans savoir pourquoi, peut-être parce que je sens que j'ai touché la merveille, et qu'il me faut le dire aux autres pour qu'ils cessent de désespérer" ("I feel like talking, maybe without knowing why, maybe because I feel like I have touched the wonder, and I have to tell others so they stop despairing") (310). Quietude thus seems to become a kind of temptation; it risks solidifying into the same kind of rigid and stifling certainty that definitive knowledge does. One cannot become self-satisfied with ignorance. In that sense, Jaccottet's ignorance is not static, as certain knowledge is, but rather dynamic in that it inspires the quest for a temporary release from itself. It is on that basis that ignorance can be affirmed, as a spur to poetic creation that is at the same time bereft of illusions about accomplishing that quest.[6] It is a kind of lucid ignorance.

It is in these prose texts that Jaccottet attempts to know what poetic experience is. Paradoxically, he affirms that poetry itself is not about knowledge but rather aims to reproduce experience (as opposed to attempting to understand it or merely representing it):

> Il ne s'agit pas pour moi d'analyser cette expérience, mais de la refaire en parlant, dans un état où la conscience claire et des mouvements plus obscurs s'associent

pour le choix des mots. Immanquablement en tout cas, et comme en premier lieu, ces mots chantent : c'est leur premier devoir. (311)

(For me it's not about analyzing this experience but of having it again in speaking, in a state where clear consciousness and more obscure movements come together for the choice of words. Inevitably in any case, and in the first place, these words sing: it is their first obligation.)

The success of a poem, on this reading, depends on its degree of fidelity to the experience, and it becomes the task of the thinker about poetry, as opposed to the poet him or herself, to define that relation between poetry and the experience it helps recreate:

Je ne fais ici, que l'on veuille bien me croire, ni théologie, ni métaphysique : j'en serais incapable. J'essaie honnêtement de savoir de quoi se nourrit le poème.... Et je sais que l'expérience, pour être mystérieuse, n'en est pas moins commune (fréquente au point que l'on oublie d'y penser). Ce qui n'est pas commun, c'est que le poème lui soit fidèle et sache en propager la contagion. (314)

(I hope you will believe me that I am not doing theology or metaphysics here: I would be incapable of that. I am trying honestly to know what the poem feeds on.... And I know that experience, which is no less common (and frequent to the point where one forgets to think about it) for being mysterious. What is not common is when the poem is faithful to it and is able to propagate the contagion.)

Jaccottet often succumbs to the temptation of affirming the possibility of transparency in these descriptions of the poem as a faithful re-creation of an experience, and thus steps back from the complexity of questions about what it would mean for a verbal experience to recreate another kind of experience. To claim that it would be impossible to articulate how that happens is to fall back into a kind of mysticism, which Jaccottet claims he wants to avoid.

He is both drawn to and repulsed by the extremes of ignorance and assurance and tempted to abandon the impulse to define poetry when faced with the impossibility of articulating his idea of poetry as experience:

Je n'ai pas appelé le poème, je ne l'ai même pas nécessairement attendu ; peut-être vaut-il mieux que je n'y aie plus pensé, que j'aie oublié ou douté que je fusse poète. Je crois même qu'à un certain moment tout cela m'a paru grotesque, ignoble, criminellement frivole et vain.... En particulier, j'aurais souhaité ne plus voir, dans les traits de certains enfants pourtant très jeunes, apparaître déjà le mélange de bêtise et d'assurance qui m'effrayait chez leurs pères. (314)

(I did not call the poem, I did not even wait for it necessarily; maybe it would be better if I no longer thought about it, if I were to forget or doubt that I was a poet. I even think that at a certain point all of that seemed grotesque, dreadful, criminally frivolous and vain to me.... In particular, I would have wished no longer to see appear, in the features of certain very young children, the mixture of stupidity and assurance that already frightened me in their fathers.)

Jaccottet appears to set up a dichotomy between thought and direct experience, claiming that the latter can only occur once the former ceases:

> Voici ce que nous avons éprouvé : que nous n'étions jamais plus vivants, plus réels, plus certains de notre réalité et de la réalité du monde que lorsque nous atteignions ce point où notre pensée s'arrête, lorsque nous atteignait, plutôt, ce lieu impossible. Oui, la seule chose qui résistât au doute, au désespoir, pour nous, il fallait que ce fût l'incompréhensible, une énigme essentiellement énigme, c'est-à-dire indéchiffrable, mais qui nous apparaissait plutôt, en fin de compte, comme la seule ouverture, la seule porte, la seule vraie source (autre et ultime contradiction, qui voulait que l'issue fût justement l'infranchissable): éternité jaillissante, désaltérante, vivifiante ... (315)

(Here's what we have felt: that we were never more alive, more real, more certain of our reality and of the reality of the world than when we attain that point where our thought stops, when we attain, rather, that impossible place. Yes, the only thing that would resist doubt and despair, for us, it would have to be the incomprehensible, an essentially enigmatic, undecipherable enigma, but which appeared to us rather, when all is said and done, as the only opening, the only gate, the only true source (another and ultimate contradiction, which wanted the exit to be unattainable): eternity gushing forth, slaking our thirst, invigorating us ...)

Jaccottet implies that attaining a point where thinking stops would be a moment of most intense living. To define poetic experience in this way is, however, to exclude the verbal, unless one were to subscribe to an idea of poetic language as purely musical and devoid of all semantic content. But in that case we return to the problem we identified in chapter two whereby poetry becomes akin to music but is thereby unidentifiable as poetry, given that pure experience must give way at some point to interpretation even to be categorized as experience. It is also important to note here the way that Jaccottet poses this issue as a question of knowing ("the only thing that would resist doubt and despair, for us, it would have to be the incomprehensible"). To posit this, however, is to place ourselves back in the realm of discourse about poetry, a fact that highlights the impossibility of dwelling in the space of direct experience which for Jaccottet would also be a state of perfect ignorance. What we see emerging here is in fact a distinction between two different kinds of ignorance: on one hand, there is the state associated with direct experience, where the question of knowing is not even posed. On the other hand, there is the more active conceptualization of ignorance, itself an active thought process by which the subject affirms lack of knowledge. This is the difference between a conscious and unconscious ignorance. While Jaccottet gives his explicit attention to describing the state of unconscious ignorance, it is in fact the state of conscious ignorance that drives him forward in the quest to know poetry and to affirm poetry's relation to a kind of knowing or unknowing. For the affirmation of ignorance is itself a knowledge claim and belongs in the realm of thought that Jaccottet claims is the opposite of the "eternity gushing forth, slaking our thirst, invigorating us" that he seeks. But if one cannot dwell in the unconscious ignorance of the direct experience, it is the second, conscious, ignorance that is the motor of the verbal quest that leads both to words about poetry and to poems themselves.

Rather than an affirmation of a nonconceptual, direct experience, Jaccottet's texts provide, both implicitly and explicitly, the space for a dynamic interplay among poetry, knowledge, and ignorance, a textual performance of his notion of poetry as "cette clef qu'il faut toujours reperdre" ("that key that you must always keep on losing"). A poem thus answers doubt's questioning by becoming a question-given-form: the poem becomes a vehicle for the expression of the question, providing perhaps some consolation in the face of doubt:

> A mon inquiétude, à mes doutes, à mon ignorance, même à mon dégoût, certains jours, ce qui s'oppose le mieux, [c'est] quelque poème long ou bref, ce poème ne serait-il pas à son tour qu'une question, la question même, peut-être, que je me posais. Pourquoi ? Parce que dans le poème la question est devenue chant et s'est enveloppée dans un ordre sans cesser d'être posée. Je dois bien constater qu'il n'est pas de réponse qui puisse abolir la question; sinon, il y aurait longtemps qu'elle aurait été donnée, et que la vie sur cette terre aurait cessé pour faire place à je ne sais quoi d'impensable; mais je dois admettre du même coup qu'une question perpétuelle, demeurant absolument sans espoir de réponse, est également impensable. Que reste-t-il ? Sinon cette façon de poser la question qui se nomme la poésie et qui est vraisemblablement la possibilité de tirer de la limite même un chant, de prendre en quelque sorte appui sur l'abîme pour se maintenir au-dessus, sinon le franchir (qui serait le supprimer); une manière de parler du

monde qui n'explique pas le monde, car ce serait le figer et l'anéantir, mais qui le montre tout nourri de son refus de répondre, vivant parce qu'impénétrable, merveilleux parce que terrible. (317–18)⁷

(What fights best against my worry, my doubts, my ignorance, even my disgust certain days, is some long or short poem, even if this poem would itself be only a question, the very question, maybe, that I was asking myself. Why? Because in the poem the question becomes song and envelops itself in an order without ceasing to be asked. I need to note that there is no reply that could abolish the question; otherwise, it would have been given long ago, and life on this earth would have ceased in order to make room for some unthinkable thing; but I must admit at the same time that a perpetual question, remaining absolutely without hope of an answer, is equally unthinkable. What remains? Only this way of posing the question which we call poetry and which is realistically the possibility of drawing out a song from the very limit, to get support from the abyss in order to stay above it, if not to jump over it (which would be to suppress it); a way of speaking of the world which does not explain the world, since that would be to freeze it and annihilate it, but which shows it nourished by its refusal to respond, alive because it is impenetrable, wonderful because it is dreadful.)

Poetry thus neither cancels doubt (which Jaccottet figures here as the "abyss") nor forces a fall into it, but rather allows us to suspend ourselves above it, and thus poetry possesses not a transformative power but a way to give form to doubt and questioning themselves, to give voice to those experiences rather than, strictly speaking, to represent them.

And yet, Jaccottet is, in this same text, reluctant to locate poetry definitively within the realm of doubt and questioning. A tension remains in his writing between needing to affirm doubt and a more nostalgic attempt to see poetry, in a Romantic vein, as the secret reflection of the world as it becomes a text to be deciphered:

Le monde ne dit pas à celui qui le questionne ainsi, cherchant la clef de sa vie, la voie juste : voici la clef, voici la voie, et maintenant ne questionnez plus (cette clef pouvant être le système qu'on voudra, naturisme, spiritualisme, marxisme). Non, le monde seulement apparaît avec la beauté des choses du monde qui n'est pas une beauté sans tache, et sa réponse est ce chant où la question continue d'être posée, mais où elle est comme portée par un souffle, allégée; sa réponse est seulement sa présence chantante, mesurée, et c'est elle que le poème traduit ou simplement répète ; le poème en lequel se retrouvent par un mouvement naturel mille rapports complexes. (318)

(The world does not say to the person who questions it that way, seeking the key to his or her life, the right path: here is the key, here is the way, and now do not question any longer (that key could be whatever system you want, naturism, spiritualism, Marxism). No, the world only appears with the beauty of the things of the world which is not a beauty without stain, and its response is that song where the question continues to be posed, but where it is as if carried by a breath, lightened; its response is only its singing, measured presence, and that is what the poem translates or simply repeats; the poem in which a thousand complex relations are joined in a natural movement.)

If the world's secret reveals itself, as Jaccottet claims here, in the poem, he does not indicate precisely how. His prose dialogue thus, like a poem, invites commentary on how it accomplishes what he claims it does. If the poem reveals the secret of the world, this prose text remains intriguingly silent on exactly how that happens, bringing us dangerously close to the mysticism Jaccottet often wants to avoid. Jaccottet goes on in this text to define poetry in terms of the secret:

> En fin de compte, peut-être la définition la moins inexacte de la poésie serait-elle celle qui embrasserait ces contraires, qui l'envisagerait à la fois comme un jeu insignifiant et comme un témoignage du secret, une façon légère qu'aurait le secret de nous parvenir.... Il n'est pas aisé d'interpréter sans emphase et sans imprécision une expérience si profonde et si dérobée ... (320)

> (After all, maybe the least approximate definition of poetry would the one that embraces these opposites, that would envisage it at one and the same time as an insignificant game and as witness to the secret, a light way that the secret would have to arrive to us.... It is not easy to interpret such a profound and hidden experience without bombast and without imprecision.)

What remains unclear is the way poetry would situate itself relative to skepticism on this view: if it reveals the secret, does it reveal the secret *as* secret or does Jaccottet envision a kind of revelatory function for poetry? The fact that the text does not make a pronouncement on this is its own secret, its own hesitation or contradiction between revelation and its opposite. By revealing what cannot be named, poetry unveils the limits of language, but it leaves in its wake a poetic record of that impossibility, which is, paradoxically, a new communicative function for poetic language. One could also describe this as a kind of knowledge in ignorance, a new awareness, and expression, of what cannot be known, the secret that names itself as such.

Here we arrive at what could be a stumbling block, a point from which we can continue no further, if poetry is ultimately destined to end in the secret. But as we have seen before, once poetry—or music, or any other art—arrives at the brink of the ineffable, it invites a continuation of discourse making sense of that ineffability, extracting meaning from it. And for Jaccottet, doubt is useful because it gives direction, or even meaning, to thought and its expression. He plays on both meanings of the word "sens" here: "dès que nous doutons, nous sommes engagés dans une aventure, c'est-à-dire entraînés dans un certain sens, vers un but qui, pour perpétuellement se dérober, n'en demeure pas moins l'indication d'un sens" ("as soon as we doubt, we are engaged in an adventure, that is, led in a certain direction, toward a goal that, even though it is perpetually hidden, still remains the indication of a direction or meaning") (324). The poem is created not in doubt's place but on account of it, as a record of it, as to some extent its product: "Je sais que demain les doutes reprendront, mais ceci aura été dit tout de même" ("I know that tomorrow the doubts will return, but this will have been said all the same") (331). Ignorance and doubt thus function together as a vehicle for poetic expression, not of the world or of experience, but of doubt about that experience. If meaning emerges, it is fleeting, but poetry becomes the space where that fleeting meaning is recorded in its very flight.

In this way doubt, rather than paralyzing poetic production, becomes the motor of it. Bringing together opposites is a key aspect of poetic activity, as Jaccottet notes in *La semaison*: "Toute l'activité poétique se voue à concilier, ou du moins à rapprocher, la limite et l'illimité, le clair et l'obscur, le souffle et la forme. C'est pourquoi le poème nous ramène à notre centre, à notre souci central, à une question métaphysique" ("All poetic activity devotes itself to reconciling, or at least bringing closer together, the limit and the unlimited, the clear and the obscure, the breath and the form. That is why the poem brings us back to our center, to our central concern, to a metaphysical question") (354). It is important to note here that poetry leads to a metaphysical question but not a metaphysics. This is a crucial distinction, given what Jaccottet and the other poets we have been considering claim about the particularity of poetry's engagement with metaphysical questions, an engagement that eschews any systematic approach in favor of one that is fed by the questions themselves rather than by a quest for definitive answers. Jaccottet wants to hold open the question of what it would mean to write in full knowledge of the illusion of transcendence: "On répliquera qu'on ne peut plus, aujourd'hui, feindre l'innocence: qu'il faut travailler (peindre, écrire) *avec* tout le savoir dont notre conscience est chargée. Mais une ignorance subsiste, quoi qu'on fasse, toujours aussi grande" ("You'll reply that today we can no longer feign innocence: that we have to work (paint, write) *with* all the knowledge with which our awareness is burdened. But an ignorance remains, whatever we do, and always just as big") (393). The distinction between innocence and ignorance highlights the fact that knowledge in this case is knowledge of ignorance as opposed to a knowledge that would replace ignorance. What has thus changed, and what defines modern or contemporary approaches to poetry on this view, is that knowledge and ignorance now coexist, with poetry giving voice to that ignorance but in a way that recognizes that ignorance feeds the poetic project rather than inhibiting it.[8]

The delicate play between knowledge and ignorance as it features in Jaccottet's writings about poetry finds an analogue in our experience as readers who are caught up in the hesitation between doubt and momentary certainty about poetry that his texts enact. In a speech given on the occasion of receipt of the Prix Montaigne in 1972, Jaccottet claims that "l'œuvre à faire, la seule qui puisse intéresser l'écrivain, commence chaque fois à partir d'une incertitude profonde, d'une sorte d'état obscur, confus, d'un manque, presque d'un égarement" ("the work to be accomplished, the only one that can interest the writer, begins each time from a profound uncertainty, from a sort of obscure and confused state, from a lack, almost from a distraction") (1335), and that it is thus no surprise that the poetic vocation often begins in adolescence, "au moment le plus trouble, le plus chargé d'espérance mais aussi de crainte" ("at the most troubled moment, the one most charged with hope but also with fear") (1336). While he claims that he is "rien moins qu'un penseur" ("nothing less than a thinker") (1340), Jaccottet implies that the way we approach questions of certainty and doubt in poetry is directly parallel to the way we approach those questions in lived experience more broadly, and that the poetic project is in that sense an amplification and extension of lived experience as opposed to an activity removed from it.[9] Thinking about poetry thus provides a model for living reflectively in the world and hints at the way doubt and certainty can be held in balance. Approaching poetry in this way provides a model for a reflective life whereby any certainties are infinitely revisable in terms of new experiences; it is a significant extension of Baudelaire's rejection of systems in favor of experience. Rather than creating a rift between poetry and thought, however, Jaccottet shows how they can be united and viewed as a similar enterprise, or in fact how poetry as he characterizes it provides the most livable option in terms of questions of doubt or certainty about the reality we inhabit;

poetry gives voice to the tentative nature of thought itself and provides a model for understanding and justifying the conceptual restlessness that thinking, as opposed to knowing, entails.[10] After having passed through the stage of "pure poetry" that would negate or at least de-emphasize the relation of poetry to lived experience, with Jaccottet the history of thought about poetry returns to a deep imbrication with lived experience which springs from the discourse of interpretation that is necessarily generated by "pure" poetry, the moment we attempt to articulate in what that "purity" would consist.

In the speech, Jaccottet describes both lived experience and poetry in terms of their strangeness. He imagines an adolescent eventually coming to maturity in his reflection on poetry:

> Loin de penser que la poésie soit, comme on voudrait le lui faire croire,… un trop beau masque sur le visage insoutenable du réel il a le sentiment qu'à sa manière, elle doit dire vrai, ou en tout cas, mentir moins que les dogmes, les doctrines. Et il en vient, beaucoup plus tard peut-être, à penser ceci: qu'a réussi à se glisser dans le texte du poème quelque chose de l'inconnu où il se sent jeté et peut-être égaré, quelque chose de la démesure qui rend sa condition si étrange, si énigmatique. De sorte que l'étrangeté même du fait de vivre, qui n'est pas mince, et l'étrangeté du poème, seraient inséparables. (1337)

> (Far from thinking that poetry is, as they would wish to make him think,… a beautiful mask over the insufferable face of the real, he has the feeling that, in its own way, it must speak truth, or in any case, lie less than dogmas and doctrines. And he comes, much later maybe, to think this: that something of the unknown where he feels thrown and maybe lost has slipped into the text of the poem, something of the outrageousness that makes his condition so strange, so enigmatic, such that the very strangeness of the fact of living, which is not small, and the strangeness of the poem, would be inseparable.)

According to Jaccottet, the next move of the adolescent on this path is to read scientists, religious thinkers, and philosophers in an ultimately vain attempt to "réduire cette étrangeté" ("reduce this strangeness") (1337). When he turns back to a poem, he finds that while it explains nothing to him and "ne lui fournit aucune clef" ("does not supply any key") (1337), it does provide "le pouvoir, obscur mais indéniable, de le maintenir en vie…. Voilà, en quelques mots, comment il se fait que la poésie et la vie m'ont toujours paru étroitement liées" ("the power, obscure but undeniable, to keep him alive…. There, in a few words, is how it happens that poetry and life have always seemed to me closely linked")

(1337). Jaccottet goes on to recount his discovery of the Japanese haiku tradition and how it cancels the silence that uncertainty risks bringing to the poet and recenters poetry on attention to the ordinary as opposed to the excessive, intoxicating, or vertiginous, "comme si à l'affirmation désespérée de Rimbaud, « la vraie vie est ailleurs », répondait non pas une affirmation contraire… mais comme une floraison de signes discrets témoignant d'une vraie vie possible ici et maintenant" ("as if to Rimbaud's desperate affirmation that 'true life is elsewhere,' responded not an affirmation to the contrary… but something like a blossoming of discreet signs testifying to a true life possible here and now") (1341). This "peu de lumière" ("little light") had a profound effect on Jaccottet because it seemed in that moment that it had something even of the divine in it. He found himself reassured by this momentary illumination "mais aussi, toujours prêts à nous être de nouveau dérobés, refusés" ("but also, always ready to be hidden or refused to us again") (1341). He finds in the haiku poets a way of being simultaneously in the world and detached from it, and perhaps a way of allowing poetry to have a transformative effect on lived experience without the potentially reactionary appeal to western-style Romantic transcendence. The haiku poets thus create a space where a new approach to poetry can coexist with a new, and similar, approach to thought without the risk of moving backwards in time or of being fixed into a systematic approach.

Jaccottet's poem "L'Ignorant," from the collection of the same name, features the interplay of poetry and ignorance by creating a space where they come together. That poetic place is literally inscribed in the poem; the poet, who begins by noting: "Plus je vieillis et plus je croîs en ignorance" ("The more I get older, the more I grow in ignorance") (154), then indicates: "Tout ce que j'ai, c'est un espace tour à tour/enneigé ou brillant, mais jamais habité" ("Everything I have is a space alternatingly/snowy or shiny, but never lived in") (154). The poem, composed of unrhymed alexandrines with capital letters at the start of some but not all of the lines, is a space situated between prose and traditional verse; its speaker retires to his room and, rather than speaking or writing, remains silent and waits.[11] After this stripping away, accomplished by the series of actions "Je me tiens dans ma chambre… je me tais… et j'attends" ("I stay in my room… I remain quiet… and I wait"), a question then appears:

> … que reste-t-il à ce mourant
> qui l'empêche si bien de mourir ? Quelle force
> le fait encor parler entre ses quatre murs ?
> Pourrais-je le savoir, moi l'ignare et l'inquiet ? (154)

> (... what remains to this dying man
> that keeps him so well from dying? What force
> makes him speak still within these four walls?
> Could I ever know it, I the ignorant and the worried one?)

Here it becomes unclear whether the poet is himself this dying man, but given that he is alone in his room, it is likely. In that case, the poetic subject is a split one, with the poet listening to his own words as if he were foreign to himself. The poem ends with the quoted words of the dying man, which become the result of an act of self-ventriloquizing as the poet reports the words which he heard himself say as he keeps silent: "Comme le feu, l'amour n'établit sa clarté/que sur la faute et la beauté des bois en cendres …." ("Like fire, love only establishes its clarity/on the fault and the beauty of woods in ashes") (154). The veracity of the claim is called into question in advance by the poet's claim of ignorance, which contrasts with the declamatory confidence of these lines. What we have in the poem is not a progression from ignorance to knowledge but rather the space wherein knowledge of ignorance itself emerges. The poem empties out subjectivity and its presuppositions in order to create the space for a paradoxical poetry of ignorance whose dynamism stems from contemplating ignorance rather than simply expressing it or attempting to overcome it. Silence turns out not to be the result of the realization of ignorance; the poetic word is not reduced to zero by it. Rather, silence gives rise to those small remains of poetic discourse, what Jaccottet calls at the start of the poem "Fin d'hiver," "Peu de chose" ("Little") (421), the incipit of that poem (at the head of the section in which it appears) that one cannot help but read as an echo or corrective to Stéphane Mallarmé's famous first words of *Poésies*: "Rien, cette écume, vierge vers" ("Nothing, this foam, virgin line") (*OC*1: 4). Jaccottet's "little" is what is left, according to that poem, to "l'âme errante" ("the wandering soul") (421), a figure who stands in contrast to the one in "L'Ignorant" who chooses to remain in his room. The errant soul is the more typical figure in Jaccottet, especially given that in "L'Ignorant" the space that the poet has is "jamais habité" ("never lived in") (154), an indication of the eternal restlessness and questioning of the poet.

Neither truth nor its opposite remains as the product of poetic production in Jaccottet. His image of the ashes which closes "L'Ignorant" finds its echo in these lines in "Fin d'hiver": "Vérité, non-vérité/se résorbent en fumée/… Vérité, non-vérité/brillent, cendre parfumée" ("Truth, non-truth/are reabsorbed in smoke/… Truth, non-truth/shine, perfumed ash") (422). The shining ashes seem to have it both ways, being fire and the end-product of the fire at once. What remains is the poem not as negation but as doubt, the trace of the dynamics of listening and speaking that bring only a reminder of the finitude that, like ignorance, spur poetic creation. As poet and critic Jean-Marie Maulpoix has noted about Jaccottet, ignorance and finitude "sont fécondes, elles fructifient et « croissent ». C'est parce que l'homme ne sait rien de sa fin que la poésie existe : elle vient occuper la place laissée vide par le savoir. Elle naît de la division du sujet, de son retournement sur soi et de son absence de maîtrise" ("are fecund, they fructify and 'grow'. It is because man knows nothing of his end that poetry exists: it comes to occupy the place left empty by knowledge. It is born from the division of the subject, from its turning back on itself and from its absence of mastery") (*Pour un lyrisme* 204). If the poem yields ashes, the perpetual ignorance of the poet as both creator and listener and, by extension, writer and reader, yields a potentially infinite return to those ashes, a perpetual questioning of the play of silence and speech that gives us ashes but refuses to see them as the end of discourse or a retreat to an ignorant silence, an idea that Jaccottet captures in these lines that conclude a section of *Airs* not with a "therefore" but a "nevertheless":

> Monde né d'une déchirure
> Apparu pour être fumée!
>
> Néanmoins la lampe allumée
> sur l'interminable lecture (440)
>
> (World born of a tearing
> Appearing in order to be smoke!
>
> Nevertheless the lamp lit
> On the unending reading)

No verb animates the last lines, which conclude without a final period. Reading is one of the only things presented as unending or as always present in Jaccottet, along with questioning; ignorance is the motor of both.

The poem "Pensées sous les nuages" works through this poetics of questioning, of what the poem sprung from ignorance would look like. In his poetry as so often in Jaccottet's thought, more traditional poetic aspirations are neither affirmed nor negated. They are relegated to a time past but evoked in their absence rather than rejected, in a way that generates poetry from that very questioning. The poem gives voice to the silence of impossible transcendence and thus reorients the act of reading and writing along the lines of the "peu de choses" and what they may offer to those newly attuned to them through their cultivated ignorance. The poem begins with a refusal of travel and an affirmation of remaining in place: "Je ne crois pas décidément que nous ferons ce voyage/… Je nous vois mal en aigles invisibles" ("I certainly don't believe that we will take this trip/… I can't envision us as invisible eagles") (718). Through preterition, the voyage is evoked under the sign of negation to mark its paradoxical presence here. The clarity of the sun is abandoned in favor of the clouds, which the poet contemplates not from his traditional position from within them but rather, like all of humanity, under them. This perspective does not cancel poetry or mourn the absence or impossibility of transcendence, but rather reframes the question of what poetry can do by offering a critique of our former expectation of transcendence or revelation or privileged knowledge in the first place:

> Il faut que nous soyons restés bien naïfs
> pour nous croire sauvés par le bleu du ciel
> ou châtiés par l'orage et par la nuit.
>
> —Mais où donc pensiez-vous aller encore, avec ces pieds usés (718–19)
>
> (We must have remained really naïve
> to believe ourselves saved by the blue of the sky
> or punished by the storm and the night.
>
> —But where did you think you were still going, then, with these worn out feet)

Poetry's role here is thus not to answer questions or attain revelation but rather to change the shape of the questions themselves by showing that what had been sought was not what was attainable in the first place, a fact which results in a misdirected question. The ignorant poet thus carries a key insight in terms of knowledge that is inaccessible or mischaracterized. This is a wise, conscious ignorance that affirms itself, as opposed to the ignorance that is under the illusion of what turns out to be false. An important aspect of the work of Jaccottet's poetry is to negotiate the difference, implicitly, between these two kinds of ignorance, a fact that echoes the splitting of the self that we saw in "L'Ignorant" between the one who keeps silence and the dying man who speaks.

In "Pensées sous les nuages" the dying disappear, and the image of ashes returns: "Leur corps est cendre,/cendre leur ombre et leur souvenir" ("Their body is ash,/ash their shadow and their memory") (719), and that ash will be dispersed by the wind. As in "Fin d'hiver," though, this is not the end of the story, because the poem introduces a "nevertheless":

> Néanmoins,
> en passant, nous aurons encore entendu
> ces cris d'oiseaux sous les nuages
> dans le silence d'un midi d'octobre vide (719–20)
>
> > (Nevertheless,
> > in passing, we will have still heard
> > these birds' cries beneath the clouds
> > in the silence of an empty October's noon)

This caveat to the reduction of all past, present, and future life to ash changes nothing about that material reduction. What becomes essential in the world below rather than above the clouds is hearing, and in particular the hearing of non-discursive sounds. Or, rather, discursive sounds in a language inaccessible to us, that of birds calling to each other in a way that is audible but, to most of us, meaningless except as pure sound. The poet at the end of the poem situates himself not only under the clouds but also under those birds whom he will have heard:

> Et moi qui passe au-dessous d'eux,
> il me semble qu'ils ont parlé, non pas questionné, appelé,
> mais répondu. Sous les nuages bas d'octobre.
> Et déjà c'est un autre jour, je suis ailleurs,
> déjà ils disent autre chose ou ils se taisent,
> je passe, je m'étonne, et je ne peux en dire plus. (720)
>
> > (And I who pass below them,
> > it seems to me that they spoke, not that they questioned or called,
> > but answered. Beneath the low clouds of October.
> > And already it is another day, I am elsewhere,
> > already they are saying something else or they are silent,
> > I pass, I am surprised, and I can say no more.)

The poem ends here. Ignorance and knowledge have seemed to disappear as explicit thematic concerns in this poem written under the guiding title of "Pensées." The birds do not participate in humanity's eternal questioning; rather, they respond, but the poet does not indicate to what they may be responding. Speaking and keeping silent are presented as equivalent possibilities at the end of the poem, and we are left with the poet in movement and wonder, both of which replace the act of saying. This, then, can be seen as the poet's own response, a response to the birds' response whose content he cannot begin to fathom.

Given that the poet records or, rather, creates this experience of passing on and wondering in a poem, the poem itself becomes that response, that act of passing, and that act of wonder. One might even conceive this active creation as a kind of happiness or at least its potential, as Serge Champeau does:

> Et le poème, indissociablement activité esthétique et éthique, maintient et accomplit dans l'équilibre qu'il produit cette promesse de bonheur. A la recherche de la vérité, théoriquement comprise, Jaccottet oppose alors celle de la justesse de l'expression, ou bien, et il n'y a là nulle contradiction si la vérité n'est plus définie en termes de théorie, il affirme que « toute vérité tiendrait en définitive pour moi dans une image ». Image qui, conformément au double sens donné à ce terme, représenterait bien ce qui est mais surtout nous ferait être. (252–3)

> (And the poem, indivisibly esthetic and ethical activity, maintains and accomplishes this promise of happiness in the equilibrium that it produces. In search of truth, theoretically understood, Jaccottet now opposes that of the trueness of expression, or, and there is here no contradiction if the truth is no longer defined in terms of theory, he affirms that "all truth would definitively be located for me in an image." Image which, conforming to the double meaning given to this term, would represent what is but above all would make us be.)

The poetics of ignorance is thus creative, attentive to the world that surrounds it, conscious of the inadequacy of attempts at knowing that world or expressing it, not to mention transcending it. As Suzanne Allaire has remarked:

> L'œuvre de Jaccottet impose à son lecteur une figure qui est celle d'un « poète de la poésie ». Et ce n'est pas là affaire de prosodie et moins encore d'éloquence…. Ecrire est d'abord affaire d'attention aux signes qui viennent du monde et de l'univers du visible. Est poète alors celui qui loin de s'évader du réel, porte sur lui un regard d'une curiosité passionnée, puis dans un mouvement d'intériorisation et de dépouillement du signe, s'attache par le surgissement de l'image, qui se fait comparaison ou métaphore, à mettre en rapport, au plus étroit, les « *contraires fondamentaux* ». (70)

> (The work of Jaccottet imposes on its reader a figure that is that of a "poet of poetry." And this is not a question of prosody and even less so of eloquence…. Writing is first of all a question of attention to the signs that come from the world and the universe of the visible. The poet is thus one who, far from escaping from the real, brings to it a gaze of passionate curiosity, then in a movement of interiorization and analysis of the sign, attaches himself, by the surging up of the image, which becomes simile or metaphor, to putting "fundamental opposites" in the closest relation.)

A focus on attention, though, cannot be the sole object or end-goal of poetry, given that attention is or at least can be wordless. The state of nonverbal attention would leave us in the same place as absolute music or pure poetry, in a wordless moment from which we need eventually to break out, via language, in order to understand, interpret, or describe the experience. And this is where the question of the definition of poetry becomes inseparable from a scrutiny of what it means to be attentive. Jaccottet's is a poetry that interrogates the possibilities of poetry at the same time that it brings the poet and reader closer to the world beyond poetry as well. Such an approach refuses either to offer conclusive insights or to abandon the questioning.[12] If the poem comes to an end in passing, wonder, and silence, it cannot dwell there, as the very act of passing itself suggests. While not a definitive conclusion, the posture of silent, moving wonder is itself a "key that you must always keep on losing," an insight that the restlessness of poetry and the creative ignorance of the poet encourage and that propels it toward the next move in the endless redefinition of poetry and reorienting of its relation to the world and knowledge of it. That reorientation takes place in the dialectical relationship between reading and writing, and the reformulation of worlds that those activites suggest. I will have more to say in the next chapter about how such an activity, such a productive ignorance, leads to the production of a literary community, one where meanings are negotiated among subjects who are defined as subjects and objects in a tentative and shifting relation to meaning that mirrors Jaccottet's approach to the only barely graspable clarity that poetry may, for a moment, provide.

A poet and critic who shares considerable affinity with Jaccottet is Jean-Marie Maulpoix, a contemporary lyric voice whose essays on poetry establish a continuity with modern poets of the nineteenth century and seek to preserve a certain, altered, form of lyricism which, like Jaccottet's, retains the voice of the poetic subject in the face of a reorienting of poetry to the here and now. He seeks at the same time a lyricism that would aspire not merely to be attentive to the present but to question it, to articulate the ways in which poetry brings a dimension of knowledge to that attentiveness and, in that way, remains unique as an exploration of doubt, knowledge, poetic creation, and living in the world. Maulpoix is conscious of the distinction between the two types of ignorance I have explored above, the first of which, synonym of a kind of naïveté and innocence, he associates with poets such as those that Rilke describes in the opening pages of *The Notebooks of Malte Laurids Brigge*.[13] The ignorance at hand in Jaccottet is, according to Maulpoix, of a different kind, a lucid ignorance:

> Il s'agit d'une ignorance *positive* en laquelle la poésie trouve sa raison d'être, et qui n'est autre que l'inaptitude fondamentale de la créature à connaître la mort, l'absolu, l'au-delà, l'infini, tout ce que fédère maladroitement le mot d'*impossible*, quelle que puisse être par ailleurs l'étendue du savoir ou de l'expérience acquise … (*Perplexe* 287)
>
> (It is a question of a *positive* ignorance in which poetry finds its *raison d'être*, and which is none other than the fundamental inaptitude of the creature to know death, the absolute, the beyond, the infinite, everything that the word *impossible* awkwardly unites, whatever may be the breadth of knowledge of acquired experience …)

On this view, nature can never be the source of definitive answers or revelations but rather an incitement to further questions even in the face of the refusal of transcendent meaning, and thus nature remains in Jaccottet's poems in order to reorient what the poet seeks in it. Maulpoix writes in *La poésie malgré tout*:

> Pour Philippe Jaccottet, la présence tranquille et tenace de la nature n'est l'occasion ni d'un épanchement sentimental ni de quelque célébration mystique. Elle est plutôt une sorte de question toujours posée et à laquelle il ne sera jamais répondu car elle porte en elle-même sa réponse. (188)
>
> (For Philippe Jaccottet, the tranquil and persistent presence of nature is the occasion neither of a sentimental outpouring nor of some mystical celebration. It is rather a sort of question always being asked and to which there will never be an answer because it carries in itself its answer.)

This approach to ignorance is part of a larger poetico-critical project in Maulpoix that seeks to adapt, as Jaccottet here does with nature, some of the ingredients of traditional lyric poetry so that they remain relevant to contemporary ways of writing and seeing the world, rather than being doomed to a reactionary style as some members of the avant-garde may propose.

To interrogate the place of lyric poetry in the contemporary world is thus to ask fundamentally related questions about the status of knowledge and subjectivity and about how the modern lucid subject can continue to write poetry, at risk of its giving seemingly vacuous expression to the unknown and the unknowable. Fundamental questioning is in fact at the heart of what Maulpoix calls *lyrisme critique*:

> Critique est ce lyrisme qui creuse plus qu'il ne s'élève et qui interroge plus qu'il ne célèbre. Critique, cette écriture qui se retourne anxieusement sur

elle-même au lieu de chanter dans l'insouciance. Mais lyrique cependant, puisque les questions qu'elle pose restent indissociables de l'émotion d'un sujet et de la circonstance vécue. (*Pour un lyrisme* 21)

(Critical is that lyricism that digs down more than it lifts itself up and that questions more than it celebrates. Critical, that writing that turns back anxiously on itself rather than singing without a care. But lyrical, however, since the questions that it poses remain inseparable from the emotion of a subject and a lived circumstance.)

He cites Baudelaire writing in 1861 as among the first to recognize a new function for the lyric to which we can continue to subscribe: "Si l'on jette un coup d'œil général sur la poésie contemporaine et sur ses meilleurs représentants, il est facile de voir qu'elle est arrivée à un état mixte, d'une nature très complexe; le génie philosophique, l'enthousiasme lyrique, l'esprit humoristique, s'y combinent et s'y mêlent suivant des dosages infiniment variés" ("If you cast a general glance at contemporary poetry and its best representatives, it is easy to see that it has arrived at a mixed state, of a very complex nature; philosophical genius, lyrical enthusiasm, and comic spirit combine there and mix together in infinitely varied doses") (qtd 99).[14] What remains of the lyric in our time is an "art du peu" ("art of little") (180), and poetry's task therefore is to reckon with that little, to question what remains and how we know that it does, and to reorient our processes of making and of knowing in accordance, not with a wholesale rejection of the poetic and conceptual past, but rather as a dialogue with it, a conceptual and artistic play with what remains, in whatever form in which it may remain accessible to us. If these formulas sound vague, it is precisely because it is the role of reflection on poetry to attempt, in an always partial and tentative way, to generate meaning from them.

This, as I have been arguing, becomes the most important task that poetry can set for itself, and it is a thoroughly epistemological quest bound up with knowledge of the world and self-knowledge of the poet and reader, as Maulpoix indicates in an essay that originally appeared in English translation: "Poetry is born out of the very nature of the divided self; it springs from the search for self-knowledge and the lack of self-mastery" ("Phillipe Jaccottet" 175). Poetry, in its restlessness, is not content merely to point to the ignorance and let us remain there; that would be a simple reinvention of the revelatory powers of poetry. Rather, as I have already argued, ignorance becomes the motor for engagement with poetry's history, which in turn pushes us to probe the depths of that ignorance, to temporarily refute it, and to evaluate the success of those attempts. To establish a hard and fast distinction between poems and writing about poetry is to discount that both forms of writing are often engaged in this same project, so that critical writing about poetry becomes itself an important form of poetic discourse, not to be dismissed as secondary to the poems themselves.

This is especially visible in Maulpoix, where so many of his sentences are attempts to describe what poetry is or what it does. He writes in *La voix d'Orphée* that "la poésie ne saurait s'empêcher d'être un savoir, même si nous la retrouvons toujours sans connaissance au bas de la page blanche" ("Poetry could not help being a kind of knowledge, even if we always find it unconscious at the bottom of the blank page") (214). Unless we were to attribute some kind of mystical revelatory powers to poems, poetry as a form of knowledge as Maulpoix describes it here must work in tandem with critical writing about poetry; otherwise we are left with a critical model that does nothing more than attempt to elucidate a directly present but ineffable truth present in the poem, a view that is arguably one of the least plausible models for poetic creation and interpretation in the modern period. If poems question at the same time as they affirm, critical writing on poetry also does the same. Both are interventions in an ongoing critical conversation. This is perhaps what can be gleaned from Mallarmé when he refuses to concede any inferiority of poetry to music on the supposed grounds that poetry requires language.[15] If that is the case, it is no coincidence that it is precisely with Mallarmé that critical writing about poetry begins to play a role perhaps even potentially equal to that of poetry itself as a source of insight and doubt about the relation among self, poem, language, and world. It is also with Mallarmé, as I have had occasion to note above, that the imperfection of language, rather than reducing poetry's potential, is actually its condition of possibility. In an analogous way, Maulpoix notes that ignorance is a motor of poetry:

> Sans doute est-il fécond pour la poésie que nous ignorions si ce monde a un sens et quand y viendra notre fin. Il est bon que l'âme demeure en souffrance, incertaine de soi, entre lumière et ombre. La poésie se nourrit d'une incertitude radicale; elle tient d'une telle absence de savoir son lyrisme et son humanité.... Ainsi chaque poème recommence-t-il dans la langue le monde à sa manière, comme à son premier jour. (*La voix* 203)

> (It is undoubtedly fecund for poetry that we do not know whether this world has a meaning and when our end will come. It is good that the soul remains in suffering, uncertain of itself, between light and shadow. Poetry feeds on a

radical uncertainty; it takes its lyricism and its humanity from such an absence of knowledge.... Thus every poem restarts the world, in language, in its own way, as on its first day.)

The lucidly ignorant poet is an example of what Maulpoix calls, in *Le poète perplexe* (2002) and following Jaccottet who coined the term in 1983, the *poète tardif*, which Maulpoix characterizes as a voice producing a song that is the sign of "son consentement à la disparition" ("his assent to disappearance") (*Perplexe* 289), a paradoxical one that "suppose une écoute plutôt qu'un parler" ("supposes listening rather than speaking") (289). This places the poet in the role of "celui qui interroge la subsistance d'une voix pure parmi la disparition des voix" ("the one who questions the continued existence of a pure voice among the disappearance of voices") (289). As we saw in the case of Jaccottet's "L'Ignorant," the poet thus characterized is a split subjectivity whose voice becomes exterior to him: "Si sa figure se trouve maintenue, c'est moins pour entonner son propre cantique que pour interroger en direction d'une parole que son cœur perçoit mais dont il ignore en quelle bouche elle s'articule: en direction, pourrait-elle dire, d'une voix sans sujet" ("If his figure is maintained, it is less in order to intone his own song than to question in the direction of a word that his heart perceives but that is articulated in he knows not which mouth: in the direction, we could say, of a voice without a subject") (289). The subject, who has not quite disappeared, is listening to its own voice, attempting to understand the splitting to which it is subject and which it directly observes. What is self-conscious here is not so much the poetry but the poetic voice, a characteristic it shares with the critical voice of Maulpoix as he describes this coming to self-consciousness.

Maulpoix thus sets up the intriguing problem of what it means to be *tardif* without being belated. The poetic voice he describes is not nostalgic for what was lost or merely taking on the voice of poets of another age. Such mythologizing of the poet would be at odds with the interrogation in which the *tardif* engages. How can the *poète tardif* build on, or against, what comes before? Would it be a reorientation of the poetic past? Or a redefinition of its vocabulary, or a reinterpretation of some of its project? The *tardif* is open to that which remains, the notion of *écoute* suggesting a particular attention to what is at hand in the poetic space the poet now occupies. As we have seen with Jaccottet, it is not enough, though, simply to be attentive. For the experience to mean anything at all, it needs to become the material of a critical reflection, an act of poetico-critical creation from the materials of what the poet attends to, the building of a lucid ignorance where questions spring from contemplating the ruins:

> Le poète tardif considère avec perplexité la double énigme de l'existence et du poème. Il se montre attentif à l'incongruité de l'existence *dans* et *à travers* le poème. Si l'existence humaine est absurde, pourquoi la poésie subsiste-t-elle ? N'est-ce pas comme une insistante réponse à cette absurdité même ? (*Perplexe* 290)
>
> (The tardy poet considers with perplexity the double enigma of existence and the poem. He shows himself to be attentive to the incongruity of existence *in* and *through* the poem. If human existence is absurd, why would poetry remain? Is it not as an insistent response to this very absurdity?)

Like Jaccottet, Maulpoix seeks to resituate poetry and reformulate the questions we ask of it so that it is no longer a question of evaluating whether or not poetry succeeds at revealing something of a transcendent world or even something about this world. These two poets shift the questions, but at the same time they demonstrate the forceful presence of the past that makes it impossible simply to abandon the old questions altogether. What they seek could be said to be a limit point for the shift, the place that gives the lyric tradition its due and recognizes the impossibility of erasing the past completely. Poetry is redescribed as the tension that exists among its possibilities, as either a questioning or a celebration of the simultaneous existence of contradictory elements:

> La poésie n'est pas l'exercice de la résignation, non plus qu'un moyen d'accession à quelque sagesse ou morale supérieure. Elle nous laisse en plan avec nos questions. Entre la victoire et l'échec elle ne choisit pas. Cela n'est pas de son ressort. Il ne lui appartient aujourd'hui que de célébrer, *en dépit de tout*, les noces du désastre et de la merveille, de la ferveur et du savoir. (*Poésie malgré tout* 22)
>
> (Poetry is not the exercise of resignation, nor is it a means of access to some wisdom or superior morality. It leaves us with our questions. It does not choose between victory and failure. That is not within its competence. Its role today is only to celebrate, *despite everything*, the wedding of disaster and wonder, of fervor and knowledge.)

Maulpoix's writings on lyricism, notably in *Du lyrisme* (2000), an expanded edition of *La voix d'Orphée* (1989), tend a bit toward the nostalgic, as opposed to the actively questioning voice of *Le poète perplexe*. Still, he associates it, like poetry itself, with that which eludes definition and whose definition is constantly changing: "Quant au lyrisme, il est de ces notions confuses qui ne font qu'approcher ce qu'elles désignent, laissent l'intelligence sur sa faim, et tombent vite en désuétude" ("As for lyricism, it is one of those confused notions which only approach what they point to, leave the intellect wanting, and fall quickly by the wayside") (*Du lyrisme* 13). He associates lyricism with joy and celebration, and distinguishes it on that basis from poetry more broadly (14). Still, it shares with poetry the common ground of the impossibility of fixed definition. Maulpoix describes it as an interrogatory mode:

> La réflexion sur le lyrisme participe de telles inquiétudes dont il ne faudrait pas croire qu'elle vienne les rassurer par quelque mystique de l'inspiration créatrice. Elle interroge la forme et le destin du poétique dont elle met en lumière la vitalité. Elle observe la manière dont le sujet s'entretient avec le réel et l'idéal, et dont le sentiment du sacré s'enracine dans l'aléatoire ou le précaire. Elle met en avant, plutôt qu'un concept, une notion fuyante dont le flou constitue en fin de compte la valeur autant que le défaut. (*Du lyrisme* 18)

> (Reflection on lyricism involves worries that one must not think it comes to smooth them over by some mysticism of creative inspiration. It questions the form and the destiny of the poetic and casts light on its vitality. It observes the way in which the subject converses with the real and the ideal and the way in which the sense of the sacred takes root in the aleatory or the precarious. It puts forward, rather than a concept, a fleeting notion whose blurriness constitutes, at the end of the day, its value as well as its defect.)

And like poetry, lyrisicm on this view is also linked to a mode of living in the world more broadly: "Sa compréhension implique une manière *effervescente* d'écrire, de lire, et peut-être d'exister" ("Its comprehension implies an *effervescent* way of writing, of reading, and maybe of existing") (*Du lyrisme* 18). That conception of lyricism allows Maulpoix to reject the standard equivalence of lyricism with expression of the personal emotions of the speaking subject.

By linking lyricism with the transitory and in turn with a certain approach to living in the world, Maulpoix is able to say that lyricism transforms, or even consumes, the self, rather than expressing it:

> Le lyrisme n'est pas l'expression de sentiments personnels: il n'a de cesse de se délivrer du fugace et du transitoire, d'échapper au moi contingent et de lui prêter un corps glorieux en l'amalgamant idéalement à la substance de tout ce qui est. Il ne représente pas l'expression plénière du sujet, mais sa dévoration. Par là, il est insatiable, tel une ferveur de parole relançant sans cesse la parole afin de la porter à son comble. (*Orphée* 13–14)

(Lyricism is not the expression of personal emotions: it never ceases delivering itself from the fugitive and the transitory, to escape from the contingent self and to lend it a glorious body in amalgamating it ideally to the substance of everything that is. It does not represent the full expression of the subject but its devouring. In that, it is insatiable, like a fervor of words relaunching the word over and over again in order to bring it to its height.)

In *Le poète perplexe* Maulpoix indicates that these definitional questions are at the heart of contemporary relation to poetry, and that the definitions of poetry and of the poet are inextricably linked:

> Interroger [la] fonction [du poète] implique d'observer ses fictions. C'est là aussi bien une manière de poser autrement la question; « *Qu'est-ce que la poésie ?* ». C'est s'inquiéter d'un vouloir et d'un pouvoir: une définition du poème est en jeu dans la représentation de celui qui l'écrit.
>
> Ces portraits du poète moderne sont donc portraits de la poésie, à l'âge de sa perplexité. Tardive et réflexive. Lorsque le *qui suis-je* du poète interroge le *pourquoi* du poème. Lorsqu'il s'agit moins de célébrer que de garder le contact avec la *question* que tout recouvre et tout oublie. (*Perplexe* 11–12)

(Questioning the function [of the poet] implies observing his fictions. That is also another way of posing the question "what is poetry?" It is to worry about a wanting and a being able to: a definition of the poem is at stake in the representation of him who writes it.

These portraits of the modern poet are thus portraits of poetry, in the age of its perplexity. Tardy and reflexive. When the *who-am-I* of the poet questions the *why* of the poem. When it is less a question of celebrating than of maintaining contact with the *question* that everything covers and everything forgets.)

Celebration has given way to questioning here, in a way that links the question of poetic subjectivity directly to the question of poetry. Maulpoix does more than simply underscore the relation between poetry and the poet; by insisting on this relation, he reshifts the question from ontological ground to that of lived experience in its contingency and its endless revision.

While this conceptual restlessness has something of the modern in it, as it seems to take its distance both from Heidegger's notion of dwelling and from the linguistic turn of the generation preceding Maulpoix, he also establishes an explicit point of continuity with the nineteenth century:

> J'appelle *lyrisme* ce mouvement qui consiste à *s'envoler vers* et à *retomber dans*. Cette obstination un peu folle de fuyard frappé en pleine course qui se relève et

qui poursuit en claudiquant. J'appelle *savoir* cette façon qu'il a de boiter, comme l'albatros, dans l'ici-bas.

« Ceux dont l'aile monte et descend », ainsi Victor Hugo définissait-il les poètes. Ceux qu'un itinéraire zigzagant conduit vers l'idéal ou vers l'abîme et qui ne parviennent à prendre une juste mesure de notre condition véritable, toujours vouée à l'entre-deux. (*Perplexe* 42)

(I call *lyricism* that movement which consists in *taking flight toward* and *falling back into*. That slightly crazy obstinacy of the runaway struck down in full stride and who keeps going, limping. I call *knowledge* that way he has of limping, like the albatross, in the here-below.

"They whose wing rises and falls," thus did Victor Hugo define poets. Those whom a zigzagging route leads toward the ideal or toward the abyss and who cannot succeed in taking the right measure of our true condition, which is always destined for the in-between.)

There is also a temporal dimension to the tentativeness of the definitional impulse in Maulpoix: he moves alternately towards and away from nineteenth-century conceptions of poetics, establishing a simultaneous sense of continuity and rupture that it is the task of the poet to elucidate. Maulpoix's elaboration of the metaphor of walking illustrates this potentially graceful but potentially difficult and awkward navigation of the space between poetic past and present and between poetry and lived experience. He conflates two common modern metaphors of the poet, the walker and the acrobat:

Cet homme qui marche sur la terre, sur la tête et sur les mains, a tout d'un acrobate. Il faut des pieds et des mains pour essayer de suivre un chemin juste. Osant le grand écart entre ciel et terre, il va boitant et claudiquant comme font les vers. La vérité du poème tient au difficile maintien de ces trois démarches : marcher sur la terre, sur la tête et sur les mains. Aller, penser et destiner. (*Perplexe* 23)

(That man who walks on the earth, on his head and on his hands, has all the characteristics of the acrobat. He needs feet and hands to try to find the right path. Daring the great divide between earth and sky, he goes along limping as lines of poetry do. The truth of the poem is in the difficult maintenance of those three walks: on the earth, on one's head, and on one's hands. Going, thinking, and intending.)

Maulpoix is thus necessarily situated as the inheritor of this nineteenth-century reinvention of the poet that is in important ways still with us, and the one charged, by virtue of the task of elucidating a definition of poetry, with accounting for the ways the poetic present joins itself to and separates itself from its modern past. Paradoxically, by pushing further the interrogative role of the poet, Maulpoix anchors himself further in the nineteenth-century tradition, as he appeals to Baudelaire and Mallarmé to illustrate important elements of his conception of the poet's task:

> Au poète qui s'envole s'est substitué le poète perplexe qui approfondit, « en vertu d'un doute », explicatif comme l'araignée, travaillant comme elle à filer le vers tiré de soi, ou le creusant et descendant comme un mineur dans le profond du langage. Pour Baudelaire, le poète moderne se doublait d'un critique; pour Mallarmé, il est un « critique avant tout ». Icare inversé, ce mineur n'est pas tombé au sol, mais rendu au sous-sol des 24 lettres de l'alphabet auxquelles, inexorablement, il conserve sa piété. (*Perplexe* 168)

> (The poet who takes flight has been replaced by the perplexed poet who deepens, "by virtue of doubt," explicative like the spider, working like the spider to spin verse drawn from himself, or digging in it and descending like a miner into the depths of language. For Baudelaire, the modern poet doubled as a critic; for Mallarmé, he is a "critic before all else." Icarus in reverse, this miner did not fall to the ground, but brought back to the basement of all the letters of the alphabet toward which, inexorably, he maintains his piety.)

Maulpoix interrogates his nineteenth-century models by claiming that the single metaphors they develop in isolation are now insufficient. He opposes Baudelaire's model of the walking poet to Mallarmé's model of the poet in his room but notes that "une telle opposition est trop simple. Elle ne rend pas compte dans toute sa réalité de cette espèce d'intime boiterie entre le dedans et le dehors, le proche et le lointain, qu'est l'écriture" ("such an opposition is too simple. It does not take into account in all its reality that sort of intimate limping between the inside and the outside, the near and the far, that writing is") (*Perplexe* 63). We cannot get past the nineteenth-century models, but they serve as the material which we need to transform in order to have a more adequate model, or rather metaphor, for the changing work of the poet.

Oppositions between poet and critic disappear here as Maulpoix works on and plays with metaphor in an attempt to seize the activity of the poet in relation to poetry, so that both are defined together, an act that negates the distinction between the subject and object of the act of writing poetry itself: "Tout poème, à la fois, est un passage et une halte, un morceau de langue remuée de rythmes mais fixée dans une forme, un morceau d'homme qui bouge, un morceau d'homme penché" ("Every poem is, at the same time, a passage and a halting, a piece of language moving with rhythms but fixed in a form, a piece of a man who moves, a piece of a man leaning over") (*Perplexe* 64). The metaphors of walking and remaining in one's room are not rejected or forgotten, but they are evoked only in order to be called into question, in order, we might say, to facilitate the kind of questioning that is constitutive of the poetic enterprise as we have been describing it. The metaphor of limping occasionally becomes one of wandering: "Errance est le nom de cette ignorance qui cherche et qui attend de devenir poème" ("Wandering is the name of this ignorance that seeks and waits to become a poem") (*Perplexe* 84); the very instability of the metaphor itself suggests the primacy of ignorance or search over knowledge and stability. The limping has, almost imperceptibly, given the use of terms borrowed from nineteenth-century discourse, changed status: from Baudelaire's limping albatross, awkward on the ground to those ignorant of its beauty in flight, we move to limping as an essential aspect of poetic discourse valued as such, as an essential function of the poet.

Maulpoix thus links the metaphorical gait of the poet to the irregular rhythms of modern poetry's claims to knowledge, and he also extends the spatial metaphor to the page itself, seeing poetry's line breaks as representative or even constitutive of its relation to knowledge:

> La poésie est un savoir fait de lignes brisées.... Qu'est-ce qu'écrire, sinon *revenir sur*. Cent fois sur le métier remettre la question, le motif. Appliquer à nouveau le fer contre la page. Jusqu'à ce que du sens s'y trame dans des figures. (*Perplexe* 41)
>
> (Poetry is a knowledge made of broken lines.... What is writing if not *going back over*. A hundred times putting the craft and the motive in question. Applying the iron once more to the page. Until some meaning hatches in figures.)

On this view, the poet gives an architecture to the void (43), in the form of the blank spaces which are the poem's silences, which for Maulpoix are not empty spaces but rather the constructed representations of our ignorance, of that productive ignorance from which the next words, the next creative act, may spring:

> Armature spirituelle du poème, le blanc est ce « significatif silence » sur lequel celui-ci se détache et dont il porte témoignage. C'est sur un fond immaculé de non-sens que vient se jouer le sens. Tel un spectacle, un drame, un coup de

dés.... Ce que nous ignorons, cette fondamentale énigme que quelque chose soit, cette ignorance donc, le poète la montre, jusqu'à souvent se faire obscur à sa façon afin que nous ne puissions y échapper. Là est son savoir: dans cette vue soudaine qu'il nous donne, ou qu'il voudrait nous rendre de ce que nous ne savons voir.... Poème est le nom de la forme entrouverte par où entre et s'en va le sens. (*Perplexe* 43–4)

(Spiritual armature of the poem, the blank is that "meaningful silence" from which the blank detaches itself and of which it bears witness. It is on an immaculate background of non-sense that meaning comes to play out. Like a spectacle, a drama, a throw of the dice.... What we ignore, that fundamental enigma that something is, that ignorance then, the poet shows it, up to the point of making himself obscure in his own way so that we cannot escape it. There is his knowledge: in this sudden view that he gives us, or that he would like to give back to us from what we do not know how to see.... Poem is the name of the open form by which meaning enters and leaves.)

One could say precisely the same about Maulpoix's attempts to capture and communicate this movement of meaning in his critical writings about poetry; an operation occurs whereby what he says about poetry becomes a description of his own attempts to make sense of it in prose. This attempt, like any other, will attempt to fill a void in meaning, or give voice and shape to that void, through an act which inspires a response in the reader, which will in turn be the reader's own critical intervention in the ongoing discourse.

There is in Maulpoix, as in Jaccottet as well, a tension between wanting to affirm poetry's power to transcend what we know about its own inability to transcend, the "salvation" of a certain instinct which we know to be impossible:

La force du poème ne réside-t-elle pas dans le prodigieux « malgré tout » qu'il oppose, de l'intérieur, à son propre savoir ? Sauver en nous, sans dieux, « l'instinct de ciel », ce n'est pas sauvegarder, en dépit de tout, la promesse, ni continuer de s'orienter obscurément vers un « ailleurs plus beau ». C'est plutôt habiter l'ici sans se satisfaire de sa platitude, et s'inquiéter de la « profondeur » sans la transformer en mythologie. (*Poésie malgré tout* 57–8)

(Does the force of the poem not reside in the prodigious "in spite of it all" that it opposes, from the inside, to its own knowledge? To save in us, without gods, "the instinct of heaven," is not to safeguard, in spite of it all, the promise, nor to continue to orient oneself obscurely toward a "more beautiful elsewhere." It is rather to inhabit the here without being satisfied with its platitude, and to worry about "depth" without transforming it into mythology.)

If poetry is ultimately doubt or questioning, then it would in fact need to be open to the at least temporary possibility of skepticism about its own skepticism, or what Maulpoix here calls its "knowledge." It is not so much a fetishistic disavowal of knowledge so much as a lucid illusion that is productive of some kind of tentative meaning:

> la poésie s'écrit « comme on ment à un mourant, et qui le sait ». Elle sait que le ciel est vide, que le visage de l'homme se dissipe, que la langue fatigue et s'éteint, que la vérité s'échappe, que le sens demeure hors d'atteinte, qu'elle n'a elle-même plus de pouvoir et ne peut rien promettre. Elle sait que depuis des années le propos de la littérature n'est plus que de répéter éperdument son absence de savoir. Elle sait le désenchantement, l'inquiétude, le retrait, le défaut. Elle a appris cela par cœur, jusqu'à l'écœurement … Et pourtant il lui appartient de continuer de vouloir *autre chose*. Ne fût-ce que pour en accuser le manque. Pour que l'homme ne renonce pas, mais reste celui qui questionne. Qu'il ne puisse jamais croire avoir réponse à tout. Qu'il ne soit pas tout à fait sa propre dupe. (*Poésie malgré tout* 254)

> (Poetry is written "as we lie to a dying person, who knows we are lying." It knows that the sky is empty, that the face of man dissipates, that language tires and dies, that truth escapes, that meaning remains beyond our grasp, that it no longer has power and cannot promise anything. It knows that for years the task of literature has no longer been to repeat madly its absence of knowledge. It knows disenchantment, worry, retreat, defeat. It learned that by heart, to the point of disgust … And yet it is up to poetry to continue to want *something else*. If only to acknowledge the lack. So that man will not renounce but rather remain the one who questions. So that he will never be able to believe he has an answer for everything. So that he will not totally be his own dupe.)

Poetry exists, then, as a safeguard against ourselves and against the potential danger of our being tempted by definitive answers and permanent forms of knowledge. Poetry is not so much an illusion as a constant recalling to mind that one must always, as Jaccottet might say, lose the key that we thought had unlocked our understanding of the world or of ourselves. By presenting transcendence as a comforting illusion, as a lie told to a dying man who knows he is being lied to, we are able to retain rather than reject that notion of transcendence, while at the same time being on guard against other kinds of fictions that may present themselves not as fictions but as truth. Poetry is knowledge of nothing so much as its own status, and is to be embraced rather than rejected for its participation in fictive notions of our relationship to the world as knowing (or questioning) subjects:

> C'est dire que nous sommes faits pour chercher et vouloir du sens, aussi bien que pour nous laisser sans cesse traverser par l'incompréhensible. Et qu'exister c'est se débattre.
>
> Le « poète tardif » n'est pas cet inspiré qui possède et manie la langue avec dextérité. Il est plutôt celui perplexe, à qui les mots viennent à manquer, celui qui fixe assez intensément et scrupuleusement le langage pour saisir combien le rien est son cœur. Notre cœur. Notre vrai cœur…. Un trou noir. (*Perplexe* 255)
>
> (That is to say that we are made to seek and want meaning, as well as to let ourselves be run across by the incomprehensible. And that to exist is to struggle. The *poète tardif* is not that inspired person who possesses and handles language with dexterity. He is rather the perplexed one, for whom words are lacking, he who freezes language rather intensely and scrupulously in order to grasp to what extent nothingness is its heart. Our heart. Our true heart…. A black hole.)

Poetic language is a source of knowledge because it reveals this void but also constitutes the way in which we account for the void, and, by accounting for it, necessarily if temporarily fill it: "La langue creuse en nous le vide qu'elle y remplit" ("Language hollows out in us the void that it fills") (*Perplexe* 333).

This vision of the *poète tardif* is sometimes at odds with other conceptions of poetry in Maulpoix's works, which echo a more traditional approach to lyricism and the poet's role. In the earlier work *La voix d'Orphée* (1989), for instance, he writes:

> Trois vertus primordiales s'attachent aux lieux lyriques: de structuration, d'intimité et d'ouverture. Elles correspondent à un triple souci du poète: organiser et interpréter le monde, y reconstruire le berceau de la subjectivité, et y ouvrir des perspectives autorisant son évasion. Cette ambition quasi prométhéenne définit le champ d'action du lyrisme. (*Orphée* 154)
>
> (Three primordial virtues are attached to lyric spaces: those of structuring, intimacy, and openness. They correspond to a triple concern of the poet: organizing and interpreting the world, reconstructing in it the cradle of subjectivity, and opening perspectives that authorize evasion. This quasi-Promethean ambition defines the field of action of lyricism.)

To this vision of the poet, however, we need to add that of the poet-who-writes-on-poetry, the critical voice of Maulpoix himself, seen not as separate from the author of the poems but as coextensive with him. Both the lyric poet and the poet-who-writes-on-poetry are characters in the drama that Maulpoix sets up across his various writings. Part of poetry's function is, as he has indicated, to create the void in order to fill it up, but what fills that void is not plenitude, wholeness, or transcendence, but rather a renewed consciousness of the fact that poetry itself depends on that void and on its own ultimate failure to fill it. Poetry articulates a desire for that fulfillment and its necessary impossibility. The model of a divided poetic self, expressing and acknowledging the necessary refusal of poetry to play its transcendent role, is the product of poetry's way of knowing here. The *poète tardif*, as a character in this drama, is also the poet who must be joined by a critical spirit, a skepticism but also a quasi-Beckettian resolve to carry on in the face of that skepticism so that something new, which is neither skepticism nor definitive knowledge, may emerge.

This instability of the poetic subject is not only what defines it but also, for Maulpoix, what defines it specifically in opposition to the subject of philosophy:

> Le sujet lyrique ne se reconnaît pas, comme le sujet pensant, dans l'unité stable du « cogito », mais se diffracte et se révèle aventureusement, au sein d'un réseau de figures qui transforment et multiplient ses traits. Il se cherche, se perd et se retrouve dans un constant jeu de miroirs et d'illusions. Plus qu'un autre, il courtise cette « maîtresse d'erreur et de fausseté » qu'est l'imagination. Déchiré par l'angoisse, submergé par l'émotion, toujours en procès avec le monde, il tâtonne à l'intérieur de lui-même,... contraint de rechercher au-dehors la stabilité qui lui fait défaut. Il n'est pas un, mais multiple, aléatoire, tel un nœud inextricable de contradictions. (*Orphée* 183–4)

> (The lyric subject does not recognize itself, as the thinking subject does, in the stable unity of the *cogito*, but is diffracted and reveals itself in an adventurous way, at the heart of a network of figures that transform and multiply its traits. It seeks itself, loses itself, and finds itself again in a constant game of mirrors and illusions. More than another, it courts that "mistress of error and falsity" that is the imagination. Torn by anguish, submerged by emotion, always litigating with the world, it gropes inside itself,... constrained to seek outside itself the stability that it lacks. It is not one, but multiple, aleatory, like an inextricable knot of contradictions.)

Dwelling in multiplicity and contradiction rather than seeking to resolve them is poetry's task, which Maulpoix explicitly opposes to that of philosophy:

> Je crois que j'appelle parfois *poésie* cela même qui résiste à la philosophie. Le travail du poème s'effectue—comme celui de la philosophie—au cœur du langage, mais en s'y alimentant des équivoques et des contradictions que la philosophie s'attache à résoudre, en tirant son énergie propre de ce contre quoi elle s'élève. (*Perplexe* 58)[16]

> (I think I sometimes call "poetry" that very thing that resists philosophy. The work of the poem is accomplished—like that of philosophy—at the heart of language, but in nourishing itself on the equivocations and contradictions that philosophy sets out to resolve and drawing its energy from that which it rises up against.)

By resisting conclusive knowledge, poetry also refuses solidly established definition, and this is what gives rise to so many moments in Maulpoix's writings where he seeks to characterize poetry in one way or another, including some definitions that establish continuity rather than rupture with traditional notions of the lyric. Those kinds of definitions exist side by side with his affirmations of questioning, leading to the perhaps paradoxically definitive characterization of poetry by negation and, ultimately, as an eternally unanswered question:

> Au lieu de ce qu'elle [la poésie] est, elle va dire ce qu'elle ne veut être. Ni discours ornemental, ni parole édifiante, ni effusion de sentiments. Plutôt un lieu critique, quelque chose comme la forme juste d'une question sans réponse. Une manière de jeter le trouble, plutôt que de fabriquer, comme naguère, l'harmonie. Une espèce de contre-savoir soulignant l'ignorance. Une façon de ne pas conclure, de demeurer dans l'entrouvert. (*Poésie malgré tout* 13)

> (Instead of what [poetry] is, it is going to say what it does not want to be. Neither ornamental discourse, nor edifying speech, nor effusion of emotions. Rather a critical space, something like the right form of a question without an answer. A way of sowing confusion, rather than fabricating harmony as in times past. A sort of counter-knowledge emphasizing ignorance. A way not to conclude, to remain in the open.)

Poetry thus becomes a dwelling-in-not-dwelling, a simultaneous evocation and negation of established definition, always offered under the sign of the question and without the hope of finding an answer. This lucid ignorance remains an approach not just to literature but to lived experience as well. Maulpoix comes back, in *La Poésie a mauvais genre* (2016), as Jaccottet and others do, to poetry as experience and as a way of life:

> Car plus que tout autre genre, la poésie est une expérience.... La poésie est le fruit tardif d'un long et lent processus d'intériorisation. Elle suppose de vivre cette vie de bout en bout, de part en part, dans ses tenants et ses aboutissants obscurs, du linge dans lequel on accueille le nouveau-né à celui dans lequel on recueille le cadavre. ... La poésie est une expérience de la vie dans la langue et de la langue dans la vie. Ainsi que le résume une formule d'Yves Bonnefoy, elle *donne à vivre* ... (*Mauvais genre* 77)

(More than any other genre, poetry is an experience.... Poetry is the late fruit of a long and slow process of interiorization. It supposes that we live this life from end to end, all the way through, in its obscure ins and outs, from the newborn's swaddlings to the clothing of the cadaver. ... Poetry is an experience of life in language and of language in life. As a formulation of Yves Bonnefoy summarizes it, it *gives and allows life* ...)

While poetry can in this sense be called a way of life, it is important to note that it does not *change* life:

> Et la poésie ne me paraît pas capable de « changer la vie ».
> Je crois tout au plus aux questions posées, étroitement nouées à des émotions, et à quelques reprises de souffle, inspirations et bouffées d'air frais, venues pour l'essentiel du sentiment d'y mieux voir et de se trouver en présence d'un monde parfois moins émietté, moins absurde, où la pensée et le visible parviendraient par instants à s'accorder, où l'interprétation se réconcilierait avec la perception ... Une autre façon d'être et de connaître, une autre respiration, dans l'intervalle, dans l'interstice. (*Mauvais genre* 75–6)

> (And poetry does not seem to me capable of "changing life."
> I think at the very most of the questions posed, tightly linked to emotions, and to catching your breath, inspirations and breaths of fresh air, which come essentially from the feeling of seeing better and finding yourself in the presence of a world that is sometimes less crumbled in pieces, less absurd, where thought and the visible would sometimes succeed in going well together, where interpretation would reconcile itself with perception ... Another way of being and knowing, another breathing, in the space between, in the interstices.)

By having humbler expectations about what poetry is capable of doing, we can appreciate moments when, at least momentarily, poetry renders the world less absurd, and when poetry can give voice to that absurdity and constitute a a questioning response to it. This is where writing poetry meets writing about poetry, encouraging us even to think about abolishing the distinction. The interrogative mode which poetry enters and which critical writing about poetry shares is precisely the mode that encourages us to question the border between poetry and writing about poetry and to favor, as Maulpoix suggests, the notion of *lyrisme critique*:

> la notion de lyrisme critique recouvre à peu de chose près dans mon esprit la part toujours possible d'art poétique, non pas normatif ou prescriptif, mais spéculatif, interrogatif, non pas extérieur et préalable à l'écriture poétique, mais qui lui soit

inhérent, et de façon telle que la chant questionne l'écriture de l'intérieur et pose ainsi des repères, voire indique au poète et aux lecteurs une direction salutaire. Ce dont il est ici question, c'est d'une poétique déduite de l'écriture, qui établirait non plus des repères formels mais des repères éthiques. C'est un type d'écriture qui questionne sa possibilité, sa nécessité, son sens, en y mettant les formes, et qui pose du sein même de l'expression lyrique—et dans la vigilante surveillance de ses excès, la question du « pourquoi » de la poésie. (*Mauvais genre* 56)

(The notion of critical lyricism in my mind covers more or less the share of poetic art that is still possible, neither normative nor prescriptive, but speculative, interrogative, not exterior to and preliminary to poetic writing, but inherent in it, and in such a way that song questions writing from the inside and establishes some points of reference, or even indicates to the poet and readers a salutary direction. It is a question of a poetics deduced from writing, that would establish not formal but ethical points of reference. It is a type of writing that questions its possibility, its necessity, its meaning, by giving form to it, and which asks at the very heart of lyric expression—and in the vigilant surveillance of its excesses—the question of the "why" of poetry.)

If *lyrisme critique* is tenuous or perhaps even ill defined as a critical concept, this is, in an important sense, the point: for *lyrisme critique* to take on conceptual precision, it would need to align itself with philosophy as Maulpoix has characterized it, rather than with poetry, and by doing so it would give up the interrogative mode which has come to define it in the first place. To that extent, *lyrisme critique* exists as question and as negation, and also as a way of writing, thinking, and living in a mode that embraces and moves within that questioning rather than seeking to move beyond it.

5

Poetry, Community, Relation

In 2016, Jean-Michel Maulpoix identified a period of resurgence of the lyric, which for him implies the poet's reconnection to the human community:

> Soucieux aussi bien de ce qu'il est possible de dire, voire de chanter encore,… il est plus inquiet que jamais du sort de la communauté humaine. S'il a encore quelque chose à écrire, c'est à propos de son appartenance à cette communauté, de sa définition, de ce qui la fonde, du silence et de la cacophonie qui la menacent. (*Mauvais genre* 31)

> (Concerned as well with what it is possible to say, or even to sing still, he is more concerned than ever with the destiny of the human community. If he still has something to write, it is about his belonging to that community, about its definition, what founds it, about the silence and the cacophony that threaten it.)

In opposition to a detached focus on language devoid of a vital relationship to its speaker, the new lyric appeals to the fundamentally human element of relation, figured either as the intimate relation between poet and reader, or more broadly as the community of those who comprise the readers of poetry and, by extension, the kind of humanity such a reading can potentially foster. The opposition I have been drawing throughout this study between the certainties of knowledge and the experience of poetry as a more humble, tentative, and infinitely revisable approach to the world and the subject's place in it has important political implications, especially if we understand politics as above all relationality.[1] An approach to politics that resonates with what we have been saying about poetry, knowledge, and ignorance would emphasize the tentativeness of political relation, its infinite potential for revision and adaptation as experience changes the ways in which we interpret the world. Christian Doumet underscores the potential for democratic egalitarianism in confronting a difficult poem that resists simplistic answers to political or literary questions:

> Rien de plus démocratique... que l'affrontement à la difficulté du poème, et c'est pourquoi il y a à s'inquiéter politiquement d'une époque qui se détourne massivement de cette sorte de désarroi et de résistance essentiels face à la langue pour cultiver la poésie facile.... Toujours, derrière l'organisation de ces amusements printaniers se tapit un pouvoir somnifère. Non que toutes les époques d'obscurantisme poétique aient été des époques démocratiques, loin de là. Mais la démocratie a inventé, depuis Mallarmé, depuis Baudelaire même qui pourtant ne la prisait guère, cette forme d'intelligibilité de la poésie fondée sur l'idée que nous détenons tous, en commun, un héritage de nuit. (14–15)

> (Nothing more democratic... than confronting the difficulty of the poem, and that is why we should worry politically about an era which massively turns away from this sort of essential confusion and resistance in the face of language in order to cultivate facile poetry.... Always, behind the organization of these springtime amusements a sleep-inducing power hides away. Not that all periods of poetic obscurantism were democratic eras, far from it. But democracy invented, since Mallarmé, and even since Baudelaire who hardly prized it, that form of intelligibility of poetry founded on the idea that we all hold in common, a heritage of night.)

In this chapter, I offer some concluding remarks in order to argue that the approach to poetry that I have been outlining can and should be extended from the epistemic realm to the domain of human relations and community. The practices of reading writing, and defining poetry generate an open community formed by poetry's call for a response and invitation to make meaning. I call on Jacques Rancière and Jean-Luc Nancy in order to identify how "literature," conceived in a very broad sense, invites us to imagine community as a notion which, like poetry, never quite coincides with itself and which lives only in our attempts to imagine it, to seize it, to interpret it and to reshape our experience in light of the ways in which we understand and claim to "know" it.

Michel Deguy has also written about a notion of poetry that implicates an epistemology and ethics, claiming that determining the relation between self and other, and by extension self and world, is a poetic task:

> Il n'est pas vrai que je sois d'abord en possession de « moi-même » en termes de connaissance, d'où procéder à la découverte de mon semblable, mon frère en le reconnaissant à partir de moi ... Découvrir l'homme en chacun d'entre nous (parmi le comme-un des mortels) comme semblable est une tâche poétique. Le semblable-à-semblable, en lui-même semblable, est à découvrir. Serait-ce la découverte la plus importante encore à venir? Le premier mot de Baudelaire serait-il le dernier? (*La raison* 35)[2]

(It is not true that I am first of all in possession of "myself" in terms of knowledge, from which I would proceed to the discovery of my fellow, my brother by recognizing him by starting from myself ... Discovering the man in each one of us (among the being in common of mortals) as a fellow, is a poetic task. The like-to-like, similar in himself, is to be discovered. Would that be the most important discovery to come? Would the first word of Baudelaire be the last?)

Making sense of such a statement requires an excursion through the ways in which "poetry" can be made to mean something far beyond the collection of verbal creations known as poems. Reading Deguy's assertion in light of all that we have been tracing of poetry's expansion in its relation to ignorance and a new kind of knowledge means attempting to assign meaning to the potentially meaningless, to see how that which is not at all "poetic" in the usual sense can come to be defined in that way.

Doing so forces a reconsideration of what we might mean by "poetic," which re-places anyone who wishes to make sense of Deguy's statement into the position of reasserting ignorance about the poetic so as to attempt to understand it in a way that accommodates the new meaning that Deguy assigns to it here. And to return to that place of ignorance from which a new definition of poetry may emerge is, as we have seen repeatedly, a poetic task, if by that we mean another intervention in the infinite task of defining poetry. Once again, the search for the meaning of "poetry" proves to be inseparable from that meaning itself. And in the context of Deguy's statement, redefining poetry is necessarily wrapped up with defining the human relation, so that it is not that a pre-existing notion of poetry helps us understand human relationality but rather that poetry and human relationality are defined together and simultaneously. What human beings may have in common, and what poetry may have in common with those human relationships, is our task to discover.

This all may ultimately sound quite vague and indeed frustrating to anyone eager to make sense of the questions of what poetry is and to characterize its relation to knowledge precisely. But the inability to be more precise and to propose conclusive answers is exactly the point: poetry's productive relationship to ignorance, as I have attempted to develop it throughout this study, makes us highly suspicious of attempts to resolve such questions definitively, and would even set those attempts in opposition to poetry as it has been characterized by the writers I have been considering. Figuring out poetry's relation to knowledge means being led to the knowledge that we cannot ultimately figure it out and that we are left instead with the kinds of pronouncements such as Deguy's, which are necessarily stated in ways that defy easy comprehension and in fact cultivate a certain vagueness when it comes to ascertaining the precise meaning of the claims. The characterizations of poetry that we have been considering are, in an important sense, variations on the unsayable, statements made in the context of a textual community of readers and writers committed to understanding what we mean by "poetry" but subscribing to a view whereby an ability to articulate that meaning would be a cancellation of that meaning itself, insofar as this conception of poetry actively resists that sort of definition. To some, that realization may be frustrating, but knowing that we can only go so far as tentative and potentially vague statements about poetry is itself an important knowledge claim, a delineation of the limits of knowledge when poetry is in question. And such an imposition of limits to knowledge is an important part of the poetic enterprise as it is characterized by those I have been considering. This is not to say that we should then be content within the bounds of our ignorance or abandon the attempt to understand poetry; rather, we can see each intervention in the dialogue as a new, tentative, interrogatory contribution to the question of what poetry is. To do so is to affirm the value of the community of those engaged in these tasks of reading and writing and to explore the bounds of our ignorance in productive ways. And such a move reinforces the importance of expanding the poetry-knowledge dyad in order to include the notion of community without which this approach to poetry could not emerge and go on.

Poetry is uniquely suited to reframe our relation to knowledge because it situates itself intriguingly between the public and the private. As shared language, poetry is inevitably public, and yet it is written and consumed largely in private, a situation which creates community from those engaged asynchronically in a momentarily solitary pursuit. As Christophe Bident observes in his study of Blanchot:

> La littérature est le lieu où le public glisse au privé sans se privatiser, où le privé glisse au public sans se dévoiler. Elle est le lieu où le rapport entre « l'immense autrui » et le moi « coriace » décide de la santé du corps. Elle est le lieu où le public et le privé s'annulent dans un état de support…, où se décide enfin l'avenir des idées, des engagements, des écrits, des passions. (286)

> (Literature is the place where the public slides into the private without privatizing itself, where the private slides into the public without unveiling itself. It is the place where the relation between "the immense other" and the "tough" self determine the health of the body. It is the place where the public and private cancel each other out in a state of support…, where the future of ideas, engagements, writings, and passions is decided.)

Literature, of which we may see poetry, as Blanchot did, as a particularly intensified form, does not participate in the public and private sphere but rather forces us to question what constitutes that distinction or the relation between those terms. Poetry's impulse to definition also extends to related terms such as public and private on which it depends when it attempts to characterize its own sphere of activity. Poetry thus establishes the space in which these distinctions are established and questioned, and that questioning in turn becomes one of poetry's defining tasks. By coming to terms with the impossibility of defining poetry, we become necessarily engaged with a larger failure to define the subject of traditional metaphysics. This is how Sylvain Santi sees poetry operating in Georges Bataille's thought in the 1940s:

> En 1948, la nouveauté consiste à penser la dépense poétique en rapport avec la communauté, avec ce qui, par définition, excède les ressources de la métaphysique du sujet. Cette mise en rapport offre ainsi la possibilité de penser la poésie, à la suite des analyses menées par J.-L. Nancy, comme une exposition des singularités, laquelle se rattache à une communication qui nous semble parfaitement cohérente avec la présence de l'autre qui s'impose à Bataille sitôt qu'il aborde la question de la poésie ou celle de sa lecture. (338–9)

> (In 1948, the novelty consists in thinking poetic expenditure in relation to community, with what, by definition, exceeds the resources of the metaphysics of the subject. This putting into relation thus offers the possibility to think poetry, in the wake of J.-L. Nancy's analyses, as an exposition of singularities, which is linked to a communication that seems to us perfectly coherent with the presence of the other which imposes itself on Bataille as soon as it takes up the question of poetry or of reading.)

In the mid-twentieth century, a portrait of knowledge thus emerges that is consistent with the shift we have been tracing in the approach to knowledge of poetry. As we have seen, the emphasis on "pure" poetry led inevitably to the demonstration of the impossibility of the very idea of such a thing and placed, in its stead, the productively endless proliferation of attempts to say what poetry is.

So too there are shifts in approaches to knowledge generally in that period that discuss it in terms that evoke the debate about poetry as well. Here, for instance, is Jean-Paul Sartre on supposedly "pure" knowledge:

> Le point de vue de la connaissance pure est contradictoire: il n'y a que le point de vue de la connaissance *engagée*.... L'espace réel du monde est l'espace que Lewin nomme « hodologique ». Une connaissance pure, en effet, serait connaissance

sans point de vue, donc connaissance du monde située par principe hors du monde. Mais cela n'a point de sens: l'être connaissant ne serait que connaissance, puisqu'il se définirait par son objet et que son objet s'évanouirait dans l'indistinction totale de rapports réciproques. Ainsi la connaissance ne peut être que surgissement engagé dans un point de vue déterminé que l'on *est*. Etre pour la réalité humaine c'est *être-là*; c'est-à-dire « là sur cette chaise », « là, à cette table », « là, au sommet de cette montagne, avec ces dimensions, cette orientation, etc. ». C'est une nécessité ontologique. (*Etre* 371).

(The point of view of pure knowledge is contradictory; there is only the point of view of *engaged* knowledge.... The real space of the world is the space which Lewin calls "hodological." A pure knowledge in fact would be a knowledge without a point of view; therefore a knowledge of the world but on principle located outside the world. But this makes no sense; the knowing being would be only knowledge since he would be defined by his object and since his object would disappear in the total indistinction of reciprocal relations. Thus knowledge can be only an engaged upsurge in a determined point of view which one *is*. For human reality, to be is to-be-there; that is, "there in that chair," "there at that table," "there at the top of that mountain, with these dimensions, this orientation, *etc.*" It is an ontological necessity. (*Being* 308))

Knowledge is never "point-of-viewless,"[3] and therefore not only the object but the subject of knowledge would disappear if this were otherwise, given that human beings are constituted as knowing subjects by their contact with culturally determined sources of knowledge which they encounter. Poetry's inability to define itself, or to define itself via that very impossibility, thus becomes a source of insight on larger epistemological questions that, from the mid-twentieth century on, complicate the oversimplified portrait of a knowing subject and the object of that knowledge. What Santi characterizes as an imposition of the presence of the other that comes about with Bataille's reflection on poetry is symptomatic of the way poetry forces redefinition of public and private, or the delineation of community, by the way it questions typical distinctions between "solitary" reading and communal implications of that practice.

This is not to say, of course, that the practice of poetry moves us to abandon notions of the solitary individual in favor of models of community. Doing so would be to replace one problematically simplified model with another. Exile is a condition that names a relation via negation, the lack of participation in a community but in a situation that defines the subject of exile by his or her very exclusion from that community. As Gerald Bruns writes: "without exile nothing can be intelligible: it is the nonrecognition from which recognition separates itself and constitutes itself. It is the condition of exclusion that defines the rule of identity and the logic of the same" (*Blanchot* 86). The exiled subject, qua exile, thus depends on the community. While the poet may take his or her distance from that community, it is the distance that defines the role of poet here. If this sounds like a hearkening back to Romantic alienation, it is with good reason, since the notion of poetry as infinite questioning does find its origins, as I have suggested, in thinkers and poets of that period who were among the first to propose the questioning of poetry as integral to our understanding of what it might be. The poet's "belonging to the outside" suggests neither a stable identity for him or herself nor a solid affirmation of identification with the other. What begins perhaps as personal problem of identity quickly becomes a epistemological problem of what it means to be constituted both via others and in opposition to others with whom we do not identify.

As readers of poetry, where does this put us in terms of our relation to exile? Do we bring back community, redefined, in opposition to exile? Do we join the poet in exile because that is the name of the "poetic condition," without which we would cease to be practicing poetry? Does community necessarily end where poetry begins, or does community newly understood only begin with, and as, poetry? Here, as in all the larger questions I have been considering, posing the question well, or differently, is perhaps all we can hope for, since our understanding of poetry makes us necessarily suspicious of answers even to questions about which we feel an urgent need for an answer. For Blanchot, it is the subject's presence to the death of another that both places the notion of the subject in question and allows for the potential emergence of community from solitude:

> Qu'est-ce donc qui me met le plus radicalement en cause? Non pas mon rapport à moi-même comme fini ou comme conscience d'être à la mort ou pour la mort, mais ma présence à autrui en tant que celui-ci s'absente en mourant. Me maintenir présent dans la proximité d'autrui qui s'éloigne définitivement en mourant, prendre sur moi la mort d'autrui comme la seule mort qui me concerne, voilà ce qui me met hors de moi et est la seule séparation qui puisse m'ouvrir, dans son impossibilité, à l'Ouvert d'une communauté. (*La communauté inavouable* 21)

> (What, then, calls me into question most radically? Not my relation to myself as finite or as the consciousness of being before death or for death, but my presence for another who absents himself by dying. To remain present in the proximity

of another who by dying removes himself definitively, to take upon myself another's death as the only death that concerns me, this is what puts me beside myself, this is the only separation that can open me, in its very impossibility, to the Openness of a community. (*Unavowable* 9)

Blanchot enacts the notion of distance from and proximity to others in the community of writers and thinkers by making these remarks in the context of a commentary on Georges Bataille. The play of proximity and distance, which implicates Blanchot and Bataille and constitutes the thematic center of the reflections on death, community, self, and other which I have just quoted, is also at stake in the relation of the reader to knowledge. If that had been implicit in Blanchot's remarks here, it becomes explicit a bit later in the same text:

> Il faut rappeler que le lecteur *n'est pas un simple lecteur*, libre à l'égard de ce qu'il lit. Il est souhaité, aimé et peut-être intolérable. Il ne peut savoir ce qu'il sait, et il sait plus qu'il ne sait. Compagnon qui s'abandonne à l'abandon, qui est perdu lui-même et qui en même temps reste au bord du chemin pour mieux démêler ce qui se passe et qui ainsi lui échappe. (*La communauté inavouable* 43)
>
> (It is necessary to recall that the reader *is not a simple reader*, free in regard to what he reads. He is desired, loved and perhaps intolerable. He cannot know what he knows, and he knows more than he knows. He is a companion who gives himself over to abandonment, who is himself lost and who at the same time remains at the side of the road the better to disentangle what is happening and which therefore escapes him. (*Unavowable* 23))

Nothing, in other words, is simple. The reader's freedom is constricted by his or her very participation in reading the work of another in a given cultural context and by the constraints that the writer wittingly or unwittingly places upon his or her reading. Several of the themes we have been considering come together in this short characterization of the reader, including solitude and community, exile and belonging (insofar as the reader "remains at the side of the road" as an interpretive strategy), and the complex relationship between knowing and ignorance, where in this case there is a knowledge unknown to the reader, a knowledge that manifests itself paradoxically in ignorance about what is known. Such knowledge, and its concomitant ignorance, can only emerge in the response of the reader to the text. That response consists of the writing or speaking of more words that emerge from the text in reply to it; they are addressed to an implied community with whom that knowledge can be elaborated in an act that does not describe the knowledge so much as change it by the intervention of new language that attempts to seize the unseizable, the knowledge of which one doesn't have knowledge.

Gerald Bruns has done important work theorizing the relationship of poetry to thinking about poetry, of poetry to the reader, and of the reader to a larger community. Following Hans Gadamer, he affirms that art effects "not just a change in one's private outlook" but "a change in one's world" (*Anarchy* 38–9). He recalls Friedrich Schlegel's characterization of the poet as "a sociable being" (*Anarchy* 84) and sees the early nineteenth century's invention of the concept of art as the moment from which "conversing about poetry with poets and lovers of poetry now becomes a condition of poetry as such" (84), a fact that forces readers to confront the fact that "as poetry ceases to be a genre distinction, poetic theories are now necessary in order to pick out a piece of language as poetic…. The distinction between theory and practice, or between poetry and poetics, ceases to be self-evident" (84). Far from effecting change merely in the individual reader encountering the solitary poet in the silence of the page, the blurring of the distinction between poetry and thought about poetry is imbricated in the idea of community. The community produced by the operations of poetry and thought about poetry is not community in a unified sense but rather a "nomadic series of associations whose sociality… is theatrical and performative in the sense that it comes together and disperses, increases or depletes itself, and never settles into place. Its form is as open as the form of its poetry" (105). Poetry thus forces a redefinition of community by the same kind of linguistic and conceptual operations through which it forces a redefinition of itself; the impetus to define poetry, itself wrapped up in the notion of the poetic, yields a reshaping not only of itself but of the relations among those who read, write, and think about poetry.

This reshaping on the part of poetry brings it back to its etymological roots as a making, an active fashioning. We can move past the simple idea that the object of poetic making is a poem by introducing the notion of making into the ongoing conversation about the relation between poetry and thought about poetry, and the role of community which we have now begun to articulate. Jacques Rancière has recently addressed "la question essentielle de ce que fait la poésie: ce qu'elle fait au langage dans la pratique du poème; ce qu'elle fait à la pensée comme intervention sur le langage; ce qu'elle fait à la politique par sa manière de mettre des mots en commun à l'adresse d'une possible communauté" ("the essential question of what poetry does: what it does to language in the practice of the poem; what it does to thought as intervention in language; what it does to politics by its way of putting words in common, addressed to a possible community") (*Le sillon* 91).[4] Our exploration of poetry's constant moving into the questioning and reshaping of its own definition has shown the way poetry works on language and by extension on thought. And in fact Rancière defines poetry as "un nœud entre une pratique de la langue et une figure de la pensée" ("a knot between a practice of language and a figure of thought") (70). Rancière's comment here, offered almost in passing, underscores poetry's relation to community by insisting that community is part of what is made by poetry. The word "possible" makes all the difference here; poetry does not address itself to a pre-existing community but rather creates its own community as part of its making. And the act of creating that community is not at all assured, as the notion of possibility reminds us. It is not that the subject enters into relation with the poem but rather that, in an important sense, the subject is constituted *as* a reading subject *by* the reading of the poem, by its own making of meaning. This notion of relationality is key to Rancière's thought about both politics and literature. His opening move in "Ten Theses on Politics," for instance, is that "it is the political relationship that makes it possible to conceive of the subject of politics, not the other way round" (27). In an analogous way, the reader is constituted via a relation to the text and by a relation or non-relation to others that is constituted, as Rancière indicated in what I have quoted above, by poetry's addressing words to a possible community. The community is, in other words, not a group who comes together to read a text but rather is formed *by* the text as it addresses itself to its readers. In this way, poetry determines rather than being determined by community and forces a re-evaluation of what we mean by community, an extension of the questions poetry forces about its own meaning.

Rancière raises the question, and keeps it at the level of a question, of poetry's status given that we are, to an important extent, past the Romantic dream of poetry but reluctant at the same time to abandon that conception of poetry and to risk substituting the full consequences of the end of art. We find ourselves, that is:

> entre le rêve perdu d'un monde qui se traduirait spontanément en formules poétiques et le rêve impossible d'une adéquation enfin trouvée de la langue à la pensée. La poésie d'après pourrait se définir comme une poésie qui sait qu'Hegel a eu lieu et qui pourtant agit comme s'il fallait, autant que possible, retarder l'heure de sa venue. (*Le sillon* 113)

> (between the lost dream of a world that would spontaneously be translated into poetic formulas and the impossible dream of a match that could finally be found

between language and thought. Poetry after that could be defined as a poetry that knows that Hegel happened and that nonetheless acts as if it were necessary, as far as possible, to postpone the time of his arrival.)

To attend to the poetic is thus never to be able to move past maintaining a role for poetry in thought; it is to resist both an affirmation of Romantic transcendence and the passing away of art into thought. Poetry's operation, defined thus as a double kind of negation, is still then fundamentally creative in that it calls its community of readers to position themselves within an ever-shifting terrain of poetry's relation to the world from which it springs and with which it interacts. Poetry's task of making thus constitutes the maintenance of the instability that comes from refusing both a nostalgic look back to earlier affirmations of poetry's power and a simple move into the realm of pure concept that would have as its goal the establishment of definitive knowledge. Poetry remains as the force that affirms the impossibility of realizing any of the goals it may set for itself, and it reshapes that impossibility as itself a kind of goal.

Such a conception of poetry working out, and in turn being worked out by, a community serves as a helpful corrective to those who would see modern poetry as having taken a hermetic turn such that it no longer refers to a world outside itself. The kind of questioning that poetry fosters would itself cause us to reject such a categorical statement, and as I hope to have demonstrated, even what seems to be the most inward-turned conception of poetry, the tautological "poetry is poetry," is precisely what returns us to the world outside the poetry at the very moment we seek to make sense of that statement. Poetry's call for interpretation simultaneously precludes its isolation from its worlds and serves as the call to potential communities of interpreters. The very difficulty that we have in enumerating exactly how this happens is indicative of the way poetry refuses definitive meanings. The impossibility of the saying is in its own way poetic. Camille Dumoulié has argued that the autonomy that comes with modern poetry's divorce from the referent can be read as an expansion of the notion of poetry, in line with the Romantics, whereby everything speaks in the universe. Infinite language "contient et exprime à lui seul la réalité dans son ensemble" ("contains and expresses in itself reality in its totality") (72). On this view, if everything is reduced to language, then language necessarily contains all the universe: "le langage fonde la communication absolue, car il exprime la communauté signifiante des hommes, du cosmos et de la société. Cette idée engage aussi bien une mystique (celle de Swedenborg ou de Novalis) qu'une politique" ("language founds absolute communication, for it expresses the signifying community of men, of the cosmos, and of the society. This idea engages a mysticism (that of Swedenborg or Novalis) as well as a politics") (72). To affirm such a view, however, is to return us to where we began as we tried to articulate poetry's relationship to the world and its knowledge of it. To say that there is a mysticism implicit in this view is to imply that we need, once again, to remove ourselves from the temptation of affirming the ineffability of poetry's relation to the world and affirm instead the move whereby discourse about poetry joins poetry in reshaping the way we understand that relation.

It is not quite enough to say that poetry "expresses the significant human community," since such a claim presupposes that there is something already given that is there to express. Poetry, rather, requires the formation of human community, as the question of what worlds poetry may create emerges from the need to interpret what poetry's self-identity might mean. There is indeed a politics here, but one that is created by poetry rather than expressed by it. This is a point made by Ulrich Haase and William Large in the context of a discussion of Blanchot:

> the language of literature is essential to the community, as all community rests on language, and as the language in question is not the everyday language of the exchange of information, but rather the language that gives rise to community. Such language articulates the relation between the members of the community rather than merely designating things. (113)

Poetry thus understood retains a kind of subjectivity in its creative function and has the power to shape a relational subjectivity in and among readers as well. To return to Jean-Marie Gleize's formulation: "nous cherchons la poésie, nous cherchons aussi à en dire, à en communiquer quelque chose (de l'ordre d'une information, d'un savoir), mais la poésie nous, me, cherche. C'est nous, je, qui sommes en cause. « Je » lis" ("Yes, we seek poetry, we seek also to say and communicate something about it (on the order of an information, a knowledge), but poetry seeks, confronts, us, and me. It is we, and I, who are involved. 'I' read") (132). Several kinds of relations are brought together and realigned here. The search for poetry is made simultaneous with the search for knowledge, the individual is found (or reimagined) in the collective which nonetheless still maintains space for the individual, and the subject/object relation implied in knowledge claims is multiplied so that poetry searches us just as we search for poetry. Here again, what this might mean is not at all immediately apparent, but nor is it completely beyond sense. Gleize's statement is "poetic" in the sense that it calls out for, demands, seeks, a response, a discourse that would seek to make sense of the utterance and, by so doing, continuing it by other means.

The community that poetry is poised to create has as its origin the absence of community, the position of exile to which poetry is forced and from which it creates. As poet Jacques Dupin puts it:

> Absente, la poésie l'a toujours été. L'absence est son lieu, son séjour, son lot. Platon l'a chassée de la République. Elle n'y est jamais retournée. Elle n'a jamais eu droit de cité. Elle est dehors. Insurgée, dérangeante toujours, plongée dans un sommeil actif, une inaction belliqueuse, qui est son vrai travail dans la langue et dans le monde, envers et contre tous, un travail de transgression et de fondation de la langue. (qtd in Gleize 144)

> (Poetry was always absent. Absence is its place, its staying place, its lot. Plato chased it away from the Republic. It never came back. It never belonged. It is outside. Rebellious, always disturbing, plunged in an active sleep, a bellicose inaction, which is its true work in language and in the world, toward and against all, a work of transgression and of the founding of language.)

A certain instability and precariousness appears in this characterization of poetry as perpetual outsider. In that sense, poetry has much in common with a certain conception of community that sees it as a space of potential conflict as much as harmony. As Robert J. C. Young writes, for instance:

> Everyone who is part of a community in a sense exists in a precarious and tangential relation to it because the community itself is a space of disturbance, disjunction, and dissolution. It is as much about discontinuity as continuity, separation and disconnection as union, conflict as harmony, silence as speech. Community is the interruption of silence, of moments of inarticulacy, of stuttering, the things you cannot say, of non-communication. (33)

This counterintuitive characterization of community resonates with the similarly unexpected characterization of poetry that we have been pursuing, one that makes room for dissonance as much as harmony, and that is aware of itself as fragile and potentially at odds with itself. Likewise, community and poetry both interrupt silence in order to create via saying, giving rise to a continual interruption of silence by the fact that each intervention calls out for an interpretive response. The responses thus belong to the poetry as well, and the act of responding together creates a community by interrupting the silence.[5]

Jacques Rancière has reflected on this kind of transformed understanding of what we might mean by a literary community: "As I understand it, a literary community is not a community of writers, it is not a community of people who do, enjoy, or teach literature. Nor is it a community represented in literary works. It is a community framed by literature" ("Literary" 93). In a characterization that echoes his notion of *le partage du sensible*, Rancière defines community as

> a certain fabric made of things that individuals can perceive as constituting their lived world, of names under which they can identify them, of forms of identification of the situations, events, and meanings which make those individuals share a certain "common sense": a broadly shared sense of what is given and what is happening. A literary community is a form of construction of such a common sense. ("Literary" 93)

Literary communities make sense not of texts so much as of the perceptual world as it is formed in the words we use to name, describe, and interpret it. They are the ground from which those words can be made to make sense. This is at one level a thoroughly literary activity. But as I have been suggesting throughout this study, it is impossible to separate the literary from the rest of lived experience on this model of poetry, and by grounding ourselves in literature defined in this way, we are also within the realm of lived experience more generally at every step. To say "literary community" is to ground oneself in a conception of literature that necessarily points beyond itself to the sense-making and attempts at knowledge of the world that literary experience more narrowly has in common with lived experience in the broadest sense. To understand how this works, one needs to alter and broaden the commonly held definition of literature, and that sort of interpretive work on language is itself a key aspect of living as part of this kind of literary community broadly defined. This is what allows Rancière to go on to affirm that "the creation of such communities is made by words. In that sense, the notion of 'literary community' goes far beyond the production of an art named 'literature.' A literary community exists whenever human beings are gathered by the power of certain words" (93–4).

One runs the risk here of defining literary communities so broadly as to dissolve the category entirely. For in what sort of community are human beings *not* "gathered by the power of certain words"? But the precariousness of the definition is a crucial aspect of it; an intervention in the act of defining either poetry or community brings us further into the balance of conflict and unity, of knowledge and ignorance, that defines each. Poetry as I have been characterizing it is an act of creation that also creates community by establishing the linguistic parameters by which we create a notion of community while also calling it into question. By calling into question the very meaning of words such as "poetry" and "community," poetry can also reinvent them. That task of reinvention becomes the task of the community that comes into being by poetry understood in this way; it is an act of literary creation that harkens back to the etymological roots of "poetry" itself. To the extent that literature and community can be thought together, we are still within what Rancière would call the "regime" of art whereby it takes on its modern identity, a development situated historically at the time of Romanticism. Paradoxically, though, the shift that allows us to think of "literature" or "poetry" in their modern sense, as opposed to something more expansive such as "les belles lettres," is at the same time the move that expands the notion of poetry so that it necessarily moves beyond the domain of verbal works of art and necessarily implies a relation to lived experience in connection with claims to know or not know the world in which one moves. Rancière underscores this historically determined aspect of literary communities: "Literature is a historically determined regime of identification of this art.... Therefore, when I speak of 'literary communities' in the narrow sense of the word, I speak of the forms of construction of the common that are specific to literature as a historical form of the art of writing, in opposition to other forms" ("Literary" 94). And yet, what is specific to poetry in the modern conception I have been tracing is its impossibility to remain within a specificity that would refuse its relation to, and embeddedness in, the world. As source of knowledge or doubt, poetry redefines the epistemological enterprise in a way that retains poetry's specificity by, in an important sense, denying it.

To begin to bring together the strands of the themes that have been central to this study, I turn to Jean-Luc Nancy's notion of the "inoperative community." Nancy shares with Rancière, as Jen Hui Bon Hoa has argued, a view of politics or community as "arising from the interval" as a "being-in-between" whereby politics "encompasses the ontology of constitutive difference that Nancy derives from the critique of the metaphysics of presence" (Hui Bon Hoa 47).[6] Nancy informs and expands the notion of subjectivity by moving beyond a distinction between subject and object in order to demonstrate how, as Simon Malpas indicates, "the analysis of existence is opened to the workings of a singularity that is always already in relation to a plurality of other singulars," resulting in "an analysis of community conceived in terms of the singular plural in which subjectivity... happens in the moments of encounter with each unique and irreducible other" (Malpas 91). Nancy's characterization of community is counterintuitive in that it is not based on shared identity. In fact, "community is made or is formed by the retreat or by the subtraction of something, which would be the fulfilled infinite identity of community" (*Inoperative* xxxvii–xxxix).[7] The impossible fulfillment of community, linked here to human finitude, is what necessarily defines community. This way of conceiving it suggests a parallel to what we have been saying about definitive truth: it is only by abandoning that notion in relation to poetry that a new and more viable notion of poetic knowledge springs forth, one that is constituted and driven by the impossibility of definitive knowledge. That this kind of poetic knowledge emerges in a community of readers, writers, and thinkers (and goes far beyond, as Rancière claims, what would constitute the literal groups of those who read and write poetry) results in a transformed notion of community as well. Poetry continues its productive function of making when it comes to community, for it is by thinking poetically that we can replace identity-based and fixed definitions of community with the tentative and open ones that Nancy proposes. Community thus never quite coincides with itself, and this is an important aspect of what it has in common with poetry, since, as I noted in the introduction, Nancy writes in a different context that "la poésie ne coïncide pas avec elle-même: peut-être non-coïncidence, cette impropriété substantielle, fait-elle proprement la poésie" ("poetry does not coincide with itself: maybe non-coincidence, that substantial impropriety, is what properly belongs to poetry") (*Résistance* 10).

There are political implications to this definition of community, in that the more common understanding of community as based on unity is tied uncomfortably to fascism according to Nancy: "the community that becomes *a single* thing (body, mind, fatherland, Leader ...) necessarily loses the *in* of being-*in*-common. Or, it loses the *with* or the *together* that defines it. It yields its being-together to a being *of* togetherness" (*Inoperative* xxxix). A community based on unquestioning being-together is no community at all according to Nancy, and thus his notion of community depends on the maintenance of difference within the members of community, allowing a space for plurality in the common or, better, allowing plurality to define the common. This kind of community is defined by a kind of difference to itself, a potentially constant transformation of itself, and this is what it shares with poetry as we have been understanding it, which stands in opposition to a potentially totalizing approach to definitive knowledge or truth.

It is not that I am superimposing the notion of poetry on Nancy's notion of community; he himself makes the link to literature which he characterizes in terms of "a bond that forms ties without attachments, or even less fusion, of a bond that unbinds by binding, that reunites through the infinite exposition of an irreducible finitude" (*Inoperative* xl). In the case of both literature and community, it is a question of working out the *meaning* of the concepts, both at the intellectual level and in terms of lived experience: "How can we be receptive to the *meaning* of our multiple, dispersed, mortally fragmented existences, which nonetheless only make sense by existing in common?" (xl). Literature has the potential to illuminate the question if not to lead to answers, or, it proposes answers in a way that simultaneously marks them as tentative, and the working out of those answers as part and parcel of what we mean by practicing poetry. An important aspect of community for Nancy is interruption: "La communauté est faite de l'interruption des singularités, ou du suspens que *sont* les êtres singuliers. Elle n'est pas leur œuvre, et elle ne les a pas comme ses œuvres, pas plus que la communication n'est une œuvre, ni même une opération des êtres singuliers: car elle est simplement leur être—leur être suspendu sur sa limite" ("Community is made of the interruption of singularities, or of the suspension that singular beings *are*. Community is not the work of singular beings, nor can it claim them as its works, just as communication is not a work or even an operation of singular beings, for community is simply their being—their being suspended upon its limit") (*Communauté* 79/*Inoperative* 31).[8] This is a productive lens through which to view the operation I have traced for poetry whereby it interrupts ways of knowing that are typically associated with philosophy and also the ways of transcendent knowing that some kinds of poetry may claim. The understanding of poetry that emerges as the paradigm I have been examining interrupts those other claims to knowledge and suspends the possibility of such knowledge, replacing it via doubt with a more tentative and fragile affirmation of a potentially infinitely revisable conception of the way we can know poetry and, through poetry, the experiential world. This discourse, I have attempted to show, does not simply cancel prior conceptions of poetry's claims to knowledge but rather allows them to coexist with their opposite, and by doing so, to suspend singularity and create a space for the being-in-common of otherwise potentially incompatible models of what poetry is and what it can do.[9]

As he explores the notion of community, Nancy considers myth in terms strikingly similar to those via which we have considered poetry, particularly in the definitional effort that springs from tautology:

> La phrase « le mythe est un mythe » a *simultanément* et *dans la même pensée* la valeur de l'ironie désenchantée (« la fondation est une fiction ») et celle de l'affirmation onto-poético-logique (« la fiction est une fondation »).
>
> C'est pourquoi le mythe est interrompu. Il est interrompu par son mythe. (*Communauté* 140–1)
>
> (The phrase "myth is a myth" harbors *simultaneously* and *in the same thought* a disabused irony ("foundation is a fiction") and an onto-poetico-logical affirmation ("fiction is a foundation").
>
> This is why myth is interrupted. It is interrupted by its myth. (*Inoperative* 55))

Tautology paradoxically establishes not an equivalence but a split. By hearing two different terms associated with, and designated by, the term "myth" (foundation and fiction), a new equivalence emerges between those otherwise unrelated terms whereby the tautology yields to a new kind of relation, in this case the fictional basis of foundation. And the interruption is here generated by the pause in the smooth functioning of tautology. The definitional plurality we have seen at play in the case of poetry makes for a comparable situation whereby poetry is interrupted by poetry, and is constituted by that interruption, by the ever-renewed impulse to rewrite the definition and thereby interrupt what had been our understanding of poetry. Nancy develops this idea in aural, musical, terms as the play of voices, noises, music, and silence:

> Lorsqu'une voix, ou une musique est interrompue soudain, on entend à l'instant même autre chose, un mixte ou un entre-deux de silence et de bruits divers que le son recouvrait, mais dans cette autre chose on entend à nouveau la voix ou la musique, devenues en quelque sorte la voix ou la musique de leur propre interruption: une sorte d'écho, mais qui ne répéterait pas ce dont il serait la réverbération. (*Communauté* 155)
>
> (When a voice, or music, is suddenly interrupted, one hears just at that instant something else, a mixture of various silences and noises that had been covered over by the sound, but in this something else one hears again the voice or the music that has become in a way the voice or the music of its own interruption: a kind of echo, but one that does not repeat that of which it is the reverberation. (*Inoperative* 62))

The comparison recalls my discussion of "pure" poetry in terms of absolute music, which I identified, paradoxically, as the point at which it becomes clear that poetry calls out for a proliferation of discourse rather than a reduction of it, that for it to be meaningful at all it requires the language through which we make tentative meaning from poetry, an act which itself becomes a crucial part of the poetic process. We can, following Nancy, label such a moment in the history of poetics an interruption in Nancy's sense, a moment that reveals figurative sounds and silences that had been covered over, in this case, by the discourse about "pure" poetry, and which allows us to see, as coextensive with that discourse, the series of attempts to make sense of what such pure poetry might be. This is, as I have suggested, a key moment of convergence between poetry and music in that even "absolute" music can only be considered meaningful, can only be considered *as* music, by that interpretive gesture which leads us, necessarily, into discourse about music.

Poetry, likewise, also becomes "the music of its own interruption," a reconception of what we thought we knew about poetry and the search for a new language with which to speak about it. It is that interruption that gets us beyond myth, beyond the fiction of a foundation as Nancy understands it. And Nancy explicitly links interruption to literature:

> On a donné un nom à cette voix de l'interruption : la littérature (ou l'écriture, si on veut bien prendre ici les deux mots dans les acceptions par lesquelles ils se correspondent). Ce nom, sans doute, ne convient pas. Mais aucun nom ne convient ici. Le lieu ou le moment de l'interruption est sans convenance.... Ce qui, de la littérature, est inconvenant, c'est qu'elle ne convient pas au mythe de la communauté, ni à la communauté du mythe. Elle ne convient, ni à la communion, ni à la communication. (*Communauté* 157)

> (A name has been given to this voice of interruption: literature (or writing, if we adopt the acceptation of this word that coincides with literature). This name is no doubt unsuitable. But no name is suitable here. The place or the moment of interruption is without suitability.... What is unsuitable about it is that it is not suited to the myth of community, nor to the community of myth. It is suited neither to communion nor to communication. (*Inoperative* 63))

Nancy's comments on the voice bring us back to Maulpoix's notion of the lucidly ignorant poet whose voice "suppose une écoute plutôt qu'un parler" (*Perplexe* 289). Maulpoix's poet, we recall, listens for signs of the subsistence of the lyric voice even amidst its supposed disappearance. That listening could also be considered an interruption, a questioning of the narrative whereby the lyric subject has become a thing of the past. To ask the question is to keep open the possibility that such is not the case; it is to interrupt an overly simple narrative whereby the age of the lyric subject has given way to something else, whether that be the depersonalized voice of some kinds of experimental poetry or the death of poetry altogether.

Nancy does not dwell within the unsuitability of the name he has just characterized. Rather, he goes on to indicate unsuitability as proper to the name "literature" itself:

> Et pourtant, si ce nom de « littérature » est toujours en passe de ne pas convenir à l' « inconvenance littéraire » elle-même, n'est-ce pas parce que la littérature a les rapports les plus étroits avec le mythe? Le mythe n'est-il pas l'origine de la littérature, l'origine de toute littérature et en un sens peut-être son unique contenu, son unique récit, à moins que ce ne soit son unique posture (celle du récitant, qui est son propre héros) ? (*Communauté* 157)

> (And yet, if the name "literature" is always in a state of not being suited to "literary unsuitability" itself, is this not because literature is so closely related to myth? Is not myth the origin of literature, the origin of all literature and perhaps in a sense its sole content, its sole narrative, or else its sole posture (that of the recitalist, who is his own hero)? (*Inoperative* 63))

Nancy raises these questions in the context of a discussion of Blanchot, for whom the terms "poetry," "writing," and "literature" are to a certain extent interchangeable. Has poetry then lost its specificity in this discussion which in Nancy revolves around the question of literature more generally? And is literature in turn tangled up in the notion of myth? What would be poetry's specificity in the context of this discussion? Once again we are brought back to the definitional concerns that have marked all of our investigation of the relation of poetry and knowledge. By turns to affirm poetry's specificity and to deny it is part of the never-ending conversation about poetry, which is an important part of poetry understood as "that key that you must always keep on losing," to return to Jaccottet's characterization. This willingness, or in fact the need, to abandon definitive foundation is what characterizes poetry. And this aspect of poetry, or, for Nancy, "literature," is what ultimately distinguishes it from myth:

> La « littérature » (ou l' « écriture ») est ce qui dans la littérature, c'est-à-dire dans le partage ou dans la communication des œuvres, interrompt le mythe—en donnant voix à l'être-en-commun qui n'a pas de mythe et qui ne peut pas en avoir. Ou plutôt, car l'être en commun n'est nulle part, et ne subsiste pas en un lieu mythique qu'on pourrait nous révéler, la littérature ne lui donne pas une voix, mais c'est l'être *en* commun qui *est* littéraire (ou scriptuaire). (*Communauté* 159–60)

("Literature" (or "writing") is what, in literature—in the sharing or the communication of works—interrupts myth by giving voice to being-in-common, which has no myth and cannot have one. Or, since being-in-common *is* nowhere, and does not subsist in a mythic space that could be revealed to us, literature does not give it a voice: rather, it is being *in* common that *is* literary (or scriptuary). (*Inoperative* 63–4))

Like Rancière, Nancy is not claiming that literature brings people together or that literary communities are comprised of those who read or write literature. The interruption of myth, according to Nancy:

n'a rien à faire ni avec le mythe de la communion par la littérature, ni avec celui de la création littéraire par la communauté. Si on peut dire, ou si du moins on peut essayer de dire, avec une pleine conscience de l'inconvenance, que l'être-en-commun *est* littéraire, c'est-à-dire si on peut tenter de dire qu'il a son être même dans la « littérature » (dans l'écriture, dans une certaine voix, dans une musique singulière, mais aussi dans une peinture, dans une danse, et dans l'exercice de la pensée …), il faudra qu'on désigne par « la littérature » cet être lui-même, en lui-même…. Le mythe est interrompu par la littérature dans l'exacte mesure où la littérature n'achève pas. (*Communauté* 161)

(has nothing to do with the myth of communion through literature, nor with the myth of literary creation by the community. But if we can say, or if we can at least try to say, while remaining fully conscious of its unsuitability, that being-in-common *is* literary, that is, if we can attempt to say that it has its very being in "literature" (in writing, in a certain voice, in a singular music, but also in a painting, in a dance, and in the exercise of thought), then what "literature" will have to designate is this being itself … in itself…. Myth is interrupted by literature precisely to the extent that literature does not come to an end. (*Inoperative* 64))

Nancy makes the move here that I have been claiming that all our investigations into the relationship of poetry to the shared world of lived experience do: what might seem at first glance to be a closing off of literature, or a definition of literature that would oppose it to the experiential world, or an attempt to make literary experience somehow more important than lived experience, is in fact the very opposite. Literature, understood as Nancy understands it here, encompasses and names the very being-in-common that resists totalization and singularity. Poetry is the mode of thinking about our being in the world that raises the very question of what that being could mean, what it might resemble, what it might oppose, and what might name it. It is, once again, a definitional concern, an approach to defining that marks it as endless.

Community is defined by that defining, as is poetry as well. Does this make community and poetry synonymous? The answer has to be some sort of mix of yes and no. And the words we need to use to make sense of such a statement bring us back to the discourse on poetry that was set in motion by poetry and continues its task. That discourse is, necessarily, communal and cannot occur in solitude. Once we tell ourselves the story of the way literature has interrupted myth, "ce qui nous est offert, c'est que la communauté arrive, ou plutôt, c'est qu'il nous arrive quelque chose en commun" ("what is offered to us is that community is coming about, or rather, that something is happening to us in common") (*Communauté* 171/*Inoperative* 69). And this is an inherently epistemological scenario:

> En un sens, nous nous comprenons nous-mêmes et le monde en partageant cette écriture, tout comme le groupe se comprenait en écoutant le mythe. Pourtant, nous comprenons seulement qu'il n'y a pas de compréhension commune de la communauté, que le partage ne fait pas une compréhension (ni un concept, ni une intuition, ni un schème), qu'il ne fait pas un savoir et qu'il ne donne à personne ni à la communauté elle-même la maîtrise de l'être en commun. (*Communauté* 171)

> (In a sense, we understand ourselves and the world by sharing this writing, just as the group understood itself by listening to the myth. Nonetheless, we understand that there is no common understanding of community, that sharing does not constitute an understanding (or a concept, or an intuition, or a schema), that it does not constitute a knowledge, and that it gives no one, including community itself, mastery over being-in-common. (*Inoperative* 69)

Does this leave no place for the individual subject? Does the writer then disappear? Nancy adamantly affirms that it is neither the disappearance of the writer nor, and here he argues against Blanchot, the disappearance of the subject. Once again, our inquiry into poetry ends up changing the questions themselves: our choice is not one between affirming the individual lyric subject or obliterating it altogether. Rather, it is a question of resituating the poetic subject, reader or writer, in the frame of the larger set of questions that poetry forces us to confront about what it means to be in common. Poetry is the vehicle by which we can realize the inadequacy of the terms or labels we have been using to name the world and our place in it. It is a realization, as I have been arguing, of lucid and productive ignorance. An affirmation of the lyric subject does not need to be nostalgic or backward-looking; rather, "lyric subject," or "writer," or "reader" can name the need to reconsider what we mean by the label itself. It is an interruption in Nancy's sense. For Nancy, the writer remains as

> ce qu'imprime, par l'interruption, le retrait de son mythe : il n'est pas l'auteur, il n'est pas non plus le héros, et il n'est peut-être plus ni ce qu'on a nommé le poète, ni ce qu'on a nommé le penseur, mais il est une voix singulière (une écriture: cela peut être, aussi bien, une façon de parler …). Et cette voix singulière, résolument et irréductiblement singulière (mortelle), il l'est *en commun*. (*Communauté* 173)

> ([that which] the withdrawal of his myth imprints through the interruption: he is not the author, nor is he the hero, and perhaps he is no longer what has been called the poet or what has been called the thinker; rather, he is a singular voice (a writing: which might also be a way of speaking). He is this singular voice, this resolutely and irreducibly singular (mortal) voice, *in common*. (*Inoperative* 70)

The writer is defined by the way in which the writer, as person or as role or as name, interrupts what we understand by the term.

And what it would mean for the writer to be a singular voice in common is left in suspension here; to say more would be to say too much and not enough. The fact that "la littérature s'interrompt" ("literature interrupts itself" (*Communauté* 179/*Inoperative* 72) is, for Nancy, what distinguishes literature from myth. What else might poetry mean? Answering that question is, as I hope to have suggested, poetry's infinite task, one that proceeds from ignorance and returns to it, in a movement that never turns its back on the world of experience but constantly seeks to rearticulate the relationship between experience and our attempts to capture it in language, and to understand something thereby, not only about the experience, but also about our capacity to know it, a capacity whose limitations poetry is always in a position to point out. Such skepticism is the motor of our attempts to understand poetry itself, and we necessarily define ourselves as we seek to understand poetry. Such a view cannot get beyond the notion of a poetic subject, nor can it ignore the ways in which that subject is anchored in a community whose existence is constantly renegotiated by those who comprise it. Rather than shutting us down, creative poetic ignorance moves us forward, creating and responding to the unsettledness that it implies. Poetry provides the lucid ignorance and the conceptual terrain from which and on which we can start to build, and question, and rebuild, an always tentative answer, something to grasp until we lose the key again.

Notes

Introduction

1. The distinction was well established by the time of Paul Valéry, who writes that "construire un poème qui ne contienne que poésie est impossible. Si une pièce ne contient que *poésie*, elle n'est pas construite; elle n'est pas un *poème*" ("Constructing a poem that contains only poetry is impossible. If a work contains only *poetry*, it is not constructed; it is not a *poem*") (2: 552).
2. See also Terence Cave on literature's potential primacy over philosophy at a cognitive level: "Literary works are too rich in complications, too densely fabricated, to allow a controlled 'experiment' in which the proposition that is to be tested can be clearly tagged and tracked. ... They improvise, or rather perhaps they model improvisation, in their own cognitive mode. Since humans wouldn't have got very far ... without improvisation, it may be that, in the evolution of imagitive affordances, what we are here calling literature may have been more central and more productive than the protocols of philosophy and science, which are after all a recent invention in the history of culture. To attempt to harness it to specific propositional content or truth values is to deprive it of its distinctive character and force: the license to think more variously, more plurally, more many-strandedly" (143–4).
3. As Jean-Luc Nancy puts it: "On pourriat dire aussi: l' « art » n'apparaît jamais que dans une tension entre deux concepts de l'art, l'un technique et l'autre sublime—et cette tension elle-même reste en général sans concept. Cela ne veut pas dire qu'il faut, ni, s'il le faut, qu'il est possible de la subsumer sous un concept. Mais cela veut dire en tout cas que nous ne pouvons pas nous éviter de penser cette tension elle-même. L'art et les arts s'entr'appartiennent sans resolution en intériorité, sur un mode tendu, étendu, en extériorité. L'art serait-il *res extensa, partes extra partes?*" (*Les muses* 16). ("One could also say: 'art' never appears except in a tension between two concepts of art, one technical and the other sublime—and this tension itself remains in general without concept. This does not mean that it is necessary, nor, if it is necessary, that it is possible to subsume it in a concept. But it does mean that we cannot avod thinking this tension itself. Art and the arts inter-belong to each other [s'entr'appartiennent] in a tense, extended mode in exteriority, without any resolution in interiority. Would art then be, *res extensa, partes extra partes?*" (*The Muses* 4)).

4   See Michel Deguy on poetry as a form of thought: "D'abord, … par « poétique de la pensée » j'entends: une réflexion vernaculaire; une détermination du penser qui pour n'être rigoureusement ni scientifique (ce n'est pas une physio-psycho-socio-logie de la pensée « cognitive ») ni philosophique (ce n'est pas une *cogitatio* de la *cogitatio* ou représentation, au long de l' « histoire de la philosophie ») n'en est pas moins une pensée de la pensée en tant que foncièrement imageante (schématistique), approximative (comparative), langagière (idiomaticité « maternelle »)" ("First, by 'poetics of thought' I mean: a vernacular reflection; a determination of the thought that, for being neither rigorously scientific (it is not a physio-psycho-sociology of 'cognitive' thought) nor philosophical (it is not a *cogitatio* of *cogitatio* or representation, throughout the 'history of philosophy') is no less a thought of thought inasmuch as fundamentally imagistic (schematistic), approximate (comparative), linguistic ('maternal' idiomaticity)" (*Réouverture* 63–4).

5   For an excellent overview of scholarly work on literature and knowledge, see Livingston.

6   On poetry as question, see also Gerald Bruns: "Perhaps the difference between philosophy and poetry is this: philosophy seeks to give reasons why (to establish that) a thing is so and not otherwise. It wants to fix things as what they are. Whereas poetry asks: Why this? Why not otherwise? (Why not nothing?) It wants to unfix things, turn them into something else, turn them loose. Philosophy settles, poetry unsettles" (*Blanchot* 41).

7   See Camille Dumoulié on poetry's taking up questions traditionally associated with metaphysics in the nineteenth century: "Par une étrange ironie de l'histoire, au moment où la philosophie annonce la fin de l'art, on assiste à la fin de l'histoire de la philosophie occidentale ouvert par Platon. Corrélativement, la littérature se libère de son assujettissement et rivalise même avec la philosophie dans sa prétention à la totalité. Désormais en charge de l'absolu, elle prend la relève de la philosophie, l'englobe, la dépasse et la sauve par ce dépassement même. Les limites entre les deux ordres du discours s'effacent au point que la philosophie devienne une zone de la littérature ou même qu'elle se dilue en elle, perdant la spécificité de son discours. Pourtant, la prétendue victoire de la littérature pourrait bien être le revers d'une nouvelle sujétion" ("By a strange irony of history, at the moment when philosophy announces the end of art, one witnesses the end of the history of Western philosophy that began with Plato. At the same time, literature frees itself from its subjugation and even rivals philosophy in its pretention to totality. From then on in charge of the absolute, it takes up the baton from philosophy, subsumes it, surpasses it and saves it by this very surpassing. The limits between the orders of discourse are erased to the point where philosophy becomes a zone of literature or even dilutes itself in it, losing the specificity of its discourse. Yet, the supposed victory of literature could well be the other side of a new subjugation") (56).

8 On competing approaches to literary truth, see Eaglestone.
9 Claire Lyu puts this in a way that links poetry directly to the lived experience of facing new, unanchored experience: "Poetry begins where solutions truly dissolve in the passage from *ancre* to *encre*: it emerges as deep immersion, dipping its pen into an ocean of ink and flowing through us, like the blood of our veins, into our lives" (147).
10 On this distinction, see Natalie Wourm: "Il existe, parallèlement, un mouvement de retour au lyrisme traditionnel, appelé « nouveau lyrisme » ou « lyrisme critique ». Espitallier explique dans son livre *Caisse à outils: un panorama de la poésie française aujourd'hui*: « [L]e lyrisme s'est lui aussi affirmé en opposition aux rigorismes de l'avant-garde, soucieux de maintenir une espèce d'essence de la poésie contre les dérives jugées impersonnelles et dangereusement asséchées. Lesquelles jouaient justement à repousser les effets du lyrisme »" ("There exists in parallel a mouvement of return to traditional lyricism, called 'new lyricism' or 'critical lyricism'. Espitallier explains in his book *Caisse à outils*: '[L]yricism has also asserted itself in opposition to the rigors of the avant-garde, concerned to maintain a sort of essence of poetry against excesses judged impersonal and dangerously dry. Those excesses tried to reject the effects of lyricism'") (Wourm 6).
11 On the way esthetics and subjectivity are bound together in new ways in modern art and philosophy since Kant, see Andrew Bowie's *Aesthetics and Subjectivity*: "From being a part of philosophy concerned with the senses, and not necessarily with beauty ... the new subject of 'esthetics' now focuses on the significance of natural beauty and of art. Reflection on esthetics does not, though, just involve a revival of Plato's thoughts about beauty as the symbol of the good. The crucial new departure lies in the way esthetics is connected to the emergence of subjectivity as the central issue in modern philosophy, and this is where the relevance of this topic to contemporary concerns becomes apparent" (2).
12 On Mallarmé and knowledge, see Campion (and the critique of Campion in Delègue 132–3) as well as Thériault 94–111: "Le savoir que [l'énigme] livre ne se laisse pas constituer à la façon des formes régionales de savoir—et c'est la raison pour laquelle il en est radicalement distinct" (Thériault 106–7) ("The knowledge that [the enigma] delivers does not allow itself to be constituted in the manner of regional forms of knowledge—and that's the reason why it is radically distinct from it"). Associating Mallarmé's approach to knowledge with the formula "Je sais mais quand même" ("I know but even so"), Thériault affirms that "nul ne peut en bonne conscience prétendre « savoir » pour de bon; le « mais quand même » dénote la résistance d'une illusion qui n'est pas de nature à se dissiper complètement, et on pourrait dire qu'il dénote aussi ... sa résilience extraordinaire" ("no one can in good conscience claim to 'know' for good; the 'but even so' denotes the resistance of an

illusion which is not of a nature to dissipate completely, and we could say that it also denotes ... its extraordinary resilience") (Thériault 107).

13 For a recent demonstration of the centrality of poetry to Heidegger's thought, see David Nowell Smith, who asks about Heidegger's philosophy: "how can thinking both define the relation between poeticizing and thinking and yet say that poetizing lies beyond the limits of thinking, withdraws from thinking's attempts to grasp it? If thinking can articulate, and circumscribe, the limits of the relation between poeticizing and itself, then this thinking cannot confront these limits, because these limits have, in advance, been assimilated with the limits proper to thinking itself. ... This also means that those moments at which Heidegger's readings will submit themselves to poetry as 'other' will only take place provided those aspects of *Poesie*—that is, those features that are central to poetic technique and yet the account of *Dichten* overlooks—come to mark these readings" (164).

14 See Alain Badiou's distinction between thought and knowledge: "at the farthest remove from knowledge, the poem is exemplarily a thought that is obtained in the retreat, or the defection, of everything that supports the faculty to know. And no doubt this is why the poem has always disconcerted philosophy" (31).

15 See also Marjorie Levinson on the interaction of what she calls "thinking with" and "thinking through": "Thinking with ... makes bid to free us from habitual ways of grasping things as they are: that is things as they are for us, or, subjectively. ... The posture of this book is that thinking with needs thinking through in that Heideggerian sense of search through things toward relations, understood as the condition of generation of the sensible: i.e., as that which brings forth objects rather than arises from them. ... [T]hinking with and through alternate over and over again, forming a pattern of thought that spirals both out and down, seeking always to expand and deepen its reach" (28–9).

16 Jacob Bittner has recently indicated in a commentary on Lacoue-Labarthe and Nancy: "Literature itself is the 'question of literature'; however, this thought is precisely what needs to be questioned, not so as to argue against it, but to understand how literature became its own question" (771).

17 Alessandro De Francesco, in the context of a discussion of poetry of the 1960s and 70s that could be expanded to the approach to poetry I will be tracing, notes how poetry can be viewed as "a cognitive means, that is, as one of the means at the human intellect's disposal for unveiling linguistic illusions in favor of a reconfiguration of the real" (115).

18 See also Gilles Deleuze's claim that "we write only at the tip of our knowledge, at the extreme point which separates our knowledge from our ignorance and makes the first pass through/into the other" (quoted in Lyu 4).

19 In this sense, poetry has a role similar to the one Zahi Zalloua assigns to theory as opposed to philosophy: "Unlike philosophy, ... theory embraces skepticism's

corrosive ways, risking its very identity, its authority and purchase on the world. Yet, while contesting philosophy's hermeneutic aspirations and biases, theory never fully adopts an anti-hermeneutics, an anti-philosophy, a refusal to understand the world. Rather, theory inventively subjects this desire to know—this curiosity—to the 'madness' of the decision" (28).

20 As Hugo Friedrich states, Romanticism "has remained the intellectual fate of ensuing generations. ... Its harmonies concealed the dissonances of the future" (13).

21 As Audrey Wasser notes: "One cannot remain self-conscious in the face of romanticism's contradictions, or adopt a steadfast, critical distance from a romantic 'naïveté,' without repeating, by these very gestures, those highly sophisticated mechanisms of irony and self-reflection that already characterized romanticism at its most characteristic moment. ... Romanticism and the critique or overcoming of romanticism—as well as the critique *of* overcoming romanticism—tend to be part and parcel of the same problematic" (19). Her own study proposes an alternate route, through rationalism, to "ask whether the constitutive tension at the heart of our received notion of literature, and of the autonomy and integrity of the literary work, cannot be reconceived more productively along non-romantic lines" (20).

22 See Anthony Cascardi's characterization: "If, in the tradition that culminated in Kant, thinking was taken as the formulation of representational ideas, then Heidegger's idea of poetic thinking is somehow to circumvent representations by moving, if not beyond them, then back before they were invented, which for Heidegger means moving back to an original (pre-Platonic) moment in Western thought" (125).

23 Jean-Michel Maulpoix notes the continuity between the project of the Jena Romantics and twentieth-century French poets in terms of establishing a dialectical relationship between poetics and thought: "Nombre de poètes contemporains continuent d'affirmer avec force combien la poésie est un espace où travaille la pensée. Ainsi Michel Deguy écrit-il dans *Réouverture après travaux*: « tâche de la poésie aujourd'hui : produire, non systématiquement, une poétique de la pensée par une pensée du poétique » (ou un penser (à) la poétique)" ("A number of contemporary poets continue to affirm forcefully the extent to which poetry is a space where thought is at work. Thus Michel Deguy writes in *Réouverture après travaux*: 'Task of poetry today: to produce, unsystematically, a poetics of thought by a thought of the poetic' (or a thought (of) poetry)") (*Mauvais genre* 13).

24 See McKeane 18–20 for an overview of Lacoue-Labarthe and Nancy's position, in which McKeane emphasizes their desire to go beyond a literature/philosophy dualism and their "mistrust of the view that would champion literature as able to resist philosophical systematization ... such a vision of 'literature' does little more than to set it up as the other of philosophy" (20).

25 See Weinstein for a study that explores, in a way consonant with my approach to poetry, how modernist prose fiction subverts the "insistence on free-standing subjectivity ... in order to reveal the human subject as situational, space/time dependent, capable of coming to know *only* if the props that enable knowing are already in place" (2).

Chapter 1

1 Further references will be indicated with the abbreviation *OC* and volume number.
2 Further references will be indicated with the abbreviation *OP* and volume number.
3 "Narrer, enseigner, même décrire, cela va et encore qu'à chacun suffirait peut-être pour échanger la pensée humaine, de prendre ou de mettre dans la main d'autrui en silence une pièce de monnaie, l'emploi élémentaire du discours dessert l'universel *reportage* dont, la littérature exceptée, participe tout entre les genres d'écrits contemporains" (*OC2*: 212) ("To tell, to teach, and even to describe have their place, and suffice, perhaps, in order to exchange human thought, to take or to put into someone else's hand in silence a coin, this elementary use of discourse serving the universal *reporting* in which, except for literature, all genres of conteporary writing participate" (*Divagations* 210).
4 This conception of poetry as an inferior translation of an experience that is more fully experienced by the mystic is developed, for example, by Henri Bremond: "Le mystique, plus il est mystique, moins il éprouve le besoin de se communiquer ; aurait-il la tentation de le faire, plus cette commuication lui paraît impossible" ("For the mystic, the more he is a mystic, the less he feels the need to communicate; if he is tempted to do so, communication seems to him all the more impossible"] (209). Bremond questions whether this implies that the mystic is therefore inferior to the poet, but concludes that such is not the case "s'il est question d'une connaissance réelle, unitive. ... [C]hez le poète, la saisie est plus supericielle que chez le mystique; moins solide, moins unifiante" ("if it is a question of a real, unitary knowledge. ... For the poet, the grasp [of knowledge] is more superficial than for the mystic, less solid, less unifying" (209–10). We will see in chapter two that Jacques and Raïssa Maritain argue specifically against Bremond's conception of poetry as an inferior sort of mysticism.
5 As Laurence Porter has noted, for the Hugo of *Les Contemplations*, "writing *is* falling ... writing constitutes a vain and paradoxical attempt to structure chaos, to deploy spatial metaphors so as to create a clear picture of our epistemological confusion" (412–13).

6 Jean Gaudon indicates that "la poésie ne peut devenir vérité que si, derrière l'image altière du mage, se profile celle d'un poète dont la parole « devient une voix / De la nature, ainsi que la rumeur des bois » ('A celle qui est restée … ')" ("poetry can only become truth if, behind the haughty image of the magus, looms that of a poet whose word 'becomes a voix / of nature, like the murmur of the woods' ('To she who stayed…')") (379). For Gaudon, Hugo's poetry in the exile years accomplishes this, but one could inquire about how this merger of the poet's voice with the voice of nature leads to legibility by the reader in ways that would circumvent humanity's ignorance as Hugo constructs it.

7 For a reading of Hugo that claims that his poetry never actually attains the external world it claims to describe and that "le texte toujours se referme sur soi-même et conclut sur son début" ("the text always closes in on itself and concludes with its beginning"), see Riffaterre 38.

8 I discuss at greater length the epistemological stakes of Baudelaire's newness in relation to Hugo in "Gautier on Baudelaire." See especially 122–8.

9 See Claude Pichois's description of the genesis of the text in *OC2*: 1378.

10 I consider the ethical implications of this stance in *The Fall Out of Redemption* 188–201.

11 For a succinct account of the way post-Kantian thought grapples with new configurations of art, epistemology, and ethics, see the introduction to Joughin and Malpas's *The New Aestheticism* 1–19.

12 See, for instance, Baudelaire's own definition in the unfinished article "Puisque réalisme il y a": "La Poésie est ce qu'il y a de plus réel, c'est ce qui n'est complètement vrai que dans *un autre monde*. Ce monde-ci, dictionnaire hiéroglyphique" ("Poetry is what is most real, it is what is only completely true in *another world*. This world, a hieroglyphic dictionary") (*OC2*: 59).

13 See Aristotle, *Metaphysics* Book 1 Part 2: "For it is owing to their wonder that men both now begin and at first began to philosophize; they wondered originally at the obvious difficulties, then advanced little by little and stated difficulties about the greater matters, e.g. about the phenomena of the moon and those of the sun and of the stars, and about the genesis of the universe. And a man who is puzzled and wonders thinks himself ignorant …; therefore since they philosophized order to escape from ignorance, evidently they were pursuing science in order to know, and not for any utilitarian end."

14 See Patrick Labarthe's reading (202–11) whereby the poem's role is to "retracer les épreuves douloureuses du moi, mais sur le mode d'une interrogation et d'une errance qui sont aussi le destin partagé du lecteur" ("retrace the painful trials of the self, but in the modes of questioning and wondering that are also the shared destiny of the reader") (211).

15 See also Anthony Cascardi, who identifies a modern split between philosphy and poetry that has its origins in "the romantic project to recover the world-in-itself," a project that "has been regarded as 'poetic' in certain essential ways" and which is "dependent on finding some term other than knowledge" to characterize the relationship between ourselves and the world in ways other than as a knowledge of objects (Cascardi 121).

16 See Catherine Witt's observation about how the *nescio* trope in Baudelaire is a "fissured site of passage that allows for the relation between writing, thinking, and being to be articulated independently of the categorical distinctions of philosophical systems. The nescio rejects the ambition of grasping the totality of knowledge but also the self as a totalizable and totalizing entity" (Witt 39).

17 I provide a more extensive reading of this poem in "Cross-Referencing Bowie".

Chapter 2

1 Gabriel Trop discusses this passage in Novalis; see Trop 123–6.
2 On the continuing relevance of this Romantic conception of the relationship of poetry to thinking about poetry, see Stefan Matuschek's comments on Schlegel's notion of the eternally incomplete nature of poetry: "That is not entirely the language of today, but it is today's thoughts—literature thought of as something dynamic, open to development, that cannot be taught in advance by theorists, but rather is always being demonstrated anew by successful examples…. Schlegel's formulation points in its own way to what I call categorical literary Idealism—the grounding of the concept of literature upon the potentially infinite reflection on literary practice and the expectations we have of it. In the 1790s, when the rules of normative genre poetry were not long gone, Schlegel's formulations were revolutionarily new. They are not obsolete even today, they have merely become a habit" (79–80).
3 See also this definition of poetry by contemporary poet Philippe Delaveau: "La poésie est une traduction de la *relation* entre le poète et le reel, par la médiation d'un langage toujours à inventer, en vue de *l'unité*. Unité obtenue selon une *intention* découverte peu à peu par le poète, au moment où il éprouve le *retour* de ce qu'il a vécu sur le mode de l'émotion, en vue d'en faire cette construction de langage qu'on appelle un poème" ("Poetry is a translation of the *relation* between the poet and the real, by the mediation of a language always still to be invented, with the goal of *unity*. Unity obtained according to an *intention* discovered little by little by the poet, at the moment when he experiences the *return* of what he lived in

the mode of emotion, in order to make of it that construction of language that we call a poem") (65).

4 Bowie goes on to underscore that an ideal achieved as ground, whether that ideal be "philosophy" or "poetry" or "self," would destroy itself. "This is why Fichte's I, as the supposed absolute beginning ... is only a fiction, not the real principle of being" (*Aesthetics* 94).

5 The original reads: "Die Poesie ist durchaus personell und darum unbeschreiblich und indefinissabel. Wer es nicht unmittelbar weiß und fühlt, was Poesie ist, dem läßt sich kein Begriff davon beibringen. Poesie ist Poesie. Von Sprach- oder Redekunst himmelweit verschieden" (*Schriften* 3: 685).

6 See also Paisley Livingston's commentary on the problem with models that claim a unique kind of knowledge that literature provides which cannot be expressed in any other way: "all such theories have the problem of making convincing claims about epistemic states that cannot by definition be restated in the nonliterary language in which the theories themselves are couched. As a result, literature's putative unique cognitive value is in danger of becoming an epistemic *je ne sais quoi* towards which a non-literary discourse can only point, this pointing being neither a literary nor a propositional form of knowledge" (256).

7 Cf. Baudelaire: "Ce serait un événement tout nouveau dans l'histoire des arts qu'un critique se faisant poète, un renversement de toutes les lois psychiques, une monstruosité ; au contraire, tous les grands poètes deviennent naturellement, fatalement, critiques" ("It would be an entirely new event in the history of the arts if a critic became a poet, a reversal of all the psychic laws, a monstrosity; on the other hand, all great poets become naturally, inevitably, critics" (*OC2*: 793).

8 The Maritains follow the lead of Albert Béguin, who had written in 1936 of the differences between the poet and the mystic in terms of knowledge and the unknown: "En un mot : le mystique suit un chemin tout opposé à celui du poète; son point de départ est la connaissance, non pas une interrogation lancée dans l'inconnu" ("In a word: the mystic follows a path completely opposed to that of the poet; his point of departure is knowledge, not an investigation launched into the unknown") (121). And again: "Le mystique tend au silence, et tout ce qui importe vraiment à ses yeux dépasse le verbe articulé. Il ne s'agit pas, bien entendu, d'établir une hiérarchie entre la mystique et la poésie" ("The mystic tends toward silence, and everything that is truly important in his eyes goes beyond the articulated word. It is not a question, of course, of establishing a hierarchy between mysticism and poetry") (124).

9 See Michel Jarrety, who notes that, for Valéry, critical readings become literature in turn: "S'ensuit pour la critique la possibilité de deux issues : être hors de la littérature et se condamner à ne pas la saisir, ou à l'inverse accepter d'entrer dans son jeu et risquer d'en être saisie" ("Criticism thus has the possibility of two ways

out: to be outside of literature and condemn itself to not grasping it, or, the other way round, to accept to enter into its game and risk being taken in there") (238–9).

10 Jonathan Lear associates irony with the kind of defamiliarization and world disruption that Valéry evokes. Lear writes: "This is the strangeness of irony: we seem to be called to an ideal that transcends our ordinary understanding, but to which we now experience ourselves as already committed. The experience of irony thus seems to be a peculiar species of uncanniness—in the sense that something that has been familiar returns to me as strange and unfamiliar. And in its return it disrupts my world. For part of what it is to inhabit a world is to be able to locate familiar things in familiar places. Encountering strange things per se need not be world-disrupting, but coming to experience what has been familiar as utterly unfamiliar is a sign that one no longer knows one's way about. And the experience of uncanniness is enhanced dramatically when what is returning to me as unfamiliar is what, until now, I have taken to be my practical identity" (15).

11 See also this indication that what has become most interesting about philosophy is the way the questions are addressed, as opposed to the answers that are generated, and the relationship of that process to writing: "La philosophie, si l'on en déduit les choses vagues et les choses réfutées, se ramène maintenant à cinq ou six problèmes, … toujours réductibles à des querelles linguistiques et dont la solution dépend de la manière de les *écrire*. Mais l'intérêt de ces curieux travaux n'est pas si amoindri qu'on pourrait le penser : il réside dans cette fragilité et dans ces querelles mêmes, c'est-à-dire dans la délicatesse de l'appareil logique et psychologique de plus en plus subtil qu'elles demandent qu'on emploie" ("Philosophy, if we deduct from it vague things and refuted things, is reduced now to five or six problems, … always reducible to linguistic quarrels and whose solution depends on the way of *writing* them. But the interest of these curious works is not as reduced as one might think: it resides in that fragility and those very quarrels, that is in the delicacy of the increasingly subtle psychological and logical apparatus that they ask us to use") (1: 1273).

Chapter 3

1 For a wide-ranging consideration of the polyvalent forms of ignorance from a variety of disciplinary perspectives, see DeNicola, who summarizes his approach this way: "Ignorance is neither a pure nor a simple concept; it has a multiplex structure and many forms. In its house are many mansions. It is both an accusation and a defense. Its practical import ranges from the inconsequential to the momentous, from the benign to the fatal, from the excusable to the unforgivable. It

is a scourge, but it also may be a refuge, a value, even an accompaniment to virtue. ... In short, ignorance is a many-splendored thing" (11).

2 Gary Handwerk links the relation of knowledge, ignorance, and subjectivity to irony: "The urge to know, which lies behind any ironic mind, leads inevitably to reflection upon the conditions of possibility of knowledge and eventually to consideration of the nature of the subject itself. Irony moves toward the negation of that individual subject as either totalized or totalizing, stressing the partial nature of all individual consciousness. For the self-reflexive quality of the mind subjects it to a paradoxical self limitation, unable to know how it can know without assuming that act of knowledge it seeks to define. Yet at the same time the falling-short that summarizes ironic insight can be taken as proof of a sense of or something beyond ironic incapacity, or else the ironists could not realize how or even that he failed" (172).

3 See for instance this affirmation of the direct relation between poetry and the real: "Qu'est-ce que la poésie, en effet ? Reprendre contact, pleinement, avec les réalités fondamentales de la vie ou de la nature, par désagrégation des représentations conceptuelles, des formulations abstraites qui réduisent ce qui est à simplement de la chose,—chose mesurable, manipulable, commercialisable, chose faite pour inciter au désespoir de la possession et à l'ambition du pouvoir, chose de mort. La poésie n'est pas la production d'un objet verbal, ... c'est une intervention dans le monde, un acte de connaissance" ("What is poetry, really? To reestablish contact, fully, with the fundamental realities of life or nature, by the disintegration of conceptual representations and abstract formulations that reduce what is simply to the thing,—a thing measurable, manipulable, commercializable, a thing made to incite the despair of possession and the ambition of power, a thing of death. Poetry is not the producton of a verbal object, ... it is an intervention in the world, an act of knowledge") (Bonnefoy 57).

4 Césaire's view places him within an optimistic perspective on poets' ability to know. He identifies the nineteenth century as the moment when "les poètes ont osé prétendre qu'ils savaient" ("the poets dared to claim that they knew") (159). At that point, "la poésie cessa d'être un jeu, même sérieux. La poésie cessa d'être une occupation, même honorable" ("poetry ceased being a game, even a serious one. Poetry ceased being an occupation, even an honorable one") (159). Still, there is an ambiguity in the essay about whether poets do in fact possess and communicate truth, which Césaire often implies, or whether poetry is (merely, we could say) "sur le chemin de la vérité" ("on the way toward truth") (167).

5 Saint-John Perse acknowledges, as Gleize indicates, an optimism inherent in that approach: "Ainsi, par son adhésion totale à ce qui est, le poète tient pour nous liaison avec la permanence et l'unité de l'Être. Et sa leçon est d'optimisme. Une

même loi d'harmonie régit pour lui le monde entier des choses" ("Thus, by his total adhesion to what is, the poet holds for us a link between the permanence and the unity of Being. And his lesson is one of optimism. A same law of harmony rules for him the whole world of things").

6 See Nancy, *Listening* for an exploration of listening as this kind of focused attentiveness that constitutes a subject. I consider the implications of this approach to listening for literature in Acquisto, *Proust, Music, and Meaning*. See especially 23–50.

7 Elisabeth Arnould summarizes Bataille's relationship to poetry this way: "L'on peut dire que la réflexion entière de Bataille naît d'un rapport à la fois critique et désirant à la poésie. … De *L'Histoire de l'œil* à *L'impossible*, le trajet de l'agnoséologie bataillienne est celui d'une pensée qui épouse la poésie pour la mieux dépasser ou qui, inversement, la dépasse pour en mieux épouser le vide" ("We can say that Bataille's whole reflection is born from a relation to poetry that is at the same time critical and desiring. … From *L'Histoire de l'œil* to *L'impossible*, the trajectory of Bataille's agnoseology is that of a thought that weds itself to poetry the better to get beyond it or which, inversely, gets beyond it in order better to wed itself to the void") ("La poésie" 782).

8 For a detailed exploration of the idea of poetry as sacrifice, see Lala, and especially this passage: "Paradoxically, [poetry] becomes the catalyst which reveals the divine part in man… and this irreducible art, which is communicated through art, eroticism and religious sacrifice, remains inscribed within man as something secret and sacred. 'The hatred of poetry' thus holds open the urgent need to respond to an *effusion*, since its sacrificial site is a part of our most intimate existence" (111).

9 I deal more extensively with Bataille's writings on the abandonment of poetry and its relationship to knowledge in "Entre Rimbaud et Bataille."

10 As Gemerchak puts it, for Bataille, "poetry is always split from itself, and that's an important part of why it can't be reduced to silence" (123).

11 See Arnould's reading of sacrifice in Bataille as marking "a limit to conceptualization and … a stumbling block to thought" and as "delineating the limit thought comes up against when it faces what it cannot think" ("Impossible" 87).

12 In this context, Gerald Bruns's comment on Blanchot, whom he reads together with Bataille as the last of the Romantics, aptly describes Bataille's conception of poetry as well: "If you ask what makes the poem possible, the answer is that there is no answer: the poem is, like the sacred, impossible. Neither the sacred nor the poem can be put into words" (*Blanchot* 13).

13 "When we think of a golden mountain, we only join two consistent ideas, gold, and *mountain*, with which we were formerly acquainted. A virtuous horse we

can conceive; because, from our own feeling, we can conceive virtue; and this we may unite to the figure and shape of a horse, which is an animal familiar to us" (Hume 11).

14 Sylvain Santi expresses a similar perspective on Bataille's "hatred of poetry": "La haine s'avère donc correlative au moins d'une attirance profonde: si la poésie est haïe, elle ne l'est qu'au nom de la poésie. Elle a le sens de la conjuration d'une absence" ("The hatred thus proves correlative with a profound attraction: if poetry is hated, it is only hated in the name of poetry. It has the meaning of the conjuring of an absence") (105).

15 Santi points in this context to Bataille's definition of poetry, one among many that he gives, as "la perversion du langage un peu plus même que l'érotisme n'est celle des fonctions sexuelles" ("the perversion of language even a little more so than eroticism is the perversion of the sexual functions") (Bataille, *L'expérience intérieure*, in *OC5*: 173, quoted in Santi 169).

16 Arnould describes Bataille's positioning of poetry with regard to to its "unworking" this way: "elle crée sa propre réalité et « n'a plus d'autre foi qu'elle-même ». Mais cette foi ne suffit pas à la soutenir. Elle n'est plus croyance dans le pouvoir ontologique de ses créations. Et si elle témoigne pour un « sacré », elle ne le manifeste pas. Elle peut en questionner l'absence et « s'abandonner » son « excès d'être », mais cet abandon même ne peut se présenter comme tel. Il n'est jamais de l'ordre d'une création et d'un pouvoir. Il est plutôt ce qui fait de l'œuvre moderne une passion désoeuvrée" ("It creates its own reality and 'has no other faith but itself.' But that faith is not enough to sustain it. It is no longer a belief in the ontological power of its creations. And if it bears witness to a 'sacred,' it does not manifest it. It can question its absence and 'abandon' its 'excess of being,' but that very abandoning cannot present itself as such. It is never on the order of a creation and a power. It is rather what makes of the modern work an idle passion") ("La poésie" 796).

17 Paul Valéry recounts the encounter: "Mallarmé lui répondit: « Ce n'est point avec des idées, mon cher Degas, que l'on fait des vers. C'est avec des *mots*. »" ("Mallarmé answered him: 'It is not at all with ideas, my dear Degas, that we make poetry. It is with *words*'") (Valéry 1: 1324).

18 Cf. Gerald Bruns's remark: "If you ask what makes the poem possible, the answer is that there is no answer: the poem is, like the sacred, impossible. Neither the sacred nor the poem can be put into words" (*Blanchot* 13).

19 Bruns identifies Blanchot's conception of poetry as a way of getting beyond a potential opposition between a Mallarméan and Heideggerian approach to poetry, and of seeing it as a kind of beginning with real reference to lived experience: "However, the Orphic and hermetic are not opposites; they are perhaps simply different interpretations of poetry's outsidedness. It is important to notice that the

disclosure of the world is not Heidegger's whole story about poetry. It remains true that poetry as *Dichtung*—literally, poetizing—is the opening up of the world; poetry is the situating of the world and of ourselves as beings in the world, where situation means historicizing in the sense of exposing us to time and history. Poetry is a name for the beginning" (*Blanchot* 11–12).

20 In this way we can avoid potential paralysis in the face of the void as Blanchot may at times conceive it. If production could be said to stem from this impasse, the impasse may effectively cancel itself. Audrey Wasser has diagnosed this problem in Blanchot as an extension of his debt to German Idealism: "Because Blanchot confronts the imperative to think creation in terms of a difference from what is, and because he cannot conceive of such difference in terms other than negation or opposition … he comes face to face with the insufficiency of the concept of possibility in accounting for literary creation. … Yet perhaps this lacuna is *not* the origin of the work, but the testament to a blind spot in this logic that is so indebted to German Idealism: a shadow that falls over Blanchot's thought in the form of its inability to account for the productivity and continuity of difference" (70).

Chapter 4

1 As Anne Gourio puts it: "Philippe Jaccottet se maintient bien sur une tension fondatrice, qui s'inscrit parfaitement dans le contexte de la poésie de la seconde moitié du siècle marquée durablement par les récents désastres humains : résister aux sirènes du désenchantement, mais se garder de toute extase lyrique; penser un possible dépassement de la finitude, mais rejeter toute illusion métaphysique. Cet entre-deux—esthétique et métaphysique—pose les conditions de l'expérience de l'émerveillement chez Jaccottet" ("Philippe Jaccottet maintains himself on a founding tension, which is perfectly inscribed in the context of the poetry of the second half of the century significantly impacted by the recent human disasters: to resist the sirens of disenchantment, but to keep oneself away from all lyrical ecstasy; to think a possible way of going beyond finitude, but to reject metaphysical illusion. That betweenness—esthetics and metaphysics—posits the conditions of the experience of wonder in Jaccottet") (186).

2 See Fabio Pusterla's characterization of the way in which Jaccottet seeks a way to preserve some role for the lyric in the decidedly catastrophic period of the mid to late twentieth century: this period "laissait entrevoir qu'il était nécessaire, voire urgent, de reconstruire quelque chose et qu'il était possible aussi, désormais, grâce à elle, de reprendre confiance dans la pratique de la poésie. Mieux même, qu'on pouvait à nouveau aborder simplement les choses du monde sans abandonner les

expériences profondes, que l'on pouvait rétablir du dialogue exaltant entre le texte et ses lecteurs, tout en restant conscient, bien sûr, de l'évidence de la catastrophe" ("let us see that it was necessary, and even urgent, to reconstruct something and that it was possible too, from then on, because of it, to regain confidence in the practice of poetry. Even better, that we could once more take up the things of the world without abandoning profound experiences, that we could reestablish an exaltant dialogue between the text and its readers, all the while remaining conscious, of course, of the evidence of the catastrophe") (34).

3   All Jaccottet references are to *Œuvres*.

4   See Jean-Claude Pinson on the link between poetry as a way of life and uncertainty: "Tenter de voir les choses autrement, de manière moins déceptive, c'est d'abord, selon moi, considérer la poésie, non plus sous l'angle théorique d'une anthropologie transcendantale, mais sous l'angle pratique de l'incidence qu'elle peut avoir sur l'existence de qui s'en occupe ou lui prête attention" ("To try to see things otherwise, in a less deceptive way, is first of all, according to me, to consider poetry, no longer via the theoretical angle of a transcendental anthropology, but via the practical angle of the effect that it can have on the existence of the one who is involved with it or pays attention to it") (*À Piatigorsk* 53). He associates this way of life with a "quête en somme de « naïveté » seconde qui est toute l'entreprise que j'appelle « poéthique »" ("quest of a second 'naïveté' that is the whole enterprise that I call 'poethics'") (50).

5   I deal more extensively with the relationship of nature, poetry, and modernity in "The Place of Poetry."

6   In this as in other aspects of his thought, Jaccottet harks back to the German Romantics. See, for instance, Novalis on ignorance as increased potential capacity for knowledge: "The more ignorant one is by nature, the more capacity one has for knowledge. Each new insight makes a much deeper, livelier impression. One notices this clearly when embarking on a new branch of learning. That is why one loses capacity through too much studying. It is a kind of ignorance that is opposed to one's initial ignorance. The first kind is ignorance from lack of knowledge—the second from excess of knowledge" (*Philosophical* 39).

7   Cf. Suzanne Allaire's comment on Jaccottet and other lyric poets of his generation: "la poésie, aux prises avec le langage, vit de le questionner, ne peut vivre que de le questionner, et d'osciller alors entre doute et méfiance ou confiance" ("Poetry, grappling with language, lives to question it, can only live on questioning it, and thus on oscillating between doubt and mistrust or confidence") (43).

8   Writing sometimes embraces that ignorance but at other times fights against it: "Tout ce que j'ai écrit, et sans doute surtout le plus clair, le plus serein, n'a été que pour repousser l'inconnu, éloigner la peur qui à présent se rapproche; et, certaines nuits, triomphe. Il n'est pas un endroit où ne nous débusque le pinceau de lumière

mortelle qui est censé nous ouvrir l'avenir" ("Everything that I have written, and without a doubt especially the clearest, the most serene, was only to push back the unknown, to ward off the fear that now is getting close and, certain nights, triumphs. There is no place where the brush of mortal light that is supposed to open the future to us does not drive us out") (*Œuvres* 401).

9 As Serge Champeau puts it: "L'expérience poétique se confond, chez Jaccottet, avec un « art de vivre » (*Eléments* 39). Il arrive certes que la transformation de soi soit pensée comme une condition du travail poétique, ou encore comme un effet de celui-ci. Mais toute l'œuvre atteste que ces deux mouvements de l'âme et du poème constituent une seule expérience personnelle" ("Poetic experience in Jaccottet merges with an 'art of living.' It certainly happens that the transformation of self be thought as a condition of poetic work, or again as its effect. But the whole work attests that these two movements of the soul and of the poem constitute one single personal experience") (243).

10 On the distinction between knowing as a world-building activity and thinking as an eternally renewable, potentially destructive one, see Arendt.

11 For an insightful analysis of the subtle changes in form and sound patterns in the collection *L'Ignorant* as distinct from Jaccottet's earlier works, see Shinabargar.

12 As Allaire puts it, poetry's role for Jaccottet is to "frayer à la parole, par le travail de la langue, les chemins d'un savoir qui interroge la totalité de l'acte de vivre, sa part d'ombre et de lumière, de plénitude et de manque, de présence et d'absence, dans l'incurable blessure de la perte de l'absolu" ("clear away for the word, by the work of language, the paths of a knowledge that questions the totality of the act of living, its share of shadow and light, of plenitude and lack, presence and absence, in the incurable wound of the loss of the absolute") (26).

13 Malte affirms, for instance: "I am learning to see. … I have an interior that I never knew of. Everything passes into it now. I don't know what happens there" (Rilke 5).

14 The passage is in *Réflexions sur quelques-uns de mes contemporains*. See *OC2*: 166.

15 Mallarmé writes in *Le livre instrument spirituel*: "La Poésie, proche l'idée, est Musique, par excellence—et ne consent pas d'infériorité" (*OC2*: 226) ("Poetry, close to the idea, is Music par excellence—doesn't admit inferiority" (*Divagations* 229)).

16 At other times Maulpoix opposes writing and university discourse in terms nearly identical to those with which he opposes poetry and philosophy: "Différence fondamentale entre l'écrivain et l'universitaire: le premier écrit pour de bon à partir de soi, de ce qu'il risque dans l'excès, et souvent dans l'outrance, *chercherie* et méconnaissance assumées, là où l'université exige à tout moment des références sûres et du savoir bien établi" ("Fundamental difference between the writer and the professor: the former writes starting from himself, from what he risks in excess, and often in outrageous excess, *seeking* and ignorance taken on, whereas the professor requires at every moment sure references and well-established knowledge") (*Mauvais genre* 46).

Chapter 5

1. See Andrew Bennett on a kind of perhaps counterintuitive relationship of democracy to a positive ignorance: "Democracy, or democracy-to-come, allows not only for 'free speech' but also for the possibility of *not* speaking. And not speaking, or speaking (or writing) in ways that amount to a resistance to speech—a resistance to meaning, to the thetic (literature as a 'suspension of the thetic relation to meaning or referent'), to making sense—is just what may be said to be instituted in and by the literary event, by the literary speech act. I want to suggest that this irresponsible or non-responsive responsibility is captured in the capacity of literature to engage with, to perform, to encompass not knowing—literature as the site of institution of 'a certain irresponsibility' (itself a high responsibility, itself involving a demand as well as a resistance) that I am calling 'ignorance', ignorance that is at the heart of the open society, of tolerance, of democracy" (338–9).
2. See also Maulpoix: "Si ce mot [lyrisme] peut nous retenir, c'est précisément en ce qu'il met en crise aussi bien l'entente de la poésie lyrique, telle que la définissait Hegel, que toute théorie du sujet. Plutôt que sur la subjectivité, il attire l'attention sur l'altérité" ("If that word [lyricism] can keep our interest, it is precisely in that it puts in crisis the harmony of lyric poetry as Hegel defined it, as well as all theories of the subject. It attracts attention to alterity rather than to subjectivity") ("Existe" 260).
3. I borrow the term from Bruner 3.
4. These remarks chime with Maulpoix's invitation in 2018 to reformulate the question of what poetry is by asking instead what it does: "Au lieu de répéter indéfiniment la question stérile « Qu'est-ce que la poésie ? », à laquelle il ne peut être apporté que des réponses partielles, peut-être faudrait-il donc se demander : Que fait-elle (avec la langue) ? Que dit-elle (de ce monde et de notre vie) ? À quoi sert-elle (surtout si elle ne sert à rien) ? Que peut-elle ?" ("Rather than indefinitely repeating the sterile question 'What is poetry?,' to which only partial answers can be brought, perhaps then we should ask: What does it do (with language)? What does it say (about this world and our life)? What is it good for (especially if it is good for nothing)? What is it capable of?") (*Les 100 mots* 32).
5. See also Philippe Lacoue-Labarthe's claim that "la poésie est l'interruption de l'art" ("poetry is the interruption of art") (65).
6. See Hui Bon Hoa 47–8 for further exploration of the similarities and differences between Nancy and Rancière on questions of whether politics produces the subject (Rancière) or potentially annihilates it (Nancy).
7. Passages from the preface to the English edition of *The Inoperative Community* are given in English only; passages from the main body of the text are given both in the original French and in translation.

8 As Simon Malpas indicates, for Nancy, "we are called upon by art to respond to its interruption of the circle of signification and its exposure of the fragility of signified sense. ... The world is constituted in and by our Being-in-common, which itself is finite and fragmented" (Malpas 92).

9 Nancy also establishes continuity with older notions of community, and another point of connection with poetry, by establishing theological stakes for the redefinition of community: "[La communauté] est le sacré, si on veut: mais le sacré dépouillé du sacré. Car le sacré—le séparé, le mis-à-l'écart—s'avère ne plus être cela dont la communion nous hanterait tout en se dérobant, mais n'être fait de rien d'autre que du partage de la communauté. Il n'y a ni entité ni hypostase sacrée de la communauté: mais il y a le « déchaînement des passions », le partage des êtres singuliers, et la communication de la finitude" ("Community is the sacred, if you will: but the sacred stripped of the sacred. For the sacred—the separated, the set apart—no longer proves to be the haunting idea of an unattainable communion, but is rather made up of nothing other than the sharing of community—there is the 'unleashing of passions,' the sharing of singular beings, and the communication of finitude") (*Communauté* 86–7/*Inoperative* 35).

Works Cited

All works in French published in Paris unless otherwise indicated.

Acquisto, Joseph. "Cross-referencing Bowie: Layers and Networks in Mallarmé and Proust." In Gill Rye and Naomi Segal, eds., *'When familiar meanings dissolve …': Essays in Memory of Malcolm Bowie (1943–2007)*. Oxford: Peter Lang, 2011, 135–50.

Acquisto, Joseph. "Entre Rimbaud et Bataille: Le salut, le savoir et l'impossible renoncement à la poésie dans *Une saison en enfer*." *Parade sauvage* 27 (2016): 131–44.

Acquisto, Joseph. *The Fall Out of Redemption: Writing and Thinking Beyond Salvation in Baudelaire, Cioran, Fondane, Agamben, and Nancy*. New York: Bloomsbury, 2015.

Acquisto, Joseph. "Gautier on Baudelaire: Lessons from Hawthorne." In Joseph Acquisto, Adrianna Paliyenko and Catherine Witt, eds., *Poets as Readers in Nineteenth-Century France: Critical Reflections*. London: Institute of Modern Languages Research, 2015, 113–30.

Acquisto, Joseph. "The Place of Poetry: Nature, Nostalgia, and Modernity in Jaccottet's Poetics." *Modern Language Review* 105: 3 (July 2010): 679–94.

Acquisto, Joseph. *Proust, Music, and Meaning: Theories and Practices of Listening in the Recherche*. New York: Palgrave Macmillan, 2017.

Allaire, Suzanne. *La Parole de la poésie: Lorand Gaspar, Jean Grosjean, Eugène Guillevic, Phillippe Jaccottet*. Rennes: PU de Rennes, 2005.

Apollinaire, Guillaume. *Œuvres poétiques*. Gallimard, 1959.

Arendt, Hannah. "Thinking and Moral Considerations." *Social Research* 38 (1971): 417–46.

Aristotle. *Metaphysics*. Tr. W.D. Ross. http://classics.mit.edu/Aristotle/metaphysics.1.i.html

Arnould, Elisabeth. "The Impossible Sacrifice of Poetry: Bataille and the Nancian Critique of Sacrifice." *Diacritics* 26: 2 (Summer 1996): 86–96.

Arnould, Elisabeth. "La poésie comme non-savoir." *MLN* 119: 4 (September 2004): 781–99.

Badiou, Alain. *The Age of the Poets*. London: Verso, 2014.

Barthes, Roland. *Mythologies*. Seuil, 1957.

Bataille, Georges. *Inner Experience*. Tr. Leslie Anne Boldt. Albany: State University of New York Press, 1988.

Bataille, Georges. *Méthode de méditation*. Fontaine, 1947.

Bataille, Georges. *Œuvres complètes*. 12 vols. Gallimard, 1970–88.

Bataille, Georges. *The Unfinished System of Nonknowledge*. Tr. Stuart Kendall. Minneapolis: University of Minnesota Press, 2001.

Baudelaire, Charles. *Œuvres complètes*. 2 Vols. Gallimard, 1975–76.

Baudelaire, Charles. *The Parisian Prowler*. Tr. Edward K. Kaplan. Athens: The University of Georgia Press, 1997.

Béguin, Albert. *Gérard de Nerval suivi de Poésie et mystique*. Stock, 1936.

Bennett, Andrew. *Ignorance: Literature and Agnoiology*. Manchester: Manchester University Press, 2009.

Ber, Claude. "Méditation de mots." In Béatrice Bonhomme and Gabriel Grossi, eds., *La Poésie comme espace méditatif?* Classiques Garnier, 2015, 17–45.

Bident, Christophe. *Maurice Blanchot: Partenaire invisible*. Champ Vallon, 2008.

Bittner, Jacob. "Hölderlin and the Romantics: The Paradigm of Writerly Necessity in Philippe Lacoue-Labarthe and Jean-Luc Nancy's *The Literary Absolute*." MLN 131: 3 (April 2016): 770–90.

Blanchot, Maurice. *The Book to Come*. Tr. Charlotte Mandell. Stanford: Stanford University Press, 2003.

Blanchot, Maurice. *La communauté inavouable*. Minuit, 1983.

Blanchot, Maurice. *L'écriture du désastre*. Gallimard, 1980.

Blanchot, Maurice. *L'espace littéraire*. Gallimard, 1955.

Blanchot, Maurice. *Faux pas*. Gallimard, 1943.

Blanchot, Maurice. *Faux pas*. Tr. Charlotte Mandell. Stanford: Stanford University Press, 2001.

Blanchot, Maurice. *Le livre à venir*. Gallimard, 1959.

Blanchot, Maurice. *The Space of Literature*. Tr. Ann Smock. Lincoln: University of Nebraska Press, 1982.

Blanchot, Maurice. *The Unavowable Community*. Tr. Pierre Joris. Barrytown: Station Hill Press, 1988.

Blanchot, Maurice. *The Writing of the Diasaster*. Tr. Ann Smock. Lincoln: University of Nebraska Press, 1995.

Bonnefoy, Yves. *La poésie à voix haute*. Ligne d'ombre, 2007.

Bowie, Andrew. *Aesthetics and Subjectivity from Kant to Nietzsche*, 2nd edn. Manchester: Manchester University Press, 2003.

Bowie, Andrew. *From Romanticism to Critical Theory: The Philosophy of German Literary Theory*. London: Routledge, 1997.

Bremond, Henri. *Prière et poésie*. Grasset, 1926.

Bruner, Jerome. "The Narrative Construction of Reality." *Critical Inquiry* 18 (1991): 1–21.

Bruns, Gerald. *Maurice Blanchot: The Refusal of Philosophy*. Baltimore: The Johns Hopkins University Press, 1997.

Bruns, Gerald. *On the Anarchy of Poetry and Philosophy: A Guide for the Unruly*. New York: Fordham University Press, 2006.

Campion, Pierre. *Mallarmé: Poésie et philosophie*. Presses Universitaires de France, 1994.

Cascardi, Anthony. "From the Sublime to the Natural: Romantic Responses to Kant." In Anthony Casacrdi, ed., *Literature and the Question of Philosophy*. Baltimore: The Johns Hopkins University Press, 1987, 101–31.

Cave, Terence. *Thinking with Literature: Towards a Cognitive Criticism*. Oxford: Oxford University Press, 2016.

Césaire, Aimé. "Poésie et connaissance." *Tropiques* 12 (January 1945): 157–70.

Chamarat, Gabrielle. "*Mémoires d'une âme* et l'épopée de la connaissance." In Ludmila Charles-Wurtz and Judith Wulf, *Lectures des* Contemplations. Presses Universitaires de Rennes, 2016, 169–83.

Champeau, Serge. *Ontologie et poésie: trois études sur les limites du langage*. Librairie Philosophique, 1995.

De Francesco, Alessandro. "Narrations multi-linéaires et épistémologies poétiques chez Jean-Marie Gleize et Claude Royet-Journoud." *French Forum* 37: 1–2 (Winter/Spring 2012): 115–27.

Deguy, Michel. *La raison poétique*. Galilée, 2000.

Deguy, Michel. *Réouverture après travaux*. Galilée, 2007.

Delaveau, Philippe. "Veiller sur la présence." *The Irish Journal of French Studies* 18 (2018): 63–74.

Delègue, Yves. "Mallarmé, les philosophes et les gestes de la philosophie." *Romantisme* 124 (2004): 127–40.

DeNicola, Daniel. *Understanding Ignorance: The Surprising Impact of What We Don't Know*. Cambridge: Massachusetts Institute of Technology Press, 2017.

Derrida, Jacques. "Che cos'è la poesia?" *Poé&sie* 50 (1989): 109–12.

Doumet, Christian. "L'incompréhensible." *L'Esprit Créateur* 55: 1 (Spring 2015): 11–21.

Dumoulié, Camille. *Littérature et philosophie: Le gai savoir de la littérature*. Armand Colin, 2002.

Eaglestone, Robert. "Critical Knowledge, Scientific Knowledge and the Truth of Literature." In John J. Joughin and Simon Malpas, eds., *The New Aestheticism*. Manchester: Manchester University Press, 2003, 151–66.

Friedrich, Hugo. *The Structure of Modern Poetry*. Evanston: Northwestern University Press, 1974.

Gasché, Rodolphe. *The Honor of Thinking: Critique, Theory, Philosophy*. Stanford: Stanford University Press, 2007.

Gaspar, Lorand. *Approche de la parole*. Gallimard, 1978.

Gaudon, Jean. *Le Temps de la contemplation*. Flammarion, 1969.

Gemerchak, Christopher. *The Sunday of the Negative*. Albany: State University of New York Press, 2003.

Gleize, Jean-Marie. *A noir*. Seuil, 1992.

Gourio, Anne. "Jaccottet, l'émerveillement murmuré." In Julie Anselmini and Marie-Hélène Boblet, eds., *De l'émerveillement dans les littératures poétiques et narratives des XIXe et XXe siècles*. Grenoble: ELLUG, 2017, 185–96.

Haase, Ulrich, and William Large. *Maurice Blanchot*. London: Routledge, 2001.
Hamacher, Werner. *Premises: Essays on Philosophy and Literature from Kant to Celan*. Cambridge: Harvard University Press, 1996.
Handwerk, Gary. *Irony and Ethics in Narrative: From Schlegel to Lacan*. New Haven: Yale University Press, 1985.
Hugo, Victor. *Œuvres poétiques*. 3 vols. Gallimard, 1964.
Hui Bon Hoa, Jen. "The Disidentified Community: Rancière Reading (Nancy Reading) Blanchot." *Angelaki* 23: 6 (December 2018): 33–51.
Hume, David. *An Enquiry Concerning Human Understanding*. Indianapolis: Hackett, 1993.
Jaccottet, Phillippe. *Œuvres*. Gallimard, 2014.
Jarrety, Michel. *Valéry devant la littérature: mesure de la limite*. Presses Universitaires de France, 1991.
Johnson, Barbara. *The Barbara Johnson Reader*. Durham: Duke University Press, 2004.
Joughin, John and Simon Malpas, eds. *The New Aestheticism*. Manchester: Manchester University Press, 2003.
Kendall, Stuart. "Editor's Introduction." In Georges Bataille, ed., *The Unfinished System of Nonknowledge*. Minneapolis: University of Minnesota Press, 2001, xi–xliv.
Kramer, Lawrence. *Expression and Truth: On the Music of Knowledge*. Berkeley: University of California Press, 2012.
Labarthe, Patrick. *Baudelaire et la tradition de l'allégorie*. Geneva: Droz, 1999.
Lacoue-Labarthe, Philippe. *La poésie comme expérience*. Christian Bourgois, 1986.
Lacoue-Labarthe, Philippe and Jean-Luc Nancy. *L'absolu littéraire: Théorie de la littérature du romantisme allemand*. Seuil, 1978.
Lacoue-Labarthe, Philippe and Jean-Luc Nancy. *The Literary Absolute: The Theory of Literature in German Romanticism*. Albany: State University of New York Press, 1988.
Lala, Marie-Christine. "The Hatred of Poetry in Georges Bataille's Writng and Thought." In Carolyn Bailey Gill, ed., *Bataille: Writing the Sacred*. London: Routledge, 1995, 105–16.
Lautréamont and Germain Nouveau. *Œuvres complètes*. Gallimard, 1970.
Lear, Jonathan. *A Case for Irony, with Commentary by Cora Diamond, Christine M. Korsgaard, Richard Moran, and Robert A. Paul*. Cambridge: Harvard University Press, 2011.
Leighton, Angela. "Poetry's Knowing: So What Do We Know?" In John Gibson, ed., *The Philosophy of Poetry*. Oxford: Oxford University Press, 2015, 162–82.
Lerner, Ben. *The Hatred of Poetry*. Toronto: McClelland & Stewart, 2016.
Levinson, Marjorie. *Thinking Through Poetry*. Oxford: Oxford University Press, 2018.
Livingston, Paisley. "Literature and Knowledge." In Jonatha Dancey, ed., *A Companion to Epistemology*. Oxford: Basil Blackwell, 1992, 255–58.
Loiseleur, Aurélie. "Le monde signé Dieu." *Fabula.org*. http://www.fabula.org/colloques/document378.php.

Lyu, Claire. *A Sun within a Sun: The Power and Elegance of Poetry*. Pittsburgh: University of Pittsburgh Press, 2006.

Mallarmé, Stéphane. *Divagations*. Tr. Barbara Johnson. Cambridge: Harvard University Press, 2007.

Mallarmé, Stéphane. *Œuvres complètes*. 2 vols. Gallimard, 1998–2003.

Malpas, Simon. "Touching Art: Aesthetics, Fragmentation and Community." In John J. Joughin and Simon Malpas, eds., *The New Aestheticism*. Manchester: Manchester University Press, 2003, 83–95.

Maritain, Jacques. *Art and Scholasticism and the Frontiers of Poetry*. Tr. Joseph W. Evans. New York: Scribner's Sons, 1962.

Maritain, Jacques and Raïssa Maritain. *Situation de la poesie*. 3rd ed. Desclée de Brouwer, 1964.

Maritain, Jacques and Raïssa Maritain. *The Situation of Poetry*. Tr. Marshall Suther. New York: Philosophical Library, 1968.

Matuschek, Stefan. "Romanticism as Literary Idealism." In Nicholas Boyle et al., eds., *The Impact of Idealism: The Legacy of Post-Kantian German Thought*, Volume III: Aesthetics and Literature. Cambridge: Cambridge University Press, 2013, 69–91.

Maulpoix, Jean-Michel. *Les 100 mots de la poésie*. Presses Universitaires de France, 2018.

Maulpoix, Jean-Michel. *Du lyrisme*. 3rd edn. Librairie José Corti, 2000.

Maulpoix, Jean-Michel. "Existe-t-il en France un nouveau lyrisme?" *Australian Journal of French Studies* 34: 3 (Autumn 1997): 259–69.

Maulpoix, Jean-Michel. "Philippe Jaccottet, 'L'Ignorant.'" In Hugues Azérad and Peter Collier, eds., *Twentieth-Century French Poetry*. Cambridge: Cambridge University Press, 2010, 174–80.

Maulpoix, Jean-Michel. *La poésie malgré tout*. Mercure de France, 1996.

Maulpoix, Jean-Michel. *La poésie a mauvais genre*. Éditions Corti, 2016.

Maulpoix, Jean-Michel. *Le poète perplexe*. José Corti, 2002.

Maulpoix, Jean-Michel. *Pour un lyrisme critique*. José Corti, 2009.

Maulpoix, Jean-Michel. *La voix d'Orphée: Essai sur le lyrisme*. José Corti, 1989.

McKeane, John. *Philippe Lacoue-Labarthe: (Un)timely Meditations*. Oxford: Legenda, 2015.

McLaughlin, Kevin. *Poetic Force: Poetry after Kant*. Stanford: Stanford University Press, 2014.

Meschonnic, Henri. *Pour la poétique V: Poésie sans réponse*. Gallimard, 1978.

Nancy, Jean-Luc. *La communauté désoeuvrée*. Christian Bourgois, 1986.

Nancy, Jean-Luc. *The Inoperative Community*. Minneapolis: University of Minnesota Press, 1991.

Nancy, Jean-Luc. *Listening*. Tr. Charlotte Mandell. New York: Fordham University Press, 2007.

Nancy, Jean-Luc. *Les muses*. Galilée, 1994.

Nancy, Jean-Luc. *The Muses*. Tr. Peggy Kamuf. Stanford: Stanford University Press, 1996.

Nancy, Jean-Luc. *Résistance de la poésie*. Art et arts, 1997.
Novalis, *Novalis Schriften*, ed. Richard Samuel, Hans-Joachim Mähl, and Gerhard Schulz et al. 6 vols. Stuttgart: Kohlhammer, 1960–.
Novalis, *Philosophical Writings*. Tr. Margaret Mahony Stoljar. Albany: State University of New York Press, 1997.
Nowell Smith, David. *Sounding/Silence: Martin Heidegger at the Limits of Poetics*. New York: Fordham University Press, 2013.
Perse, Saint-John. Nobel Prize Speech. December 10, 1960. https://www.nobelprize.org/prizes/literature/1960/perse/25384-saint-john-perse-banquet-speech-1960/.
Pinson, Jean-Claude. *À Piatigorsk, sur la poésie*. Nantes: Éditions Cécile Defaut, 2008.
Pinson, Jean-Claude. *Habiter en poète: essai sur la poésie contemporaine*. Editions Champ Vallon, 1995.
Porter, Laurence M. "The Fall into Narrative: Negative Verticality in French Romantic Poetry." *Nineteenth-Century French Studies* 22: 3–4 (Spring–Summer 1994): 404–16.
Pusterla, Fabio. "Promenade sur une colline." In Philippe Jaccottet, ed., *Le combat inégal*. Geneva: La Dogana, 2010, 30–41.
Rancière, Jacques. "Literary Communities." In Thomas Claviez, ed., *The Common Growl: Toward a Poetics of Precarious Community*. New York: Fordham University Press, 2016, 93–110.
Rancière, Jacques. *Le sillon du poème: En lisant Philippe Beck*. Nous, 2016.
Rancière, Jacques. "Ten Theses on Politics." In *Dissensus*. London: Continuum, 2010, 27–44.
Ray, Lionel. *Le Procès de la vieille dame*. Editions de la différence, 2008.
Réda, Jacques. *Celle qui vient à pas légers*. Fata Morgana, 1999.
Reverdy, Pierre. *Œuvres complètes*. Flammarion, 2010.
Riffaterre, Michael. "Sémiosis hugolienne." In Jacques Seebacher and Anne Ubersfeld, eds., *Hugo le fabuleux*. Paris: Seghers, 1985, 38–57.
Rilke, Rainer Maria. *The Notebooks of Malte Laurids Brigge*. Tr. Stephen Mitchell. New York: Vintage, 1990.
Royet-Journoud, Claude. *The Whole of Poetry is Preposition*. Tr. Keith Waldrop. Iowa City and Paris: La Presse, 2011.
Sacré, James. *La poésie, comment dire?* Marseille: André Dimanche, 1993.
Santi, Sylvain. *Georges Bataille, à l'extrême fuyante de la poésie*. Amsterdam: Rodopi, 2007.
Sartre, Jean-Paul. *L'Etre et le néant*. Gallimard, 1943.
Sartre, Jean-Paul. *Being and Nothingness*. Tr. Hazel Barnes. New York: Washington Square Press, 1993.
Schlegel, Friedrich. *Philosophical Fragments*. Tr. Peter Firchow. Minneapolis: University of Minnesota Press, 1991.
Shinabargar, Scott. "Effacement Eclipsed: The Texture of Voice in Jaccottet's *L'Ignorant*." *Symposium* 65: 4 (2011): 290–306.

Stout, John C. *L'Énigme-poésie: Entretiens avec 21 poètes françaises*. Amsterdam: Rodopi, 2010.

St. Clair, Robert and Ross Chambers. "Incipit: On Reading (Chambers)." *Nineteenth-Century French Studies* 45: 3–4 (Spring–Summer 2017): 116–32.

Thériault, Patrick. *Le (de)montage de la Fiction: La revelation moderne de Mallarmé*. Honoré Champion, 2010.

Trop, Gabriel. *Poetry as a Way of Life: Aesthetics and Askesis in the German Eighteenth Century*. Evanston: Northwestern University Press, 2015.

Valéry, Paul. *Œuvres*. 2 vols. Gallimard, 1957.

Walsh, Dorothy. *Literature and Knowledge*. Middletown: Wesleyan University Press, 1969.

Wasser, Audrey. *The Work of Difference: Modernism, Romanticism, and the Production of Literary Form*. New York: Fordham University Press, 2016.

Weinstein, Philip. *Unknowing: The Work of Modernist Fiction*. Ithaca: Cornell University Press, 2005.

Wilson, Catherine. "Literature and Knowledge." In Eileen Johnand Dominic McIver-Lopes, eds., *Philosophy of Literature: Contemporary and Classic Readings*. Oxford: Blackwell, 2004, 324–28.

Witt, Catherine. "Passages through Baudelaire: From Poetry to Thought and Back." In Joseph Acquisto, ed., *Thinking Poetry*. New York: Palgrave Macmillan, 2013, 25–42.

Wourm, Nathalie. *Poètes français du 21e siècle: Entretiens*. Leiden: Brill/Rodopi, 2017.

Young, Robert J. C. "Community and Ethnos." In Thomas Claviez, ed., *The Common Growl: Toward a Poetics of Precarious Community*. New York: Fordham University Press, 2016, 17–38.

Zalloua, Zahi. *Theory's Autoimmunity: Skepticism, Literature, and Philosophy*. Evanston: Northwestern University Press, 2018.

Index

absolute music 15, 145, 180–1
adolescence 137–8
Apollinaire, Guillaume 23, 49–52
Arendt, Hannah 201 n.10
Aristotle 192 n.13
art, definition of 54–5, 186 n.3
attention 145

Badiou, Alain 189 n.14
Bancquart, Marie-Claire 86–7
Barthes, Roland 61
Bataille, Georges 12, 19–20, 85, 96–108, 167, 170
Baudelaire, Charles 18, 21, 23, 37–49, 81, 137, 147, 154, 155, 164, 194 n.7
 "La chambre double" 23, 47–8
 "Laquelle est la vraie?" 23, 46–7
 "L'art philosophique" 37–9
 "Notes nouvelles sur Edgar Poe" 40–3
Blanchot, Maurice 12–13, 19–20, 85, 108–20, 169–70, 182
Bonnefoy, Yves 90
Bremond, Henri 191 n.4

Césaire, Aimé 90, 196 n.4
Char, René 57
clarity 39
community 5, 16, 22, 163–4, 172, 175–9, 184, 203 n.9
conclusions 43–4, 108
contemplation 128–9
contingency 3, 4
Courtade, Fabienne 89
creation, poetic 50, 98, 144, 177, 198 n.16
crisis 91–3

death 118, 169
defamiliarization 100, 195 n.10
Deguy, Michel 8, 22, 57, 164–5, 187 n.4, 190 n.23
Deleuze, Gilles 189 n.18

democracy 163–4, 202 n.1
Derrida, Jacques 7
doubt 21, 30, 35, 90, 120, 125–6, 132–4
Dupin, Jacques 175

enthusiasm 42–3
epistemology 18, 49, 105
ethics 9–10
exile 168–9
experience, lived 8, 16, 18, 20, 22, 67–8, 84, 114, 120, 126, 130–1, 137–8

fascism 178
fiction 63, 78, 86
Flaubert, Gustave 83–4

Gadamer, Hans 171
Gaspar, Lorand 10
Gleize, Jean-Marie 57–9, 91–3, 174–5
God 26, 34, 100–1

haiku 139
Hegel, G.W.F. 98, 172–3, 202 n.2
Heidegger, Martin 8, 15, 152, 189 n.13, 190 n.22, 198–9 n.19
Hölderlin, Friedrich 60
Hugo, Victor 17–18, 23–37, 153
 Les Contemplations 17, 23, 26–37
  "A Madame D. G. de G" 26–7
  "Ce que dit la bouche d'ombre" 36–7
  "Je lisais. Que lisais-je ?...." 28–31
  "Les Mages" 35–6
  "Magnitudo parvi" 31
  "Pensar, dudar" 24–6
Hume, David 105

Icarus 154
ignorance 10–11, 17, 19, 30, 35, 50, 66–7, 68–9, 86, 89, 95–6, 116–17, 130–3, 147–9, 195–6 n.1, 202 n.1

impossibility 103–4, 109, 113, 123
ineffability 30, 62, 66, 69–71, 74, 96, 103, 136
inner experience 12–13, 20, 114–15
interpretation 27, 28, 30, 112, 173
interruption 180–1, 185
irony 29, 195 n.10, 196 n.2

Jaccottet, Philippe 4–5, 21, 86, 121–46
    Airs 141
    Eléments d'un songe 129–36
    "Fin d'hiver" 140–1
    La Promenade sous les arbres 123–8
    La Semaison 121, 136
    "L'Ignorant" 139–40, 149
    L'Obscurité 127
    "Pensées sous les nuages" 140–3

Lacoue-Labarthe, Philippe 14, 15, 54, 190 n.24, 202 n.5
Lautréamont, Comte de 5–6
limits 10, 20, 33, 96, 99, 105, 136, 166, 189 n.13
limping 153, 155
lyricism 120, 145, 150–3, 158, 188 n.10, 202 n.2

Mallarmé, Stéphane 8, 17, 24, 32, 50–1, 69, 75, 93, 110, 140, 148, 154, 164, 188 n.12, 198 n.17, 201 n.15
Maritain, Jacques and Raïssa 3, 64–6, 191 n.4
Maulpoix, Jean-Marie 8, 21, 86, 141, 145–62, 163, 190 n.23, 202 n.2, 202 n.4
meaning 3, 22, 24, 58, 62, 69–70, 79, 90, 92, 111, 119, 136
metaphor 73–4, 154
music 62, 70, 132, 136, 148, 180
Musil, Robert 119
mysticism 65, 99, 113, 131, 135, 173–4, 191 n.4, 194 n.8
myth 179–83

Nancy, Jean-Luc 14, 22, 54, 94, 164, 177–85, 186 n.3, 190 n.24, 202 n.6
nature 17, 24–5, 28–9, 146, 200 n.5

neuter, the 115, 117
non-knowledge 20, 96, 97, 98, 100
nostalgia 122, 126, 173
Novalis 16, 18, 53, 60, 61–3, 122, 173–4, 200 n.6

obscurity 17

painting 38
philosophy 2, 5–6, 80, 108–9, 119, 159–60, 179, 187 n.6, 187 n.7, 189–90 n.19, 190 n.24, 193 n.15, 195 n.11
Pinson, Jean-Claude 56–7, 200 n.4
Plato 175, 187 n.7, 188 n.11
plurality 178
Poète tardif 149–50, 158–9
poetry, definition of 2–3, 40–1, 64, 66, 77–80, 102, 105–6
poetry, hatred of 6, 20, 105, 107, 197 n.8, 198 n.14
politics 172, 174
Proust, Marcel 17
pure poetry 74–5, 138, 145, 167, 180–1

questioning 13, 59–60, 82, 89, 108, 133, 141, 160

Rancière, Jacques 22, 164, 171–3, 176–7, 202 n.6
Ray, Lionel 86–7
Real, the 54–9, 78, 123–4, 189 n.17
Réda, Jacques 15
Reverdy, Pierre 18, 53–6
Rilke, Rainer Maria 145
Rimbaud, Arthur 99–100, 118, 139
romanticism 5, 7–8, 21, 49, 53–4, 60, 86, 122, 169, 190 n.20, 190 n.21, 200 n.6
Royet-Journoud, Claude 88–90

sacred, the 198 n.18, 203 n.9
Sacré, James 66–7
sacrifice 85, 96, 98–9, 197 n.8
Saint-John Perse 90–1, 196–7 n.5
Sartre, Jean-Paul 167–8
Schlegel, Friedrich 6, 10–11, 53, 171
science 90–1

secret, the 135–6
silence 15, 29, 66–7, 90, 98, 101, 103–7, 112–13, 118, 128–9, 140, 175, 194 n.8
skepticism 27, 34, 45, 135, 157, 159, 185
subjectivity 146, 188 n.11, 191 n.25, 196 n.2, 202 n.2
subject, poetic 8, 16–17, 93, 122, 145, 159
sublime, the 47

tautology 18–19, 60–1, 63, 81, 173, 179–80

thought 7, 108, 132, 137–8, 187 n.4, 189 n.13, 190 n.23, 201 n.10
translation 17, 28, 33, 35
truth 5, 18, 23, 39–42, 44, 63, 178, 192 n.6

uncertainty 122, 200 n.4
unknowing 8, 94–5

Valéry, Paul 19, 68–84, 186 n.1, 198 n.17

wonder 45, 47, 199 n.1
writing 112–13

www.ingramcontent.com/pod-product-compliance
Lightning Source LLC
Chambersburg PA
CBHW052041300426
44117CB00012B/1922